To
Margaret
Every Good Wish
Ann Wheal
March 2013

A
Scrapbook of WW2 Memories

Second Edition

A collection of personal stories of life during WW2

Ann Wheal

Published by:

Brinton Cottage Publishing
Brinton Cottage
Bull Lane
Waltham Chase
Southampton
SO32 2LS

tel: 01489 892601
email: bcpublishing@btinternet.com
web: www.brintoncottagepublishing.co.uk

June 2011

British Library Cataloguing-in-publication Data:
A catalogue record of this book is available from the British Library.

ISBN: 978-0-9555988-2-1

Printed by:
Digital Print FX Ltd
Unit B3,
Segensworth Business Centre,
Segensworth Road,
Fareham,
Hampshire,
PO15 5RQ

This book is dedicated to my grandson

Jamie Bray

who died so tragically on July 13th, 2010, aged 8 years

Contents

Acknowledgements

A book such as this would not be possible without the help of so many people. Firstly, I would like to thank all those who willingly gave of their time to tell me about their experiences as well as those who provided me with written material. Without these people this book could not have been written. The list below is in alphabetical order.

I would also like to thank Sue Eggleston and John Barnard of Court Lane Junior School and the many people from The Lee on the Solent School for their help and guidance. Tracy Thompson has provided valuable help and support as well as acting as a critical reader along with Kathy Estcourt, Jan Boram, Catherine O'Mahony, Heather Rayner, Shelley Ducarreaux and Eve Lemm.

Thanks are particularly due to all the children who helped in many ways and to Samuel Thompson and Molly Wheal for their help.

Finally, as always, I would like to thank my husband for his patience, tolerance and love.

Contributors:

Iris Andrews, Roy Andrews, Kathy Arnold, John Arnold, Joan Baker, Keith Barnard, Sylvia Barron, Jean Batchelor, Maud Beaman, Bob Boother, Jan Boram, Laurence Bray, Pat Caine, Rosemary Clarke, Hilary Cole, John Cole, Christine Cooke, Alan Corbishley, Ted Cottle, Micky Cottle, Richard Davenport, Freda Davis, John Davey, Ron Dugan, Hilda Dugan, Gladys Eadon, Doreen Embling, Jean Emery, Desnia Ford, Sybil Foster, Sylvia Glew, Ken George, Beryl George, Vernon Gibbons, Helen Glantz, Harold Goodwin, Brigid Goldsmith, Gill Gould, Kath Graham, Mary Grant, Evelyn Gray, Harry Hargreaves, Beryl Harris, Leslie Harrison, Mary Hill, David Hill, Pamela Houghton, Norah Hull, Les Jackson, Grace Kattenhorn, Arthur Kemp, Ron Keyte, Joan Keyte, Sylvia Lacoski, Jean Lawson, Jean Lawson (yes, there are two Jean Lawsons!), Gwen Lawrence, Do Lemm, Sam Lipfriend, Win McCurrach, Colin Martin, Bob Middlebrooke, Vera Moody, Jimmy Naylor, Roy Nemko, Catherine O'Mahony, Steve Park, Betty Parker, John Parsons, Megan Paxman, Dorothy Pelosi, Dennis Pink, Maureen Pritchard, Dave Rackham, Heather Rayner, Olive Robinson, Jean Robertson, Alan Robertson, Joan Roper, Barbara Rudd, Peggy Rutherford, John Shaul, Michael Sparrow, John Stirling, Audrey Spiers, Fred Steel, Harry Steward, Alex Stockwell, Warwick Taylor, Betty Thompson, Peter Tosdevine, Danny Trainer, Bill Turner, Thelma Turner, Charles Underwood, Peter Wheal, Steven Womack, Eileen Young.

Sadly, Freda Davis and Charles Underwood died before the book was published.

About the book

World War 2 was a dreadful time for anyone involved in the fighting and also for the people who lost loved ones. When a war is declared people worry as to how it might affect their families and themselves. For some it means being called up to fight in many different ways from being on the front line shooting guns; flying planes and dropping bombs; being captured and sometimes tortured and many more. The bravery and heroics of these groups has been well documented.

There were many people who were not directly involved with the fighting but who also had difficult times; there were people in the forces who were not on the front line; there were those who were unable to join the forces who did other worthwhile jobs; there were women doing 'men's work'; and so many more. All these people have stories to tell.

This book is for old and young alike. The stories are in the people's own words and own style.

The book is a collection of stories and quotations of people's lives during WW2. It is the result of extensive research by the author who has carefully woven the material into a cohesive book.

All the people whose material has been used in the book were interviewed face to face; talked to on the telephone or they sent written accounts or emails of their lives and experiences. All the stories are from people who are now in their 70's, 80's and even in their 90's. Factually there may be a few minor inaccuracies but these people's memories are as clear today about their experiences as they were when they occurred nearly 70 year's ago. The ratio of women to men contributors reflects the fact that women outlive men by approximately 7:1.

Appendix 1 is a list of terms used by the story tellers should a query arise as to a meaning of a word or phrase such as ack ack.

At the top of some pages are boxes that contain quotations from mainly from people who were children during the War. There are many more children's quotations in section 3.

Catherine O'Mahaney, a contributor and critical reader noted:

I enjoyed being reminded of my childhood years, but even more so reading the accounts of those children who, almost overnight, had to become adults and fill jobs left vacant by servicemen and women. The adult's stories are really interesting, some sad, but the vast majority full of optimism and enjoyment. They showed that having lots of money wasn't a pre-requisite for happiness.

At the end I felt enormous pride in our country. Everyone played a part in victory, although at the time they were just existing from one day to another.

Introduction

Many years later I met the captain of the submarine that torpedoed the SS Benares that I was on. He said if he had known that there were children on board he wouldn't have followed the orders to torpedo the ship.

One of my sons asked me one time: "Mum, how did you handle living like that?" I replied that we didn't know we were 'handling' anything, it was our way of life. We just got on with it.

When they tested the sirens after the War, I stopped to listen in case it wasn't a practice. They tested them for some years afterwards and I always stopped in case, even though I knew the War was over.

War is a terrible thing. It is cruel. It is violent. All people, civilians as well as soldiers, sailors and airmen must obey orders even though sometimes they do not wish to do so.

World War 2 (1939-1945) was the largest armed conflict in human history. It covered six continents and all the world's oceans. The War caused an estimated 50 million military and civilian deaths, including those of six million Jews.[i] People lose their lives. Women lose their husbands or boyfriends; children lose their fathers or mothers, aunts or uncles, brothers or sisters; families are broken up; houses and treasured possessions are lost. All of this is through bombing, rocket and gunfire from the enemy.

The people knew about sirens and what that meant; they knew the dreadful noise of the doodlebugs or the V2s; sometimes they saw dead bodies in the street and they knew too that sometimes these might be their friends or relatives – yet they carried on their lives as normally as possible. Despite all of this, people survived. People made the most of their lives.

Did you know:
- women had to give up certain jobs or leave the services if they became pregnant, whether they were married or not married?
- unmarried women were often cast out by their families if they became pregnant. To this day many women who became pregnant or had babies out of wedlock during the War do not admit to it. The shame is still there for them.
- women had to give up their jobs when the men came back from War?
- women who did the same job as men were paid sometimes less than half the amount that men were paid?
- when they were 18, some young men had to go down the coal mines and learn to become miners if they were unlucky enough to have their name 'drawn out of a hat' rather than be called up to join the services? They were called Bevin boys after the minister who introduced the scheme.
- many boys did jobs that would normally have been done by men, often working long hours, in dreadful conditions so there was money in the family?
- men who wanted to go to war were not allowed if they were in what the Government defined as protected occupations?
- men who chose not to go to war because of their beliefs, conscientious objectors, were often treated very badly and given the worst possible jobs to do instead? People thought they were cowards and to this day many are still scarred by the treatment of those who came in contact with them.

There are many more issues discussed in this book.

Part 1

Life during the War

I was only six when the War started and on the 'Day that War Broke Out'...I was playing in a park some miles away from home with friends, when a man said, "YOU KIDS BETTER GET HOME, THE WAR HAS STARTED"...It didn't mean too much to me – but it did to my mum when I got home!

During the War everyone was always smiling. There was always something going on. I wouldn't have missed it. Everyone seemed really friendly; more trusting. You took anyone in who needed a house or just needed a meal.

I DO remember sitting on the bunk at the front of the Anderson shelter near the doorway and counting the bombs coming down (ignorance is bliss!).

Later I found out that my classroom had taken a direct hit. The adjacent room used by the ARP wardens was also flattened, sadly along with the wardens themselves.

When War was declared by Britain in September 1939, and even during the War, people often didn't understand what was going on. People were asked to do very different jobs, to make sacrifices and to do all they could to help the war effort.

The war effort

Everyone, including children, was given an identity card which they had to have with them at all times. Many people still have their cards today.

Gas masks were given to everyone, even babies. The one on the right opposite was known as 'a Mickey Mouse mask' as it had a flap at the front. It was for younger children. The one for babies (opposite left) meant the baby had to go inside the whole thing as shown by the doll in this one.

A Hull fishing trawler taken over by the Royal Navy to act as escort/minesweeper in the North Atlantic. Note the gun added at the front.

The sickening smell of the rubber and the claustrophobic feeling of having the heavy mask on my face have stayed with me forever.

Our teacher showed us how to put on our gas masks. She said "You must not laugh when wearing them." Of course, we girls giggled which made them vibrate. This caused a very rude raspberry noise which made us laugh even more!

If you blow whilst wearing your mask it makes a really horrible whistling noise.

At school we had to parade around the hall with our gas masks in the boxes and then take them out.

A gas mask for babies

A Mickey Mouse Gas Mask

Rationing of food, clothing and heating fuels was introduced adding extra pressure on those still at home. Rationing meant that you were allowed a certain amount of food each week plus a small amount of coal to keep the house warm and a very limited amount of clothing. Children often became good at finding things to burn and mothers learnt to manage very economically. This, in part, was encouraged by promotional material from those running the war effort.

© Imperial War Museum

Some of the suggestions as to what people might do to help the war effort were serious, such as keeping children and families healthy. Other suggestions were not always realistic, such as 'Dig for Victory' which, if you lived in a town without a garden, was just not possible. Another suggestion was that people should collect metal so that it could be used to make guns. Park railings were taken by the Government, to be made into weapons, and metals of all kinds were collected. People felt they were helping the war effort but many of these piles of metal were never used.[ii]

© Imperial War Museum

I wasn't evacuated as my parents wanted us to stay together as a family. In our local park all the metal railings were taken away so anyone could go to the park whenever they wanted. The only things that were left were the park gates. These were opened and closed every day so that the people knew when the park was open and closed!

My mother sold our clothing coupons to give us some extra money for food.

My job was to collect as much wood as possible during the week for the fire. There was usually plenty around because of the houses being bombed.

The Government introduced a scheme to try to help children and students keep safe, known as evacuation. They were sent to different parts of the country as well as overseas. Some parents chose for their children to stay at home with them. Some people went with the children as helpers and teachers went too.

Sometimes people had to sell things to help them survive. Children and adults alike became very good at earning a little money, getting things cheaply or selling anything they had, or could make, so there was enough money for food.

© Imperial War Museum

The black market

Many people talked about the 'black market'. What it means is that if someone had say petrol coupons, that they did not want, then they either exchanged them for goods they wanted or for money to enable them to buy what they wanted.

People throughout the War always seemed to know exactly where a certain item was available, or who to contact and how to get it. The feeling was that everyone used the black market. In reality this was not the case but what was true was that people were always willing to help each other out and to share what they had with others.

Being creative

The average person in the street became very creative in 'making do and mending', as the saying goes. They repaired their own shoes, darned socks and patched clothes, made clothes, made wedding dresses from parachute silk, skirts from blackout curtains and cupboards from

old wooden boxes, to name a few. People even made rugs from old rags. Nowadays people do this as a hobby, as the picture on the left shows, but in WW2 it was essential.

People in authority were also creative. Probably, the most important war time creation was the prefabricated house – known as the 'prefab'. These houses were not made in the way houses had been made before the War. They were made in parts which were bolted together, rather like a jigsaw.

My sister had a really frightening experience during the War. Only recently she told her family about it for the first time. They thought she was going mad. At first they didn't believe her.

When I knew I was going to Israel, I took my grandchildren with me so they could see the Holocaust Museum. Here they tell the story of what happened to the Jewish people during the War. I wanted my grandchildren to see for themselves what we, the Germans, did. I hope that they will make sure such dreadful things never happen again.

When I visited the museum in the town in Poland called Auschwitz, I was stunned into silence. None of the films I had seen or books I had read really showed what happened. Everyone was crying, especially the children, as they couldn't understand how their grandfathers could have been part of such dreadful things

People needed somewhere to live as quickly as possible so a way was found to build temporary buildings very quickly. They were cheap to build, easy to install and were warm and cosy for the occupants. They also had running water, electricity and inside toilets that was more than many people had in their previous homes. Families thought themselves very lucky to be offered one in which to live. They were meant to last ten years but a few are still being used today.

Families whose country was at war all suffered

War impacts on everyone. For example, we were at war with Germany yet their rationing system was apparently much harsher than in the UK. Families went hungry because of the lack of food. Many other countries at war with Germany were also hungry.[iii] Poland was probably the country that was bombed the most during the War. Whole towns were completely destroyed and whole families were killed.

People were often affected by what they saw but sometimes managed to make themselves believe that nothing had happened.

People did not always treat other people very well and did not understand about their race or culture. This meant that there was a lot of prejudice throughout the world, that today we would find difficult to understand. In the American Army, black and white soldiers never mixed and were in separate units. In the UK the upper classes were usually the officers. Although these ideas were terrible they were nothing compared to the idea of the German leaders that the whole of the Jewish people should be exterminated. The ordinary German people themselves usually did not know that this was happening. To this day, many of the people who were children during the War in Germany are finding out as much as they can about what happened. Many have said how sorry they are for what happened in the concentration camps, such as Auschwitz in Poland.

The War at home

There was a positive side of war. It brought people together – rich and poor, educated and not educated, working class and upper class. Many large houses were taken over by the people running the country for the war effort, so the rich and poor all missed out. The rich and poor served together in the forces as well as in the factories and on the land. Friendships were made that have often lasted to this day.

> *I kept in touch with Mr and Mrs Judd after I came back from being evacuated with them. I was so homesick for my evacuation home! They came to my wedding.*
>
> *The War gave me the chance to have a wonderful childhood.*
>
> *I don't know how my mother managed. There were five of us children and we were all living in a two-bedroom house which had an outside toilet. We slept four to a bed, two at one end and two at the other so we were head to toe. The baby slept with my mother.*
>
> *There were no men where we lived - they had all gone to war.*

Life was very different:

- there were no televisions
- there was no central heating. The houses were really cold. Usually only one room was heated
- quite a few houses didn't have electricity or running hot water
- many people had baths in front of the living room fire once a week with everyone using the same water
- some houses had outside toilets with no flush
- very few people had a car
- there was very little money about
- even if there was money there was very little choice in the shops anywhere
- families' lives were changed forever

Yet people still smiled and tried to make the most of their lives.

Women

The women left at home

Men volunteered or were enlisted into the Army, Navy or Air Force. Many women also joined the forces and it was a life changing experience for them.

For most of the wives who were left at home this was often the first time they had been on their own, having gone from living at home with their family to being married and living with their husbands. Now they had to make decisions about all matters relating to their home and their children. This was as well as managing the household budget which was often much less than before.

The changing role of women

Women without children or those with school age children were asked to work in factories, often those making ammunition. They also did other jobs that had previously been done by men such as delivering milk to the houses.

Women who lived in rural areas were also asked to work on the land as many of the male workers were away at war. These workers were called the Land Army. The valuable work they did during the War was only recognised in 2008 by the Government.

> *After my husband died I got my papers to say I had to do a war job. They always said if you had a child under a certain age you could choose. I wanted to join the forces, but because mum was looking after my child they offered me different jobs, and welding was one of them. I became a welder.*
>
> *We had uniforms and dungarees, boots with corded trousers for best. The first time I wore trousers was when I went on the farm.*
>
> *"If it was good enough for your sister it's good enough for you," my father said, but I had different ideas.*
>
> *We went to the marine's barracks. How many of you have been to the toilet where a man sat outside with a fixed bayonet as there were no women's loos.*

After the War it was very difficult for these girls and women to come back home and to take on the mundane jobs, which they might have done before or to not to work at all. The younger girls also saw the differences in their sisters and realised there might be better jobs for them too so they started to rebel.

Another problem for families was that when the men came back from war they often wanted to carry on their family life as they had done before which was often difficult as the wives had been making all the decisions for years. Many of the men too had changed and often found it difficult to settle back into the routine of working in a regular job and being a family man.

Those who didn't go to war

Men who had particular skills did not get called up to go to war. Also, people who were disabled who could not fight and people who were older also stayed at home. These people were given jobs, often more than one, to help the War effort. For example, a butcher would do his own work during the day and then in the evening, or during the day if there was an emergency, he might be an ARP warden or fire fighter Women also did this work.

Certain people were in what was known as 'protected occupations'. This meant they were not allowed to go to war as they were needed at home. These jobs were builders who had to make houses safe or rebuild damaged properties after the bombings; electricians, plumbers and gas fitters; shopkeepers such as grocers and clothing store workers; the person delivering coal; doctors and nurses; council officers who helped to run the War effort in their town and farmers who supplied the food for the country.

During the War several voluntary organisations also helped out including the Salvation Army (the Sally Ann), the Women's Royal Voluntary Service (WRVS) and the Red Cross. These groups collected clothes and furniture that people didn't need, so that if a whole house was bombed, for example, they would provide items needed to enable the families to carry on with their lives. They also ran stalls offering hot drinks and snacks both for the workers to buy and for people who had lost their homes. The Red Cross gave first aid and family help, and also worked in hospitals.

Another group who stayed at home were conscientious objectors (CO).These people claimed the right to refuse to perform military service on the grounds of freedom of thought, conscience, or religion. Some conscientious objectors consider themselves pacifists. In the UK during the War conscientious objectors were given alternative civilian tasks as a substitute for conscription or military service. A nurse in Portsmouth told of how the COs were made, day after day, to move the dead bodies and to collect up the body parts and move them to the appropriate places Stories are also told of the abuse these people received as many people saw them as cowards - a view which still exists to this day.

> *When people got bombed there were little shelters set up at the end of the road so people could get a cup of tea or cocoa. So, as kids we would go and get in the queue to get a free drink.*
>
> *When I took a banana into school the teacher put it on her desk and the whole class filed past as no-one had ever seen a banana before.*
>
> *When I had an apple to eat, all the other children rushed round me and said, "Baggus the core." In other words they wanted the core to eat when I had finished with the apple.*
>
> *My mother managed to get us an orange at Christmas.*
>
> *One memory is of our next-door neighbour returning from a visit to the country where he had bought a dozen (very expensive) eggs, supplied as usual in a paper bag. As he closed his front door, an anti-aircraft gun fired a salvo of eight shells right outside his home. It so startled him he dropped and broke all the eggs.*

Food and drink

When thinking about being a child and the War, many people remember their daily dose of a spoonful of cod liver oil (horrid) and a spoonful of malt (some children quite liked it). Children were also given daily doses of orange juice, which was very thick and needed to be watered down – you either loved it or hated it.

One of the things that stay in people's mind is SPAM. It was various left-over pieces of meat with many additives made into slabs of a pinky coloured mixture. Spam is meant to stand for "**S**piced **P**ork **A**nd ha**M**". However there were probably more jokes about SPAM than any other food – 'Something Posing As Meat' and 'Spare Parts Animal Meat.' You had cold spam, hot spam, fried spam, spam in batter, diced spam, sliced spam. Spam was used in so many ways, often disguised, as it was cheap and easy to use and obtain.

As food was rationed parents were very careful with their purchases and learnt to make things last. For instance, a pot of tea might be drunk fresh, then next time heated up with more water added, often more than once until the tea was so weak it had hardly any flavour. Evaporated or condensed milk was used which made the tea taste very sweet and sickly. Bread with sugar on or bread with dripping (the fat left over from cooking meat) was popular for tea. Beetroot sandwiches also come to mind with the beetroot making the bread a purplish red colour and rather wet.

If you were able to grow your own fruit and vegetables you were lucky as at least you had plenty to eat. People did go hungry though, often mothers, who made sure their children had enough to eat.

School and education

Going to school, for some children, was not important for their families during the War. Sometimes children were kept off school to help in the house or to help with their younger brothers and sisters. If they were older they got jobs to bring money into the family budget.

I had 14 schools in 4 years.

Writing books were scarce and precious, so the youngest children used slates for writing and sums.

Eventually, we found a little school in someone's front room. There were about eight children. When we went back one morning nothing was there. The people running the school had been arrested as they were spies.

My parents didn't want me to be evacuated. There were hardly any children where I lived so for some time I didn't go to school. I then had some lessons in the village hall before going to an all-boys' school where they laughed at the huge Navy blue knickers that I wore for PE!

In some areas whole schools were evacuated to another part of the country, which meant the schools closed down. In some towns every school moved away so if a child came back from being evacuated there was no school for them to attend. School uniforms were very formal as this picture shows. Often, children who were evacuated would be homesick or their mothers would miss them so much that the children didn't stay away very long. Gradually, schools would start to open up again if there were enough children though sometimes it was quite a few weeks or months before a child got back into school.

The children who were evacuated often had to share their schooling with the children who were already living there. This may have meant having half day schooling each day, or say two days a week. It often meant having more than one class in one room. The children soon learned to ignore the other group and get on with their lessons.

During the War there was a selection process still running which became known as 'the scholarship' and later the eleven-plus (the 11+). This was a way of sorting out the brighter children and teaching them in grammar schools – this system continued for many years in the

UK. Despite all the upheaval of the War, the selection and examinations still remained. Many children were coached to pass this exam, with parents sometimes borrowing the money to pay for the coaching. They saw it as a way of helping their child to get a better start in life than they had.

The boy wearing the sailor suit in this picture had a schoolteacher who was fond of smacking boys on the legs if they misbehaved. Being smacked or hit with a stick at school was normal at that time. The boy decided to wear the bell-bottom trousers to school – tucked into his Wellington boots. When he mis-behaved the teacher had to struggle to pull the trousers out of the Wellingtons, then roll the trousers up to show his legs. By the time she did all this she was so exhausted she couldn't smack him very hard!

It is really surprising that, despite all of this disruption, children still seemed to manage to get a good education – at least that is what we are told!

> *We went to the local school; the boys and girls were separated even at lunch and playtime by a high wall. This encouraged my sister and I to play truant some afternoons – taking comfort in each other's company- for we were treated as unwelcome intruders by the other children and bullied.*
>
> *Within a week they'd erected new buildings at Eastfield Road School. They were the prefabs. We were the 'prefab kids'. At first, we, of Miss Woodhead's class, attended mornings only, and the next week it was afternoons. The buildings were just temporary, though I believe some still exist.*
>
> *We continued our main education. I swapped two pieces of worthless Costello AckAck shell for a large piece of land mine from the little kid next door. He'd got it from the rubble of six houses on Council Avenue and the fool didn't know it was worth a bomb.*
>
> *My sister's teacher was a grumpy man. Once when Shirley had a bad headache in school, he banged her head on her des, so mum went to the school to complain.*

Having fun

Life was pretty grim during the War no matter how the memories deceive us. In order to lighten their lives people were always looking for an excuse to have a party or at least to have friends or family round for tea. Everyone had to make their own entertainment. Toys were often hand made using scrap pieces of wood, metal, wool or old cloth. Toys were nearly always handed down from child to child until the toy was completely worn out.

In the evening, the whole family listened to the radio – especially to hear news of the War. The radio was powered by a battery/accumulator for those who did not have electricity. There were two parts to the radio; the actual set where the programmes were tuned and the speaker. The set was powered by the accumulator (a large heavy battery) which had to be charged every week at a local shop – sometimes a bicycle shop – while the household's other accumulator was being used. The speaker was powered by the battery, which had to be renewed as necessary.

Families tried to behave as normally as possible and, as now, weddings were a good excuse for a party. It wasn't unusual for there to be a page boy in a military uniform. Most bridegrooms wore their uniform for their wedding. The bride's and bridesmaids' dresses were often made from parachute silk which everyone rushed to get when a parachute came down. The leftover bits of silk were used to make underwear.

Many families had someone who could play a musical instrument so sing-songs were a great way of forgetting your troubles. Quite a few houses and pubs had a piano or a piano-accordion where people gathered round and sang both old and new songs. Children and adults were encouraged to learn to recite poems, tap dance or sing songs to entertain everyone else.

The War was over, so we made a huge bonfire with an effigy of Hitler sitting on an armchair.

I can remember the day the War ended there was a party in the street. I had a big Chinese hat on. I thought I might not get invited but I did. On VJ day we went on holiday to Norfolk and hired a typical seaside country shack, which we learnt later was made of asbestos.

To celebrate the end of the War, the few children left in our street went to Chessington Zoo. I hated it. I had never seen real animals before.

We had a fantastic street party. The whole street got together, brought out tables and chairs. My sister, who worked in a factory, had brought home little round things which were scrap. We covered them with bits of material and made them into hats.

Short and fat, long and thin, we all had fun. Hats out of paper, people recited poems, sang songs and did the conga.

As soon as people realised that the War was ending they started making plans for huge parties – for friends and families, for neighbours and also for the men coming home from War.

Conclusion

To this day, if someone is in need, such as if the house is flooded for example, people rally round and help out. It is sometimes referred to as their 'war effort'. This spirit of supporting and helping others is what many people remember about the War. By having fun and seeing children enjoying themselves it made the dreadful side of the War just a little easier to bear.

8th June, 1946

TO-DAY, AS WE CELEBRATE VICTORY, I send this personal message to you and all other boys and girls at school. For you have shared in the hardships and dangers of a total war and you have shared no less in the triumph of the Allied Nations.

I know you will always feel proud to belong to a country which was capable of such supreme effort; proud, too, of parents and elder brothers and sisters who by their courage, endurance and enterprise brought victory. May these qualities be yours as you grow up and join in the common effort to establish among the nations of the world unity and peace.

George R.I.

The Government acknowledged the end of the War by giving every child a copy of this certificate.

Part 2

Personal stories

The best part of keeping chickens was the eggs they laid. They were lovely, I can almost taste them now even though we usually had one egg between two of us as we sold the rest. Before we kept chickens my mother had to use powdered eggs as our normal ration was two eggs a week for our whole family.

On bath days, usually once a week on a Friday, my mother had to heat the water on the stove (usually over the open fire but sometimes on the gas cooker if we were short of wood or coal) to fill a tin bath which was kept in the garden and brought indoors to use. We all bathed in the same water, including my mother when we had gone to bed. We bathed in front of the fire as that was the only room in the house that was heated. We got out, dried ourselves, put our pyjamas on plus a jumper on top and socks and ran upstairs to bed as fast as we could so as not to get too cold.

When I was evacuated, I remember having to race home from school with four other kids as the last one home got to go in the tin bath last. I was the youngest and littlest – so guess who always got the cold dirty water?

Life at home during the War

During the War, life was very different for everyone, even when they stayed at home:

- windows were boarded up
- blackout boards and/or curtains covering every piece of light in a house that might show through
- 5-watt light bulbs, if you had electricity installed
- gardens dug up and Anderson shelters built
- blast walls built in some gardens
- no lights on vehicles or on trains
- severe food shortages
- everything rationed from food and sweets to clothes and furniture
- bombings and being blitzed
- people being killed everywhere

…and yet some families chose for their children not to be evacuated but to stay at home. Other children did go away but were so homesick that they were not able to stay. Others were ill-treated so were brought home, often by a parent who went to fetch them.

There are many stories of people keeping chickens and rabbits in their garden with the idea that the families would get the eggs from the chickens and eventually the animals could be killed and eaten to add to their small rationed supplies. As most people had never owned animals before these were not always cared for as they should have been.

The most difficult thing was when the time came for the animals to be killed for eating. Some people just could not do it. It upset them too much. There was also the problem of plucking the chickens or skinning the rabbits. Some people had local butchers who were willing to help out in exchange for a share of the meat but often the chickens and rabbits just stayed in the gardens as pets.

As the War continued so those running the country needed more money. The Government felt that the people of Britain would be happy to make sacrifices for the War so they reduced the money people were given even more. Money was really tight.

So which was right? Staying at home or being evacuated?

It is not possible to know whether it was best for a child to stay at home or be evacuated. Every parent made their own decision based on what they thought was best for their particular child.

Certainly the children who stayed at home saw dreadful bombings, saw houses being blown up and people being killed. These children mainly had their parents close by and so could feel their warm affection. Children who were evacuated were physically safer but usually lacked, and often missed, the closeness of home.

In the remaining part of this section there is a series of people's own stories of their war time experiences.

Staying at home

John Parsons stayed at home but had evacuees in his house - One nation two cultures!
In 1940 I was six years old, living with my mother, my newborn baby brother, Keith, and our family dog, 'Smut', in an isolated cottage, 'Kitescroft', in the hills above Westbury, Sub-Mendip, Somerset. Dad was a seaman in the Royal Navy.

Kitescroft was a 'two rooms downstairs, one and a half upstairs' stone cottage, a mile from the centre of Westbury village. It was the highest house in the village. In good weather the view was splendid, but the cottage had no electricity, water or gas at all. Cooking was by oil-stove or the kitchen range, heating by the range or wood/coal fire. Lighting was by oil lamp or candle. The toilet was a bucket under a seat in a shed in the garden. Water came from the well down the road.

The nearest home to us was the farm owned by Mr Allen, down the lane and on the junction, with a dead-end side lane. Next to the farm, Mr and Mrs Spearing and the boys lived in part of a cottage owned by Mr Allen and both adults worked at the farm. Mr Allen's pigman, a strange and solitary man, lived in the smaller part. He preferred pigs to people and nobody seemed to know his name. An elderly couple, Mr and Mrs Franks, lived in a bungalow at the end of the lane. Mr Franks kept bees and supplied honey. Across the main lane and slightly nearer the village, a Mr Conway had a bungalow. He was rarely at home and was rumoured to be a Methodist minister.

It was into this environment that, unannounced, a family of evacuees arrived one day.

Mum had taken a long time to recover her strength after Keith's birth and was just getting back to normal when the arrival of the evacuees in late summer of 1940 completely changed our lives. Thinking back and having read books and seen TV on the subject, I believe this first batch of evacuees was a trial run, especially as after several months they all returned to London.

Cars up our lane were a rarity, and as in 1940, British servicemen were being killed regularly in the War, a car containing a policeman and a suited official stopping outside was dreaded. So when a car came up our lane and stopped outside, mum went into an instant panic. She told me to come and stand by her saying, "Something terrible has happened to dad." Luckily, the police sergeant knew the family and shouted: "Don't worry, May, Stan's OK. We're here about something else." The man in the suit was familiar but I didn't know his name. Some other people were still in the car.

The sergeant waited outside while the man talked to mum, who then took him inside and upstairs. After a short while they came back down. Mum then explained to me that the people in the car were going to stay with us. I'd have to give up my little room and sleep in the big room with her and Keith and the new people would use the little room. She said they'd been evacuated from London. A woman and a boy, a little older than me, then got out of the car carrying suitcases, which they took indoors. Mum started to make a cup of tea and I was told the boy's name was Robert and the lady, Mrs Richards.

The official and the policeman went to the car and brought in some folding beds and piles of blankets which they took upstairs. They rearranged the furniture in both bedrooms and put up the beds. Mrs Richards and Robert had been on trains and buses all day and went up to bed straight after having tea. Mum and I went to bed just before it got dark, our usual habit in the summer.

Mrs Richards was not very pleased when she came downstairs next morning. Like many Mendip cottages the floors in the bedrooms in Kitescroft were rough cut planks. The gaps allowed light and heat from the room below to rise up and avoided the necessity of lighting bedroom fires. Over the years, Kitescroft's boards had worn pretty smooth but could still produce splinters. Moving the furniture could have exposed areas that were usually covered and Mrs. Richards had found splinters in her feet.

She was even less happy when she discovered that if she wanted hot water to wash, and to have tea, it meant heating two lots of water on the Primus stove. Mum had already been down to the well to bring her a fresh bucket of water.

Her visit to the toilet raised the temperature even more – she didn't like the smell or choice of toilet paper, ranging from pages of shiny catalogues, newspapers to tissue paper. The weekly emptying and burial of the contents of the toilet was another blow to her.

Robert slept late, but when he came down seemed quite happy not to have a morning wash! He made his first mistake when I was giving Smut his breakfast (our scraps plus dog biscuits). Smut approached him to make friends but Robert kicked him away. Smut did not retaliate directly, but for the rest of his stay Robert had to walk round him!

Mum showed Mrs Richards how to operate the bucket in the well, and after everyone was washed, dressed and breakfasted, took Mrs Richards and Robert round to meet the neighbours. I think Mrs Richards thought they were country bumpkins, but she soon learnt that both Mrs Allen and Mrs Franks were better educated and from a higher class than herself. Robert met Pete and Arthur Spearing for the first time.

Mr Phelps, or one of his staff, had delivered our usual quantity of milk that morning, but with two extra people it was used up by the afternoon. Mum sent me down to Mr Phelps farm at evening milking time for an extra can of milk and told me to show Robert where to go.

In the field that surrounded Kitescroft on three sides, Mr Phelps had put his recently weaned young cows. With Robert, I crossed the stile in our fence and started walking down the slope to Phelps farm. The young cattle saw us and, as often happens, started following us. As they came nearer, Robert became terrified and said, "The 'bulls' are chasing us." He stayed with me and we reached Phelps' farm. I asked one of the milkers for mum's extra milk and he filled the can. He then asked me and Robert if we wanted a drink of milk and filled two mugs straight from a cow. I drank mine, but Robert said, "This isn't proper milk – milk comes from a bottle." And refused to drink.

We started walking back up the slope for home and the calves had spread out in the field. Robert stayed with me most of the way, but as the young cattle started to follow he became more nervous. About 100 yards from our fence he bolted full tilt. Of course, the young animals followed at a run.   When I reached home a few minutes later Mrs Richards was screaming at me that I had risked her son's life taking him through a herd of bulls. After suppressing her laughter, mum finally convinced Mrs Richards that the calves were no risk.

Mrs Richards wanted to go to the shops and on Thursday, the day mum drew her allowance for dad's pay, mum, with Keith in the pram and me walking, took Mrs Richards and Robert down to the village. After drawing her allowance mum usually left her shopping list in the shop, then went up to Mr Fisher's cycle/battery shed to charge her accumulator which we needed for our radio. She then collected her groceries on the return journey. Mrs Richards also ordered her groceries and ordered 'delivery'. The fact that the shop didn't deliver surprised her.

Things settled down a bit after a couple of weeks but Mrs Richards didn't seem content. After a few clashes with Pete Spearing, Robert seemed to be adjusting to our small gang and had realised that even Arthur Spearing, the youngest could outrun, outclimb and knew the countryside better than he did.

When the autumn came school started. Robert, and about six other five to eleven-year-old evacuees, had to join the village school. Over-eleven-year-olds had to catch the train to Wells each morning and return in the afternoon. The village school had six classes in two classrooms, being taught by a headmistress and one other teacher. The headmistress lived on the school premises and taught five, six and seven-year-olds in classes one to three. Each classroom had three columns of desks with the junior classes on the teacher's left. In autumn 1940, I was in class two and sat in the middle row. Robert was placed in class three in the right hand column. Writing books were scarce and precious so classroom one used slates for writing, sums etc. Mrs Richards did not approve of this and complained to the headmistress, to no effect.

The headmistress was a disciplinarian and stood for no nonsense. A list of sanctions was operated in classroom one – standing in a corner, staying in at playtime, smacked bottom (boy or girl) or finally being sent home with a letter for parents.

Each child was allowed one toy in the classroom and Robert incurred a smacked bottom for hitting a girl and taking her toy from her. Most children did not tell their parents about a smacking as parents would probably provide a second dose. Robert told his mum and a heated exchange with the headmistress occurred.

Robert continued to learn a bit of country lore as the autumn progressed and after two painful experiences accepted that young Arthur Spearing was right to walk around the stinging nettles rather than use the short route straight through them. However, as the nights drew in he made himself a source of ridicule by telling a couple of his fellow Londoners that we had wolves around Kitescroft. The story spread and the Spearing boys and I were asked to confirm it. Of course, we couldn't as we knew the noises were made by foxes.

Mrs Richards, however, made a more serious mistake. The blackout was in existence and enforced by the ARP warden. One evening, the local ARP warden, in his navy blue battledress called and said it had been reported that someone at Kitescroft had been flashing lights at night, perhaps to the Germans. As mum and I only had an oil light or candles we obviously couldn't flash a message. Robert gave the lead to the answer – he said Mrs Richards had a torch. She hated going to the toilet in the dark so had bought a torch and used it when walking down and coming back from the toilet. The warden stared at her and I believe threatened her with court action. She observed the blackout after that.

The evacuees were organised by the gentleman who had supervised Mrs Richards' and Robert's arrival. He still had his normal job (a clerk in a solicitor's office, I believe) so the evacuee office was only open Saturdays, when buses didn't run to Wells. The evermore-disgruntled Mrs Richards wanted to see him to change accommodation to live in Wells and asked mum how she could get there.

Farmer Allen had a putt – a one-horse general purpose cart with vertical sides and back about 18 inches high, which then sloped outwards – which he, Mrs Allen or one of his men drove to Wells market each week. If the bed of the cart was loaded, passengers could lean against the sloping boards with their feet on the load or if the bed was clear, plank seats could be placed across. After Mrs Richards' request, mum said she would speak to Mrs Allen to see if a lift to Wells was possible. It was and Mrs Richards was told to be at the farm by 7.00 am on Saturday. I don't know if mum told Mrs Richards that it was a horse-drawn vehicle or not but Mrs Richards apparently thought it was a motor car.

Mrs Richards and Robert left early in the morning. She returned that evening in a flaming temper.   As luck would have it some piglets that had just been weaned from their mother, were being taken to market and were in the putt. 'Pigman', with his own smell, was also making one of his rare trips to Wells. One of Mr Allen's workers was driving that day and only a couple of other ladies, whom Mrs Richards did not know, were passengers.

Mrs Richards apparently did not get much satisfaction from the evacuee office, but the drivers, 'Pigman' and the ladies had enjoyed the market with its extended licensing hours. On the return journey a comfort stop was needed – to Mrs Richards' outrage, the driver had a 'pee' by the nearside wheel whilst still holding the reins. In fact this was the legal requirement.

After a strained weekend, Mrs Richards and Robert left Kitescroft early on Tuesday morning and did not return that evening. When mum looked, their packed suitcases were in the room. These were collected by the evacuee officer some days later, together with the folding beds and blankets. Mum was told that Mrs Richards had decided to go back to London.

Mum, Keith and I lived at Kitescroft for another 18 months before we had to leave it empty. Mum, a known needlewoman and seamstress, had been directed to work sewing uniforms in a factory in Wells. This made living in Kitescroft impossible so we moved to my grandfather's house in Wells.

The other evacuees around Westbury also returned to London, soon after Mrs Richards. The next wave of evacuees was much better organised.

Rosemary Clarke - *On wash days there was always an unforgettable smell of boiling clothes*

My mother lived with her parents and her brother, Will, in Hatfield Road, Ipswich, in what was probably quite a 'smart address' when they first lived there! Will moved away and we didn't have much contact with him during my childhood.

I understand that my grandfather (whose family were crofters on the Isle of Lewis, Outer Hebrides) lost his job and then became ill. He died in 1940 following a fall downstairs. This left my grandmother and mother, who had to move from Hatfield Road into a council house in Rands Way, Ipswich. My mother worked to support herself, her mother and later, me. She worked until she retired in her late 60s.

At some stage, my mother met her future husband, James Hepburn, who was seven years younger than she was. He served in the Merchant Navy. I can only assume that she met him when his ship docked in Ipswich. I was born on 26 November 1941, apparently the night of the first serious bombing of Ipswich Docks.

The nursing home was only a couple of hundred yards from the docks. Mothers and babies were taken down into the basement of the nursing home for protection. When I was naughty as a child, I can remember my mother saying, "They must have mixed you up with another baby as you are far too naughty to be mine." As I was the only baby born that day who had ginger hair, she guessed they must have got it right.

I understand that my father chose my name (Rosemary = Remembrance). I know that my father did see me once when his ship brought him to England. His ship was torpedoed three times, once off Harwich after sailing out of Ipswich. The third time was off Tristan da Cunha. His parents received a letter from the ship's carpenter saying he had seen my father in charge of a lifeboat, smiling as he always did, but nothing more was seen of him. The ship is recorded as having been officially lost on 31 October 1942, just before his 26th and my first birthday.

As a child, nothing was said about my father. He was certainly not forgotten, as photographs were displayed around the house and I was allowed to see his war medals (which I still have). I can only assume that life was so difficult and the grief so deep for my mother who was trying to bring up a small child and look after her mother whose health was failing.

Eleven Rands Way was a typical council house but to a small child, it seemed huge! We had a cupboard with a triangular door under the stairs in the hall. I remember locking my grandmother in the cupboard, then going out to play in the garden, leaving her to wait for my mother to come home from work. This must have been when I was very young as she died during the hard winter of February 1947 when I was just six.

In our house there was a front room which we hardly used. The back room where we lived had an open fire. This led into the kitchen, where we had a copper for doing the washing.

The copper was used on Mondays, whatever the weather, to boil up the water. I remember my grandmother pounding the washing with a copper stick.   We also had a mangle. This had two rollers and you pushed each piece of washing through as you turned the handle. The idea was to get as much water out as possible.

On wash days there was always an unforgettable smell of boiling clothes which went right through the house. The clothes were put out on the washing line, if the weather was good, but the line often broke as the washing was very heavy. If it was raining the washing was draped around furniture and the open fire. This made the house feel damp.

Two steps down from the back door there was the garden. My mother spent a lot of her spare time gardening and I had my own little plot which I can remember digging. I had a friend, Peter Downs, who lived next door and we would talk through the hedge. I remember the secrecy and mystery surrounding the birth of his younger sister – such matters were not discussed!

On the other side was Mr Daldry, with his unmarried daughter, 'Auntie' Muriel, who looked after him and her brother, Fred. Her eventual husband, Uncle Charlie, visited for tea every Sunday, wearing his best clothes.

One of my great delights was to spend time with Mr Daldry and his chickens (most of the neighbours kept them), seeing how brave I could be and how fast I could run when the cockerel chased me. Occasionally, Mr Daldry would kill a chicken and I was allowed to help pluck and draw it (take out the inedible part).

The chickens and their food scraps encouraged rats and I decided I would catch one, using an old paint tin with a piece of bread as bait. I checked the 'trap' every day, but no success, although I can remember the rats running between the gardens.

I was fascinated to watch Mr Daldry shaving with a cut-throat razor, sharpened on a leather strop. The strop was hung on the back door. There was lots of lather which I think came from t

A cut-throat razor and strop

this soap for most things, not just clothes. We had a laburnum tree in the garden and I knew this was a dangerous tree and not to be touched. We also had a large, flourishing, blue hydrangea beside the front door. The property and the garden had to be kept neat and tidy or residents risked being evicted.

The horse-drawn delivery carts were part of our life – the greengrocer, the coalman, the milkman. The horses could be left unattended whilst deliveries were made, standing quietly, munching from their nosebags. Neighbours were 'digging for victory', so everyone collected horse manure. I remember the gardeners rushing out with their buckets to collect the stuff. Sometimes there would be an argument as to which house had the manure outside – making it theirs!

On cold nights, my pyjamas were warmed in front of the fire. I got ready for bed, then raced up to my bedroom to dive under the blankets and the silk puffy eiderdown and search for the stone hot water bottle. Next day's clothes were left under the bedclothes, at the foot of the bed, so they would be a slightly warm in the morning.

I don't know how often we bathed (certainly not every night), but we had a geyser in the bathroom. I would not want to light it if I had one now. I remember my mother approaching it with a taper. It would then roar as the gas caught alight. I wonder how safe it was – but we survived! We cleaned our teeth using a brush and solid blocks of Gibbs toothpaste - which came in different coloured tins.

We had a cupboard at the top of the stairs where the gas masks were stored. I can remember being made to try one on – the sickening smell of the rubber and the claustrophobic feeling of having the heavy mask on my face remain with me.

I can't remember much about wartime food (perhaps because it was so forgettable). I do remember being given stewed eel for my first school dinner. We were made to eat it, because there was nothing else. I do remember going into the hall cupboard under the stairs and drinking vinegar from the bottle, and have always loved it since! We are told that my generation has probably got better teeth than later generations because we didn't have sugar or many sweets.

Across the road was a Co-op (which I remember calling the 'Cop Stores'). This had an arrangement for moving cash from the tills to a mysterious office on the first floor. You put the money in a container, attached the container to a wire, pulled a handle and the container was carried along the wire to the office.

I was allowed to run errands for the neighbours who would reward me with the occasional ration token to spend on sweets, but this was a very rare event! Children were supervised but I think we had much more freedom than children these days. Once we had learned to cross the road, we were allowed to go to the shops and to the local recreation ground.

I can remember the sound of sirens and of aircraft engines, and the shade of the central light in my bedroom swaying in the night air. I can remember going down into the Anderson shelter, which was in the Abbotts' garden, next door but one. Before going down into the shelter, my grandmother was sitting under the kitchen table, clutching her handbag, which apparently contained her pension book.

Mary Hill - *the GI's were rushing around wildly, trying to catch the escaping animals, with more enthusiasm than skill!*

I was born at Blackdown Farm, Upham, Hants and lived there during the early part of the War. In 1940, we moved to Pastures Farm, East Meon and then to Comphouse Farm, Southwick, in 1942. At that time all of this area was subjected to many air raids because the accuracy of the bombing was not very good.

When we moved to Comphouse Farm, several bombs had fallen close to the farmhouse. Fortunately they didn't cause too much damage. To everyone's great relief there were no more close by. My best friend was called Pat and she lived on another farm about two miles away. We cycled to visit one another very often.

Southwick House, which was next to our farm, was taken over from the Thistlethwaite family in the early part of the War, and became known as HMS Dryad. It was chosen to be the centre of the D-day operations.

By April 1944, the preparations for D-day were well under way. I was eleven years old and a pupil at the local secondary school. A great many troops had already moved into the area, ready for the invasion of France. There was a British gun emplacement at Pinsley, about half a mile away, and a small Canadian emplacement at the end of Pitymore Lane (the way to the farm).

One damp April afternoon, when I got off the bus, my mother had come to meet me, which was most unusual. I soon discovered the reason – the American Army had moved in – chaos reigned! An American lorry had collided with a lorry full of pigs and the GIs (the nickname for the American soldiers) were rushing around wildly, trying to catch the escaping animals, with more enthusiasm than skill!

One American found time to greet my mother, "Hi, mam, do you have another daughter about 18?" My mother declined to reply. However, generally, the soldiers proved to be polite and friendly. We got on with them very well.

In the next few days, the surrounding woods became full of American troops, busy setting up camp, making concrete hard standing for the vehicles and cinder roads. The lane to our farm was closed, so the only vehicles allowed were the milk lorry and occasionally the vet.

Our groceries and bread had to be left at the shepherd's cottage about half a mile away. Although my father still had his car, we all made most of our trips to the village by bicycle. Bicycles were the main means of transport for most people in those days. My friend, Pat, and I still managed to meet regularly and made the most of these exciting times.

By this time, General Eisenhower was established in his headquarters in Sawyers Wood, about a quarter of a mile from the farm. He lived in a type of mobile home/caravan.

The entrance to our farm had become a three-way junction. With so much traffic a military policeman was always on duty. Pat and I sat on the garden fence after school, especially on Thursdays, when the soldiers received their sweet ration. Needless to say we were given quite a lot!

General Montgomery was living two miles away, at Broomfield House. The King, Winston Churchill and many other important service chiefs came to Southwick House regularly. When they passed by our place on the way to Broomfield House, we sometimes caught a glimpse of them, in huge staff cars with motorcycle outriders.

When the Americans moved in they took over our barn as a concert hall for the soldiers. All sorts of entertainment took place. The best bands played there and films were shown before they were released for the public to see.

There were also dances, to which the local WRNS (Women's Royal Naval Service) and ATS (Auxiliary Territorial Service) girls were invited as well as Pat and me when it was deemed suitable. Rumour has it that Glen Millar performed there.

My mother would leave the front door open, and put newspapers and magazines in the sitting room so that some of the soldiers could come in and have a quiet time. On one occasion, Sergeant Don Hillier, whom we had got to know quite well, pointed to a headline in the Daily Mail that referred to SHAEF (Supreme Headquarters Allied Expeditionary Force). "That's us, you know." he said.

On one occasion, I had not been well, and had a few days off school. Eisenhower's cook, known as Ike just like the General, came round with a box of chocolates that he himself had made for me. They were made of plain chocolate that I didn't like, so the adults ate them. Chocolates at that time were unobtainable, so the present was much appreciated. I often wish I had kept the box.

Another time some of the men came round with a bag of corn. This puzzled my mother, so she said she would give it to the chickens. The Americans were horrified. It was popcorn and considered a great treat. We had not come across it before so they cooked it for us. We didn't like it much - but didn't tell them.

Sargeant Don Hillier with Peter the kitten, Pat and Rosemary

We used to get a lot of air raid warnings, both day and night. I think the first of the doodlebugs (V1s pilotless planes) were coming over by then. It was very worrying as we didn't know where they would land once the engines cut out.

The American warning siren was higher-pitched than the civilian one, and often went off a few minutes earlier than ours. Our little terrier, Jock, knew all about the American siren – I wonder if his ears were more sensitive to the sound? If the siren went off when he was out in the fields, he would race home and go straight into the cupboard under the stairs that we used as an air raid shelter. He was not above hitching a lift on a passing jeep, which the soldiers found most amusing.   They were always happy to pick him up.

I remember D-day because at sunset on 5th June 1944, the sky was full of gliders. On the morning of 6th June when I was on my way to school there was an unusual amount of activity everywhere and staff cars were rushing about at high speed. At mid-morning, our head teacher came into the classroom and said, "This day will be very important in history, the D-day landing has begun."

Most of the Americans left soon afterwards, though some stayed well into August. When they had all gone, black American soldiers came to do the clearing up. They too were friendly, not at all intimidating. We found it difficult to understand that black and white soldiers were simply not allowed to meet.

That was it really. By mid-autumn all the American soldiers were gone, the air raids were easing off, and I settled down to life as before.

Bob's Middlebrooke's memories from the diary he kept - The end of the War celebrations

The main events of 1945 for me were the two-stage ending of the War. We must have known it was coming because my friends and I were busy collecting wood for a bonfire. I had never seen a bonfire before. Our source was Boothferry Park, the uncompleted base for Hull City AFC. It was started before the War and the stands were rough hills set with old railway sleepers to stand on. The sleepers were heavy but burned extremely well. Bunkers Hill, as we called the complex, was our playground.

I remember VE (Victory in Europe) day we had a party in the street. All my uncles could play instruments. We brought the piano into the street and we had a party. I remember my gran had a dress made from a Union Jack.

On Tuesday 8 May, it was VE Day. I went to school and they marched us off to a church service but then we had one and a half days' holiday. My diary says 'we nailed Hitler to a swastika and lit the bonfire at 9.30 pm.' We need not have bothered lugging sleepers for the fire. All the grown-ups arrived carrying wooden blackout shutters freshly taken down from the windows.

VE Day bonfire party with an effigy of Hitler nailed to a wooden swastika

A few weeks later it was the 'Peace party' in our street. The grown-ups had a sort of fire-watching and refuse-collecting committee. One day, a marquee arrived on our field. At the party we started with a 'Punch and Judy Show' followed by a tea, which mainly consisted of cream cakes, custard, jelly, blancmange and iced chocolate buns. Then we had races followed by a concert with music provided by a hired band. I remember a lady accordion player whose surname was Dixon. We sat by yet another bonfire and had free ice cream, sweets and lemonade.

Then there was more wood-collecting. No wonder Boothferry Park was a year late in opening! On 14 August it was VJ Day (Victory in Japan) and yet another bonfire.

More was to come. Saturday 1 September was the Seaton Grove VJ party. We had races. I came fourth in the flat and second in the sack race. Then there was a fancy-dress parade. My mother dressed me up as Little Lord Fauntleroy, a character I'd never heard of, nor had anyone else. I had my best suit on with bits of lace pinned to the cuffs and collar. I won a painting set and one shilling and sixpence. I then had a really jolly hour with the magician and his conjuring tricks. There was ice cream, lemonade and apples. After supper we all sang songs and I went to bed at 3.00 am.

There was one final party. My friend Gordon's father arranged for us to attend the Sons of Temperance party at a chapel, down St. Georges Road. I remember the jelly and custard. I never knew what temperance meant.

The end of the War is very vivid: bonfires, (and my parents dancing around one). The bonfires terrified me. We had bunting, the street lights came on for the first time for years, there were street parties and a lot of drunken revellers. I also remember signs, soon afterwards, on the houses to greet returning soldiers. 'Welcome home, Jack' and queuing for those exotic bananas and oranges which we hadn't seen for years.

Jean Emery - *All the tanks came zig-zagging along as the soldiers couldn't drive very well*

We lived in Shedfield, Hampshire when the War started and then moved to Curdridge, close by. Throughout the War we went to Curdridge school but my brother stayed at Shedfield school. When we went to school, if the sirens sounded, we had to run into a ditch or to someone's house.

Around 1940 my family took in evacuees. We had five families in our house at one point. We had twenty rooms and there was a big tunnel under the house which we used as a shelter. All my father did was to get some tree trunks to strengthen it.

We had a family from Gosport, and my mother, thinking they would be OK, gave them her bed, but they were filthy and in less than two weeks they had wrecked the lot. Mum had them thrown out. A lot of people had trouble with evacuees. Us country children had not experienced anything like it, the evacuee children were fighters. After that dreadful experience, my mum only had business people to stay. Waller's supermarket people came and we had no more problems.

At the top of the four-story house, there was a magistrate from Southampton. She used to come downstairs with her candle. We'd tell her to hurry up as we were just going to put the lights out. Luckily, my mother didn't hear us as she would have gone mad.

People were often desperately poor. That's why the people in the big houses took on girls as servants and boys as gardeners – it gave them a chance in life.

In 1942 we had all the soldiers around in the copses next to us – English. The Canadians were down the bottom end of Curdridge, then some Poles came to Outlands Lane to learn to be pilots. The soldiers by us were there for quite some time. When we used to go to school we couldn't go along certain roads when the soldiers were having deliveries. This particular afternoon, in June, it was very hot, the soldiers tried to stop us going through. Apparently Churchill and Montgomery were there in the officers' tent but we didn't take any notice – they were planning for D day we learnt later.

In the evening the soldiers came to our house for strawberries and cream. The sad part was, when they left the area they put a plaque up in Churchill's walk - Montgomery's Leap - by a ditch. That was there for 40 years. The people who, later, bought the land, cut the tree down, threw away the sign and that was history lost. People in Curdridge knew nothing about it.

The Americans were in Bishop's Waltham, Medstead and Newbury so the locals there had lots of food because the Americans had plenty and shared it out.

When they went over to France, all the soldiers who were by us were killed. We used to ask them their names - Kendrick and Western were two - and I can remember them today. When they arrived, they filled in the ditches. Another time we were in the field, whilst the soldiers were with us. An aeroplane was on fire. The soldiers jumped over the gate to help. It was a terrible experience

At school we had 48 in the class. The evacuees used to frighten us. They loved fighting. They were so dirty, full of flees and lice.

When we went to school we could look out over Eastleigh and see all the barrage balloons. It was a lovely sight. One morning I thought I would go looking for chestnuts. I was in the copse when the siren sounded and I thought nothing would see me. The plane was coming over dropping bombs. Luckily I rushed to the nearest building, which was a cow shed. I got in trouble from my father for not going home. Another time, when I was making daisy-chains, a dog-fight started and I had to run into the cow pen. We experienced an awful lot in those days.

I can remember when they took the gliders to Arnham. The sky was black with gliders. "Come out here mum, there are a lot of planes in the sky." I said. Those boys who went over were all killed within about three hours.

When we were at school, the siren used to sound and the teacher was so frightened she hid in the cupboard and we had to tell her when it was all clear. We just stayed in our chairs. One day, the teacher said to us "Tomorrow, there is going to be a lot of tanks through here so, when they come, jump in a ditch or in the field." All the tanks came zig-zagging along as the soldiers couldn't drive very well - they crashed into the baker's van and killed a girl. There is a memorial stone in Botley.

One morning a doodlebug came and then the engine stopped. Then suddenly there was a terrific bang. The doodlebug had landed on a pig farm in Curdridge. There were dead pigs all over the road. What a mess that was.

Our teachers were very poor. Towards the end of the War better teachers came back from war or evacuation and got their jobs back. They were as brown as berries.

Clothes were mainly handed down and anything new was bought using coupons. I remember tearing my dress on a tree and was given a good hiding. Living in the country we missed out because there were no shops. One time we went to buy shoes but there was nothing left. We used to have to wear our clothes until they were really old and faded – even if we didn't like them. We never threw anything away. My mother bought boys' shoes for us as they lasted longer.

My father ran the farm so he was not called up. We had an allowance for food but, because we had animals and vegetables on the farm we were very lucky. My father used to give a lot away to the poor. We were brought up to work on the farm. As the War ended, I can remember we had the Navy lads sent along as we had no labour. I can see them now – cropping beans.

At the tail end of the War we had the Italian and Germans helping us on the farm. The Italian POW camp was in Newtown, near Bishop's Waltham. The Germans were in camps all over the place and were brought to the farm by lorry. Some stayed in the farm buildings. Initially they were guarded with guns as they worked. The Germans were also at Fairthorne Manor. Lots of Germans surrendered so they could get out of the War. They didn't want to fight. The Germans worked very hard. They loved playing instruments and my father used to go to Southampton to buy accordians for them. We had lovely evenings listening to them playing. That was their pleasure after they had been working. The Germans and the Italians worked hard. Some brought their families over after the War, and my father paid them well and he got the benefit from them because they worked so hard.

As the men came back from the War, lots of them worked in factories as they could get more money and we had to rely on casual labour and family labour – like me when I got home from school! It was hard work but we enjoyed it. We planted potatoes by hand, then, when the machines came out, we no longer had to do it.

Celebrations? We didn't really have any in Curdridge. We were always too busy to celebrate. My father was always working. I hardly ever saw him.

After the War we didn't keep in touch with anyone because everyone was doing their own thing.

John Stirling - *so I volunteered for the air force but by the time I got kitted out the War was over*

In 1939 I was 12 years old. We lived in a tenement building outside Glasgow, six miles outside the city centre. My father was a coalman, going round selling coal. In order to supplement the family income I became a caddy at the local golf club.

Most people went to War, but there were still some golfers left. There were no trolleys or buggies. I was paid two shillings to carry the bag of clubs plus 6d tip if the player did not lose the ball that he started with.

I was a good footballer but gave it up. I sold my boots to buy two second hand golf clubs - a 4 iron and a 7 iron. A man gave me a putter. In the long clear evenings when the members had finished playing I used to go to practise as far away as possible from the clubhouse.

I left school at thirteen – the normal leaving age was fourteen, but because I could already write and spell, the teacher got me to help the other children. The Head came around the class and asked why I was walking around? The teacher told him. I was moved up so I was a year ahead and so left school a year early.

My family couldn't afford to advance my education so I went to the golf club to see if I could get a job. The professional had gone to war. The green keeper said "I need some help, can you start on Monday?"

There were only two of us. We kept the course in good order. We cut the greens, Mondays, Wednesdays and Fridays. We cut the tees and the approaches on Tuesday, and the fairways once a fortnight as fuel was strictly rationed. All the other machinery we used was hand pushed. I used to go home at night absolutely exhausted. The groundsman and I had nothing in common, so I took sandwiches and practised chipping and putting at lunchtime as he was so boring. We worked 7.30am to 6pm, five and half days a week. On Saturdays, we swished the greens, trimmed the holes and raked the bunkers ready for the day's play.

There had been an assistant at another golf club who had access to the lockers there – members paid for shoe and club cleaning. He knew the names of members who had been killed during the War. If no-one collected the clubs after six months he sold them. I bought some from him - mine cost £10. Then I won a competition and the first prize was John Letters woods – I wore the driver out. I loved practising. My idea of golf is to go to a quiet corner to try to do different things with a ball.

I was always practising whilst working as a green keeper. One day the captain asked me if I would like to play a few holes. Later he asked me how I'd learnt to play the way I did. I told him that I'd been a caddy. "We must have you as a member of the club", the captain said. I replied that I could not afford the entrance fee and subscription. He told me not to worry – he would arrange everything. By the time I was sixteen, I was club champion and held the course record at Eastwood Golf Club.

I worked so hard as a green keeper and the work seemed interminable so I volunteered for the air force but by the time I got kitted out the War was over. I was kept in and went to the Middle East but there was no golf there.

When I was demobbed I was entitled to return to my job but I wanted to be a golf professional. I played the West of Scotland championship, thanks to a wealthy butcher who sponsored me, but the desire to be a professional was ever present. After playing an exhibition match with John Panton and Bobby Locke and a Walker Cup amateur, I told Bobby Locke I wanted to be a professional. John Panton advised me to go to England. I took his advice and with £10 in my pocket, my demob suit plus my set of clubs I left. I bought Golf Illustrated and answered an advertisement for an assistant at Roehampton Golf Club. They said if I went along I could meet George Gadd, the professional, who had played in the first Ryder Cup team. He took me on and that was the beginning for me.

I never fulfilled my ambition, of playing in the Ryder cup but I have played with Gary Player and Peter Alliss.

I have no regrets.

Sylvia Glew - *For every dance, I made a corsage of flowers to go on my black dress which was the only dress I had.*

I left school, aged 14, with no ambitions. My mother was in service and she was determined her daughter would do the same. She found me a job - 4 hours in the morning - looking after an elderly couple. I hated it and was determined to get away. I had a cousin who was a butcher boy and he heard of a couple looking for a maid. So my mother sent me there. They were policeman's parents and I worked from 8am – 2 pm. When I was 16 I had a friend who got a job in Southampton High Street and I said I would like to go there. The restaurant owner said they would train me to be a silver service waitress. The bombing started, the café got a direct hit so we were both out of a job.

At that time we had an air raid shelter and when you went to the cinema and there was a raid, they closed the cinema so we walked home through the bombing. I knocked on the front door and no-one heard me, so I went round the back through the terraced house next door. I was going round there and I heard this funny noise like a swishing of paper so I jumped down, then I heard the earth quake and it all went quiet. I got up and went to the shelter but instead there was a big hole where an unexploded bomb was and I fell down on top of it. The dustbin fell on top of the bomb and I fell down inside the dustbin.

I was shouting and yelling and everyone came out. I was annoyed as my hair had just been washed. "Get away from the top of the hole as you as you're making my hair dirty." I said. Someone tore a clothes line down and put a loop on it and they pulled me up. My family was in the air raid shelter and my brother was 9 months old. My mother was nursing him in the shelter and when the bomb dropped it blew him out of her arms. Then she heard me shouting and I stopped. She's dead, I know she's dead but the women next door took me into her house and she gave me half a glass of whiskey and I fell asleep and went to work the next day as though nothing had happened.

We then had to be re-housed so we moved into my aunt's house about a mile up the road. Opposite my aunt was a girl who was in the NAAFI. As I didn't have a job or a home I joined.

The NAAFI was a sort of canteen and a sort of shop for forces personnel. You had to live on the camp site. You cleaned in the morning before breakfast, doing floors etc. then the canteen opened up for a couple of hours, then you had a break and you started work again at 6 until 9 serving in the café. We sold tea, cakes, chocolates and cigarettes on ration so they had to give up their coupons. Then after 9 o'clock you were free to go out. Me being a 'baby' I was in the care of the manageress so I had to be in early at 10 pm. I didn't like that.

There was dancing in the village in Netley. I started to learn to dance but my mother wouldn't let me go to dancing "As only wicked girls did that." I thought up a scheme whilst in the NAAFI - I used to go to bed fully dressed and when everyone was in bed I sneaked out of the window which was quite low, closed it again afterward. I only went dancing until 11 pm. One night someone split on me so the manageress pushed a wardrobe across the window so I was confined to my room for a while.

One of the NAFFI girls was an old maid. At least she looked pretty old to me but I was only 17½. She had grey hair, pulled back in a bun, she never smiled and she served on the corporal side of the bar. She was so slow that all the corporals used to come to our side of the counter as we were very quick at serving. I could pour 3 cups together, 2 in my right hand and one in my left hand.

Then there was a fellow who used to come and play the piano and the guys used to sing. He was married but we used to walk around the grounds at night. He was faithful to his wife but we had a lot in common. We used sit on the grass. That was the most romantic scene of my life. The moon was shining; he sang to me 'You would be so nice to come home to.' It was so romantic and I wished he was not married. One of the girls who served on the corporal side met a man and they courted and married in the chapel at Netley hospital.

I used to serve tea and cakes for the cricket match and they used to collect up some money to give me a tip. They had dances in the NAFFI after the bar was closed. For every dance I made a corsage of flowers to go on my black dress which was the only dress I had. I used to make them for others too.

I used to wander around the grounds at night but there was barbed wire around the beach where we weren't allowed to go. I suppose it was mined. I was always happy there. Everyone who had been there said what a lovely place it was.

The Yanks came and took it over and they didn't exactly pull the NAAFI down but wanted to run it their way - so I was sent to a gun site, at Taunton school.

Working in the NAFFI was great fun. At Netley hospital I befriended a bugle boy and we used to go to the local pub most evenings. There was a civilian sergeant on the gate and he used to tell us to come back sober but we never were - we always rolled back. My bugle boy went to Aldershot and then we lost touch and all the others we knew dispersed to war.

Food rationing – you could get sausages as they were not rationed. We couldn't get nylons so we used to paint our legs with a black line on the back. Girls used to get parachutes for the white silk to make their wedding dresses. If you were getting married you got a few extra coupons for a few eggs but mainly we had dried egg. For a wedding cake you had a tiny fruit cake then you had a bigger one made from cardboard which was iced to look like a real wedding cake. Petrol was rationed.

Signposts were taken down because of spies. We all had identity cards. There was a complete black out, no street lights. Car lights were masked, but there were not many cars. There were doodlebugs, incendiary devices, air raids, sirens went off when enemy planes were sighted. These doodlebugs, you used to hear the engine but when the engine stopped you knew it was time to run as they would hit the ground. Land mines would be dropped by parachute. Incendiary bombs set fire to everything. The ARP warden told you to put lights off if it showed. The home guard patrolled the railway stations and the docks or helped out where they could or if anyone was suspicious they asked for their identity. Girls used to take their gas masks out of the box and then used it to carry make-up in it but people thought they were being good. On Southampton Common there was a prisoner of war camp. There were also lots of the American lorries and small tanks just before D-Day as the overhanging trees camouflaged them.

I think it was the art school near the cenotaph in Southampton that got a direct hit. All the children were killed so they sealed it up. There is a plaque in the park to say what it is.

In Woolston, the super marina - where they built the spitfires - that got a direct hit. There's a tunnel there and it is said that they were bombing the railway line and people in it got hit too. There is a plaque there too.

Where we were staying with my aunt, another time the bombs dropped, one dropped right outside my aunt's house and it blew the soot down over my cousin and girl friend and they managed to run down to tell us they were all right.

I met another soldier in the Royal Engineers, and I ended up marrying him and I went into a civilian job. He went to France but after about a year I got a letter from him saying he wanted a divorce to marry a German girl. Eventually I divorced him – I wasn't going to give him his freedom – him on desertion. Later, I joined the Air Force. As fate would have it I was stationed near where he lived. I was still friendly with his sister and I was still seeing her. Eventually he wrote to me and said he would like to meet me to pay half his divorce fees. We met him and he put his arms around me which I didn't like.

I met another fellow, Peter, and we eventually got married. We had to find a place to live and found a bungalow in Bishopstoke. That was a happy marriage.

Vera Moody - *Everything was so uncertain; you never knew what would happen.*

I was 19 when I got married. I was working in a hotel, waitressing, but I had been in service. Later on I did dinners at The Guildhall, Southsea, and also worked in a restaurant in Osborne

Road. No matter how much money the owner had, when he opened his mouth he wasn't going to be a gentleman! You had to stick up for yourself otherwise they took advantage of you. I worked at the Worth Hotel where I used to do bedrooms, go home for a few hours, and then back and do the dinners. Another job I did I worked at the Beach Hotel where they agreed to pay half my health stamp. I also worked in a hospital. Many nurses didn't get married. They often came in to the hospital when off duty to read to children or look after patients.

I was going to marry someone, but I kept thinking to myself that he would be lowering himself to marry me. He was in the medical corps, training to be a surgeon.

Then I met Eric in a pub (port and lemon 9d) and my dad was talking to him and asked him round for meal. Next time I saw him he was with a girl and was engaged but I still fancied him. He was a Plymouth rating. We were only going together for six weeks before we got married on 2nd December 1939. I wasn't pregnant or anything it was just that the War was on.

You had to save up for everything. If I had a white wedding dress I couldn't have a suit. My whole outfit cost £5. I shopped in C & A for a hat which cost 1/6d. It had lots of specks of yellow and red. I had a real satin blouse which cost 2/lld, shoes 3/- and stockings cost 6d from Woolworths.

My dad paid 30 shillings for the wedding cake which was as big as a dart board.

We went to the marines' barracks. How many of you have been to the toilet where a man sat outside with a fixed bayonet? There were no women's loos!

We were bombed out on 10th January, 1940. My dad had been through two wars and came back from both. Our house had three floors. They dropped bombs on it which went straight through the roof. It was really cold. We had said to my mum "You need a new pair of slippers." When she came out the house she had these old slippers on. There were bricks falling, glass falling yet she never cut her feet. My gran lived next door. Her dog came out and got in the way so was kicked - but it still followed us. A local shop had fur coats where people put them for the summer. This shop was blown open and people were stealing the coats. We were opposite the Garrison church and a vicar was standing outside. He said "Where you are going? You can come and stay in my cellar which is clean and strong."

The Garrison church was hit. We got on a bus, but in the meantime, my husband was coming home but we didn't know that. He got panicky but eventually found us. There was a child staring at us and he remembered us. His mum said "You come home with me to Crofton Road, Milton." We went round and looked at this house, she gave us blankets and a few things from the second-hand shop so we landed up there and that's where we stayed.

The most wicked thing in the War was when they bombed St Thomas Church and the electricity station. They also machine gunned us. The garages had holes in. Neighbours used to help each other even if only providing drinks of water. Our cat and dog survived the War.

My son was born in 1942 in St Thomas Street in Portsmouth. I paid half a crown (2/6d) a week to Landport Bazaar for the pram which cost £5. My husband was killed in 1943. I was out when the telegram came 'missing presumed killed'. I had a good mum but my son doesn't remember his dad.

My friends and I used to go to the 'shilling hops'. I danced with Canadians, but didn't like the Americans. The Canadians always showed you photographs of their families - they just wanted company.

After my husband died I got my papers to say I could do a war job. Because mum was looking after my child they offered different jobs. They said if you had a child under a certain age you could choose. I wanted to join the forces, but instead I became a mechanic – then, later, a welder.

The first job I had was as a car mechanic. I didn't worry about the dirt. No men there. I was once working under a car when I saw that the jack was old and was coming down so I got out quickly.

I was allowed to change to become a welder in the dockyard. I can read anything but I am not a good speller. I had to go to classes for two weeks. Two young lads helped me with writing my notes. Then this bloke asked me a question and they helped me pass. I was given trousers that were far too large, huge gauntlets and a duffle coat that went down to my knees.

I did my first jobs on barges. I had one or two accidents. You had to hold the welder in one hand and the mask in the other. You had to get a wire brush to clean off round where I was to weld. In these landing barges, they were making a hole down one end so they could put a little ladder there. "You'll be alright Vera you can do it." They said. They used to give me a mug of tea.

I always told the foreman I would never work on a Sunday so I could be with my son. He said that was OK. There was one other woman working there. The foreman asked me if I could come in one Sunday as it was urgent. I went in but the boat hadn't arrived so I was told to lose myself. I went up the ramp, under this big ship. It was as big as a liner. No-one stopped me. I told the foreman but he said there was nothing you can do.

My mum brought up my son whilst I was working. Some of the women had to take the children off early. Everything was so uncertain; you never knew what would happen. You just got on with it. I was with my mum for years. Len, my son, went to Naval boarding school but didn't join the Navy.

One day at work some fellers gave me some butter. It was a big piece – too big to go in my tiny sandwich case so I shoved it down the front of my trousers. At the gate I was stopped by an enormous woman. The boys had given me cigarettes too and some sweets for the children. I thought I was going to prison. She was searching me, hitting me all over. She said I could keep the sweets for the children but not the cigarettes. Luckily, she didn't see the butter. The men in the dockyard thought it was a real laugh and kept asking if I'd like a few rashers - but I turned them down!

I went in again the next Sunday but was told to 'just potter around'. "Vera, can you cook?" someone said. There was a lovely piece of beef on the bone and they asked me if I would cook it and make them a batter pudding. The other women couldn't cook so she did the vegetables. Suddenly everything went really quiet. I was basting this beef when this bloke said "I am going to enjoy my lunch today." He had more gold bars on his uniform than any one I'd ever seen!

I stopped welding in 1946. I couldn't be a welder because the men came back and took over the jobs. I then had to do two jobs a day. I went to the greengrocers at Eastleigh in the morning and then on to the cinema as usherette. I woke my son Len up so I could talk to him.

Our milkman's wife took over the milk round during the War, then, when her husband came home he took it back. There was a neighbour who went into the RAF and when he came out he couldn't get a job as his work was not needed any more. You weren't guaranteed a job you when you came out.

I couldn't celebrate the end of the War because I was too sad about my husband. He would never argue. He had been an orphan so had a poor life. I was saying goodbye to him once and he said "It's alright my darling, I'll be back" - but he wasn't.

I did meet someone from New Zealand towards the end of the War but my dad wouldn't let me marry him.

I was never out of work. I then started in a sausage factory where I was paid £7 per week for 46 hours including Saturdays. The working conditions were terrible; we were always wet down our fronts which seeped right through to our underwear. We were given clogs to wear on our feet

as the floor was also soaking wet. Later I was chosen to work the machine that made beef burgers instead. They were a very happy bunch of girls; we were always singing and laughing. We had to scrub the place clean every evening.

If I thought I wanted two weeks off I'd leave a job as there was no

holiday pay in those days. I then went to the labour exchange. I always found some job. I always made sure my health stamps were paid when not working to ensure me and my son had health care.

Michael Galvin - Sparrow is the Irish translation - *They had difficulty understanding me and I couldn't understand them*

I was born in 1923 so was sixteen when war broke out. There was the National News Service in Ireland but people relied a great deal on the BBC Home Service.

The history of Ireland is that in 1922 they came to an agreement on independence headed by Eamon de Valera. At the outbreak of war the Irish Government decided to be neutral during the War.

Ireland relied on Britain for trade interchange. Britain exported all day to day needs into Ireland because at that time there was little Irish manufacturing. The immediate effect of war was that there was a shortage as things were needed for the war effort in UK. The UK Government introduced rationing on certain things but Ireland was not as well organised - rationing sort of happened.

They did make a few changes. One of things they did (Ireland relied on imported wheat in order to make bread) was to start making a sort of wholemeal flour. People used white flour for soda bread even! We got a substandard sort of flour. Day to day things were in short supply - like bicycle tyres – it was almost impossible to get them.

My wife came from Northern Ireland. She told me later that it was difficult to get radios (battery operated) but these were easily available in the Republic because Pye was based in Dublin. People used to go over the border to try to get what they needed despite lots of controls - but smuggling still existed.

The first concern of the Irish Government was security. The Local Defence Force (LDF) was set up. This was similar to the Home Guard in the UK. Just before the War the ports had been handed back by Britain and Winston Churchill made strenuous efforts to get access to the ports because it would make life a lot easier for the British Navy working in the Atlantic. The greatest threat was on the southern and south west coast of Ireland which was undefended. Ireland had a very small army plus a few motor boats but nothing elaborate and the air force hardly existed. Consequently we had to rely on the LDF at the ports at night to watch the coast line. You heard lots of rumours which exist to this day that German U-Boats used to land in Ireland.

Petrol was something that was in very short supply but there were not many cars so it was not too bad. There was no great shortage of clothes and shoes but foodstuffs were a different matter. There was a huge black market in tea - people sold it at enormous prices.

One left school at sixteen but could leave at fourteen. If going on to secondary education your choices were technical schools or to academic college. Education had to be paid for so it was the privilege of the wealthy. Ordinary people couldn't afford to stay on. Books were very expensive. Most colleges had boarders. The convent schools played a big part in the education of girls; most of the teachers were religious. In those days the predominance was that girls went on to religious/caring professions and the boys to the priesthood. The aim was always for the eldest boy at least to become a priest.

In the 1930s, 40s and 50s there were seminaries all over the place. The big drive in those days by the Catholic Church was the conversion in other countries. All the priests from UK went to China to raise funds for the mission. They also went to Middle East countries too.

I left school at fourteen and my father had a small farm. My job was helping him. Farming in those days was mostly rearing of livestock and growing crops. There was a big drive for people to grow more food and be more self-sufficient.

One of the things that the Eamon de Valera Government did was to try to increase the output from the land by prohibiting people leaving so you couldn't emigrate if you lived on the farm, girls were OK but not men. Immigration has always played a big part in Ireland especially in poorer parts. Most families had eight or ten children in those days. Many of girls went into nursing during the War years. Four of my cousins came to England in 1930s to be nurses.

When my brother grew up it was obvious the farm wasn't going to be able to support us both. In Ireland in those days it was tradition that the eldest son would inherit the farm but I decided I would go to England. I wrote directly to the department in Dublin explaining the family circumstances and eventually got a passport. When you got a passport you then had to have an offer of work. I got an offer from an Irishman who was running a pub in Bermondsey and in due course got a visa to allow me to travel. The pub was called The Adam and Eve in Bermondsey. I came in January 1945 and initially stayed with relations in Crystal Palace and travelled to work each day. When I arrived at the pub, the domestic help took me to the town hall to get a ration book and identity card. The next thing to do was to report to the police and they allowed me a three months stay. Eventually I was allowed to stay permanently.

Naturally it was vastly different coming from Ireland. Surrey Docks and Rotherhithe Docks were close by. It was a very poor area. The biggest change, apart from the hustle and bustle of life, was the cockney accent. They had difficulty understanding me and I couldn't understand them. I did find them very warm-hearted and friendly. It was one of the best experiences of my life. Things to a large extent were better than in Ireland.

Rationing was very strict. Where I worked you lived in, so not much experience of the shortages because the pub catered for me. Pubs generally provided cheese rolls at lunch time for people to buy. The pub was the hub of that area, weekends especially. You would know the dockers by day as they came in and out. The dockers came flying in at lunchtime and downed their beer and dashed away to get back. Their break was half an hour. Weekends were different. You saw them in their 'Sunday best'. On Friday and Saturday nights they came to the pub with their wives.

The women who came into the pub would occasionally organise an outing in a coach. They would talk about it for weeks afterwards.

For music, we had a chap who came in and played a dulcima (keyboard) and he would entertain the patrons with songs such as 'She's My Lady Love' and 'Down At The Old Bull and Bush'. In the summer months people went hop picking in Kent. – During the month of July and a lot of August the pub would be very quiet because all the women had 'gone hopping' and many men joined them at weekends.

Sometimes there would be a short supply of beer so it was limited and some times we ran out of beer. If the landlord saw this, he either tried to ration it for regulars or shut down the pub!

Drinking habits were different in England. For starters, in Ireland it was a rare thing for women to be seen in a public house - but in England they came. The pub was divided into three sections. 1d extra in the saloon bar, then the private bar, then the public bar - that's where men went to play darts, shove ha'penny and dominoes. During the day some men came in and stayed all day with just a half pint. You had regulars - the labour exchange was right opposite us so at lunch time the labour exchange people would come in for half of bitter and a cheese roll.

The other thing about the pub was that the publican was very fastidious about glasses, windows, brasses etc.

At the back of the pub there were 'maisonettes' – flats. Lots of the people lived there. The surrounding streets were terraced houses. Very early in the morning, women would be out putting whiting on the doorsteps and cleaning brass knockers. The other thing that I did find very different was the fogs!! Everyone had coal fires in the area so the fogs were so thick – 'pea soupers'. I can remember on occasions we went down the street and had difficulty finding our way back.

Coal and the coke were delivered to the gas works. Many people did an early morning run to see what they could collect from what had been dropped to fuel their own fires. A man we knew had converted a push chair into a cart to carry coke from the depot!

There were no fridges so huge ice blocks for the pub came regularly on a lorry.

The nearest hospital was St Olave's. The first experience I had of the War was that a rocket fell in the grounds. The impact woke me up. The dock area got quite a pasting. The planes used to follow the contours of the Thames. The other big disaster was Dock Head which is quite near London Bridge. The church there took a direct hit in March 1945. It was totally demolished and three priests were killed. The only other experience I had of the bombing was when visiting my families at Crystal Palace – two bus journeys – I saw all the bomb damage.

The War was tapering off. The Doodlebugs had more or less finished and then the rockets started. The first rocket was dropped in Orpington.

One of the things that even to this day intrigues me was that despite there being a war on, public transport functioned pretty well. The buses always ran to a schedule.

I remember the VE-Day. It was one of the busiest days in the pub. They stayed open all day and very late at night. The other big day was the VJ-Day.

Staff were strictly not allowed to drink, and could not accept a drink or tips from anybody.

We got one day a week off, mine was nearly always Tuesday. I seldom got a weekend off unless we were out of beer and that only happened a few times. Normal chores in the morning, like cleaning the cellar, finished by about 10.30. We always started at 7.30am and Sunday mornings started earlier because it was customary for pubs to be washed through once a week. Every barmaid/ barman longed for a weekend off.

I hardly ever went back to Ireland, except for a couple of weeks each year.

I think it is very sad that the docks have been wiped out on a par with mining. The way of life due to the docks ensured a close knit community.

Jean Lawson - *I have no photographs, no history of the War.*

My mother was very self-possesed and she always went her own way. During our period in India, (now Pakistan) she took food to prisoners even though she was not meant to. We lived near Lahore. I remember coming in from school and the bearer would be there to look after me and putting my food in front of me. The Indians just disappeared. Then the RAF would come round the perimeter of our bungalow. It never bothered me. No-one was allowed in or out. During hot periods we went into the hills. My happiest times were in India. I had lots of freedom. I went to an army school in Kohat. In 1938 we came back from India because war was expected. My father had wanted to stay there. We were taken to a castle where we were going to be stationed but mother insisted on coming home. We came back through the Suez Canal and my mother contracted malaria and was in the ship's hospital. We were on HMS Dorchester. I remember going through the Suez Canal. We had to stay below deck with all daylight blocked out.

War was imminent. My father was a regular airman. He was in air-sea rescue. He was a warrant officer engineer. My mother was always saying, go for a commission. He used to say 'I am the only one on the camp, I have people working for me and that's how I like it'

We arrived in England just before Christmas and stayed in a place called Bridge with my grandparents. The place had thick, thick snow and men came to the station and brought out sledges for the luggage and me.

The first war posting was to Sheerness. I went to school but it made no impression on me whatsoever and I know I went to the church there. We had rooms with a Mrs Cat on the seafront - very comfortable; then to Thorny Island in 1939. We lived on the island and I loved it. We went to school there. I hardly saw my father. I was 10, an only child. I went off on my own a lot. I looked after myself. My first memory was of English flowers and the hawthorn bush.

Because of the War we had to move off the island and lived in Emsworth. We were living in there when war broke out. I can see us sitting round the radio when the announcement was made. The two people we had digs with were crying. One was an ex Naval captain. We then moved to Southborne to a fairly large modern house converted into two flats. Evacuees came to the area and I went to school in Southborne. The school was only for evacuees and I went there as I was considered to be one. The evacuees were horrible to me and bullied me.

Education was not important to my family so we just moved and moved.

We then went to Aylsham in Norfolk and my father was stationed at Blickling Hall, a large house. We went to shows there and saw stars such as Bebe Daniels and Ben Lion. I was confirmed in 1942 in Aylsham church. Aylsham was a small marketing town and we had rooms in the High Street. A beautiful house. I went to school locally.

We then lived in Little Sutton in The Wirral in Cheshire. There was definitely bombing there. I went to school in Elsmere Port and spent most of our time in underground shelters as there was so much bombing. We stayed with Mr and Mrs Parry and their daughter Joan, who was about my age. I went to a private school in Chester.

At one time we lived in Leamington Spa. We were bombed, bombed and bombed again. We had all our windows smashed out. Eventually I was put on a train with my little suitcase and I went down to Kings Cross on my own. My mother gave the guard a packet of cigarettes to look after me. I went on my own on the underground to Paddington then on to Baltimore in Berkshire to stay with an aunt and uncle and two cousins as it was too dangerous in Leamington Spa.

We also went to Wick in Scotland as my father was stationed at Stornaway. We had rooms in Wick with a bank manager and his wife who were very kind to us. I was nearly twelve I so I went to the high school. Before I went to the school I saw the headmaster – he was called a rector. He was quite horrible to me and he said he didn't like children who had been to private school. It was a very Scottish school where we as English people weren't recognised. I got into trouble for writing an essay about English history and I got called up to the front and told that "WE DO NOT DO ENGLISH HISTORY". I couldn't tell my parents. No one did in those days, you just accepted what teachers said.

All this time we had a car we bought it in Sheerness - an Austin 8. We travelled down from Wick by car in the middle of winter and ended up in a snowdrift near Catterick. We slid straight into it and I can remember a farmer and his wife coming down the lane and collecting my mother and me and taking us to the farm house and giving us hot drinks. The car got pulled out and went to the garage. Dad went to his camp. Mother and I lived in a boarding house. The people there were very kind.

My mother and I came back to live with my grandmother in Mortimer near Reading. My father was sent away to Ireland and we couldn't go. I went to a small private school in Reading. During the War my mother never wore utility clothes. She always went to a top shop and paid top price for shoes, hat, coat, everything. Always good makes. She was happy for her daughter to wear utility clothes and often second hand clothes. I was always clean and smart but not dressed as well as my mother.

One time we went to London to a zoo, even though I didn't like zoos – they never asked me! They didn't have a good memory for faces. We were walking along and I said to my father "That's Mr and Mrs Yew." "Oh, don't be silly" he said and then realised it was them. My father shook hands. Much later, they came to live in Reading but my parents never really kept in touch with them.

Later my mother was in the Royal Berkshire hospital for 2 months as she had cancer. I was put with a great aunt and uncle. I was 16 and locked in my room every day. They were kind but horrid. My mother recovered but she was quite cantankerous after that.

Then we went to a military station at Thornby on Tees and that's where we were for VJ-Day. VE-Day I was in Kent. My life was very unhappy so I left and got a job in Middlesborough as a nanny. I told my employers I was qualified but I wasn't.

My father came out of the forces in 1945/6. He was a very unhappy man because he couldn't settle. He had been in the services for twenty six years. Eventually he got a job auditing school finances which he loved because he was out and about. He lived in Reading.

I think my mother had always been difficult.

I have no photographs, no history of the War.

My parents NEVER discussed or told me anything.

Richard Davenport - *I can play the piano so we had sing-songs, there was much camaraderie*

I was born in Hucknall, Nottingham. It was a mining town, there were two collieries with deep mines of about 20,000 people. We also had an RAF station and a Rolls Royce factory where they did a lot of work on the Merlin engine. Also there were many hosiery manufacturing places on the outskirts of Nottingham. It became the centre of manufacturing as it was where the machines were made.

There was quite a lot of poverty among the pit children, where the amount of coal was limited as in the general recession in 1929. Things gradually improved in the 30's then in 1936 the Government started to take more interest in the rearmament situation and also in the preventative side – what happened if we were attacked. The ARP was formed in 1936. It later became Civil Defence. Each authority made their own arrangements with the view to training people on overcoming the effects of war and rationing. They were also training people as ARP wardens. When I was fourteen I became a young boy messenger.

The boy messenger role was to get on your bike and be prepared to carry messages around if communications were disturbed. Age fourteen was the earliest we could volunteer for anything. I'd been in the scouts but a messenger boy was a recognised role in the survival arrangements. We were suitably trained in survival techniques. We all assumed that gas would be used and were instructed on the type of gas that would be used. We had the same gas masks as the police and ARP and had instructions on how to behave. I do recall there was a gas van. The idea was that you were to go into this van and put your respirator on quickly and walk through the van and take off your mask at the end. I had a badge and felt quite important. People generally, felt very patriotic.

My local authority was an urban district and organised all civil defence, ambulance and police. We had periodic meetings and instructions plus simulated activities which went on until 1939. We young chaps realised that we would be conscripted or volunteer for the various services.

In 1938 I injured my leg playing rugby and had to go into hospital. At that time because of the poverty and lack of food we all had a third of a pint of milk each day at school. I drank gallons of milk as I was a short chap and thought it would make me grow. Milk then contained organisms and bacteria. One of these was TB. The bacteria adhered to injured joints – which I had. My doctor could see something was wrong so sent me to hospital. I had osteo-myelitis (OM) – in the bone marrow. That meant I was treated with a sort of disinfectant which was nowhere near

as powerful as antibiotics. OM is an abscess in the bone marrow which is not easy to get rid of so I needed an operation. I came home after 2 months and went back to school for less than a year and then clearly things weren't right so on May 24th 1939, Empire Day, I went back into hospital. I had to be completely fastened down, in plaster to stop the infected joint moving. If it didn't stop naturally it meant amputation.

It was no use having an x-ray in less than 4 months as I was on a frame and bed splint; the idea was to keep you taught so there was no movement at all. Important people came round, it was like a zoo, as it was a new type of treatment for bone diseases. Colliery people with bone problems were there too – the photo shows the layout of the hospital. We used to tell outrageous lies about coal seams and crippled miners and they went away believing us.

I do remember Chamberlain's speech at 11am that Britain had declared war. The hospital prepared for war casualties; then followed the 'phony war'. Everyone was getting prepared for a mighty attack, aircraft were being improved and the collieries were working hard as it was realised that coal was needed to service boilers and factories. Instructions were issued regularly to all homes. There was a great deal of glass around the hospital so masses of tapes were put on all the windows. The fear was that the War was imminent. The alarm went off around the country. It was a practice but everyone thought it was real so they panicked.

The first war casualty to come to the hospital was an RAF pilot, a Cambridge undergraduate. He trained as a pilot at 21 and then when the War broke out the Volunteer Reserve was incorporated into the RAF. He was flying a Hawker Hurricane and though not well trained he was number two in a patrol of three. They had tried to shoot down the Germans but without success and he was shot in the leg. As I was an old hardened patient I told him about the food and the nurses. He then moved on to another RAF hospital. His parents were obviously well off and gave me the largest box of chocolates I had ever seen.

War casualties came and went and eventually the surgeon realised that my hip had seized up. I was seventeen and was so disappointed as I desperately wanted to join up.

The first conscription was in May 1939 for militia – all twenty year olds. We all wanted to contribute, especially air crews. Then casualties came in fairly regularly. In 1940 the blitz started just as we had been lulled into a complete sense of complacency. We had thought WW2 would be like WW1. Everyone thought we would soon finish off the Germans, then attacks started through Belgium then Holland. Then came Dunkirk where the British army had to get out. Several casualties came back to my ward.

After I came out of hospital when I was getting more mobile in 1941/42 there was a recruitment campaign in the town. Knowing some of the chaps in the Home Guard, I said "Can I do anything?" "Come on in you can be storeman/clerk at the company office." It was a paid job where I worked every morning and every evening. I had to type out all the information that came out and send it to different platoons – we had six platoons consisting of about twenty-five men in each. Rolls Royce had its own platoon. The platoon commander was the test pilot at Rolls Royce. My job was given the rank of sergeant but was later re-assesssed to lance corporal. I also answered the telephone and received weapons, grenades and uniforms. These were intended for use by the Home Guard against the enemy. The theory was that the Home Guard knew the local territory. Sometimes the HG manned the antiaircraft guns. My role was the focal point around the captain and other officers. We also had some exercises with professional soldiers over weekends.

We all had a desire to do something but there were many different personalities and plenty of bright ideas. Everyone had to feel they were doing something.

In the evening there were exercises. I was deferred to as I had information and all materials. However, we all met in the pub afterwards. Really it was playing at soldiers. The guns we had were mainly WW1 stuff. By 1942 the Home Guard was more militarised and under the regular army who supervised and trained us in the area. We had a shooting competition against the RAF. We had a colonel who was useless but it was quite a jolly period for me.

I had hopes that because of my service in the Home Guard I might get into the regular army. I was very fit and strong so could disguise my limp – much to my parents' dismay. We all thought that, with the Home Guard well trained, it would be in the second front. I was then twenty when a friend of mine who worked in the local council health department joined the forces so his job was vacant. He said I should apply as I couldn't get into the forces. So I cut my losses and decided to get some qualifications before he came back. I then had to join the Civil Defence. I was progressing in my career and during that time the urban district council was dealing with billeting. We were an overspill area for evacuations plus the Bevin boys who worked in the coal mines.

There were many fire watching rotas, movement of troops to and fro but my main role was to look after my friends when they came home on leave. I arranged the nights out! I can play the

36

piano so we had sing-songs, there was much camaraderie. I can never remember being hungry. We grew vegetables. We worked together.

We could hear bombs going off around about but there were not many Anderson shelters in our area as we were not considered too vulnerable. Everyone was given a booklet on how to behave.

The air force station was part of the elementary flying scheme so there were many Polish men learning to fly.

I remember VE-Day. I was with my friends and we were in Nottingham and had to walk home – about ten miles. I usually got free beer when I played the piano. An ATS girl sang and they passed the hat round so I got paid as well!

Everyone was involved in WW2 in some way. My father was a special constable. We were better fed during the War than after when things got really short. We were hungry and cold. I moved to Kettering where it was so cold and I was only allowed four inches of water in a bath!

The worst thing for me was the frustration at around seventeen to know that I would be disabled and I would not be able to play an active part in the War.

Win McCurrach - *Things would never go back to where they were before the War, when women had no rights at all!*

The day war was declared in September 1939 everything was suddenly closed down and it seemed to me that we were all waiting an eternity for something to happen.

Local halls all kept functioning, except the cinemas closed at 9pm and the buses stopped then. If we wanted to go dancing, we had to walk home and I have walked many times from Southsea to Copnor even during air raids. They would stop the music and tell everyone the sirens had just sounded if a particularly heavy raid was expected. As we walked along, the shrapnel was pinging down all around us. It seemed we became impervious to the danger. After dancing all evening then having to walk home was very hard on the feet!

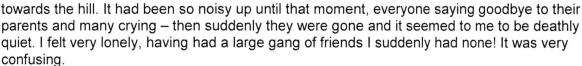

In the morning the schools were closed. The coaches were lined up outside the schools where the children were waiting to board them. The teaching staff was there to help. The children were carrying their boxes and had a tag giving their names and addresses pinned on their lapels. I did not go having point blank refused, saying I would run away if they ever sent me. A letter had been sent to each child's home and the parents had to give their consent in writing.

So I, being thirteen at the time stayed at home. All my friends went and I remember watching the coaches drive away and disappear towards the hill. It had been so noisy up until that moment, everyone saying goodbye to their parents and many crying – then suddenly they were gone and it seemed to me to be deathly quiet. I felt very lonely, having had a large gang of friends I suddenly had none! It was very confusing.

That all happened in September and my fourteenth birthday was the following month. I was told very firmly by my mother that I could not stay at home and it was arranged for me to start working in the office of the family business. We lived in the flat above the shop. My mother continued working in the family business as she had always done. She worked a long day 6.30 am until 9 pm - sometimes later. My father left for the pub at 7pm sharp and returned home when it closed. Nothing changed. I was paid fifteen shillings per week and the arrangement was that I would bring my own clothes and shoes but was helped if I needed a new coat. Looking back, it was amazing that I managed quite well to afford to go to the pictures or dancing when I was fifteen or sixteen.

Portsmouth was full of foreign service people. As each country in Europe was overrun by the Germans - many escaped and made their way to Britain. They either joined our own forces, or were allowed to form their own battalions under British command. Portsmouth was perfect for accommodating them – so much room in the many barracks we had then. The Poles escaped in their own submarines and operated them alongside the British.

The girls had to be particularly careful and we (sisters, cousins etc) always stuck together for safety. Those foreign accents and, seemingly having more money than our men, tempted many a girl. In those days it was still a sin if you became pregnant if you were unmarried. It was very tough on women and there was a surge of unwanted pregnancies and broken marriages when lonely young wives of service people went astray.

There were no ante-natal clinics in Portsmouth and birth control was spoken about in whispers. I found out that there was a clinic in London (the Cecile Booysen Clinic) run on a voluntary basis by a group of women doctors. You paid according to your means. They were quite happy to fix me up, even though I was only engaged at the time. They did marvellous work among the poor in London. My mother and her sisters and, I guess, most women of their generation, were very ignorant about sex.

We were still waiting for something to happen for at least six months of the War, until the bombing started and then it was a regular occurrence. Sometimes the planes passed over the town towards London and other cities and often a lone bomber would fly overhead, so high that the guns could not reach it and it was just a tiny glint in the sky. Then we would all wait for the pilot to unleash his bomb load indiscriminately. Everyone soon learned the difference between the sound of our own and enemy planes. It was interesting to note that many people completely ignored the sirens, until the bombing became heavy but others took shelter immediately. At my home we could not have an Anderson shelter because the gardens were all concreted over and the family had built a huge brick store across the back of the three original houses. So, if things got a little noisy we sheltered under a very substantial oak dining table. Surface brick shelters, reinforced to withstand bomb blasts, were built on many street corners and people could take shelter during the raids.

When a bomb was dropped, the blast was very dangerous and often rocketed from one side of the road to the other, blasting in windows and doors. Many people would be cut badly, as well as suffering blast injuries.

The King's Theatre remained open throughout the War and there was only the odd amateur performance because of the shortage of actors, but we still had treats, such as two weeks of opera and ballet and I went two or three times during their stay. Also, I remember seeing 'Flora Dora' and Gilbert and Sullivan. Another treat was given by a wonderful orchestra provided by the Royal Marines, who played the classics every Sunday afternoon. The conductor was Captain Vivienne Dunn, a very handsome soldier with whom we all fell in love!

Ration books were issued very soon after the War started. Meat, bacon, butter margarine, lard, tea, sugar and eggs could only be purchased through the points system. Everyone was encouraged to grow as much as possible in their gardens. Public parks were dug up. Recipes were broadcast regularly on the radio. There was often a shortage of eggs. It became quite a challenge to make decent edible scrambled eggs from the man-made powdered egg on offer. Babies were issued with a ration book which entitled them to special rations including orange

juice. Of course, this spelled the end of the hundreds of small corner shops. Everyone had to register with a grocer and supplies were allocated according to the number registered.

The big treats - tinned fruit, salmon, other fish and jam - were also divided up according to the numbers registered with each shop and this system encouraged people to register with the larger shops. This system allowed managers of shops to be very influential and I would say it was the beginning of the black market. If you happened to hold an important position with influence then getting rations was no problem, after which, of course, a favour could be asked such as letting you off prosecution or a fine. The Chief Constable reigned supreme.

Conscription started immediately war was declared and was organised in age groups. There was already a very active Territorial Army that had been meeting at least twice a year on training manoeuvres. By law, employers had to release these men and, as many could not afford a holiday, it was a very attractive solution which gave them a break. What happened was that immediately the 'call-up' began, the Territorials who happened to be on active service were immediately drafted into the army and some immediately transferred abroad.

There were exceptions to the call-up but I do not remember any details. However, where moves immediately caused a shortage of able-bodied men, everyone (men and women) were directed into jobs which supported the War effort. Women could be called up when they reached the age of eighteen. I had made up my mind to join the ATS, but was married at the age of eighteen which let me off the hook. The job market was wonderful, everyone could find employment. Women began to show their worth in the factories and the forces. They were running the balloon barrages along Southsea front, flying planes from the factories to air bases. They excelled at engineering and anything else they were directed to carry out and at long last their contribution had to be recognised by the men. Things would never go back to where they were before the War, when women had no rights at all!

It was a hard slog to reach where we are today and things could slide back very easily if we took our eye off the ball. Immediately after peace was declared, women's worst enemy was Winston Churchill. From being such a wonderful inspiring war leader, he wanted everything to go back to what it was in 1939. However, this time the men who had been fighting the War wanted something better and felt they deserved it – so did the women. I think from his privileged position which he held all his life he regretfully just did not understand the hopes and dreams of the ordinary men and women of this country. Thankfully, the establishment is gradually losing its control, although we still have a long way to go.

Portsmouth town, before, during and immediately after the War was mainly run by the top business people and as far as politics were concerned definitely Conservative. The mayor and many councillors were wealthy business people and as far as I know they belonged to the town's Masonic Lodges. During the War in particular they looked after each other and wanted for very little. I know it was quite common for these people to call at a family business premises even though they were not registered with the firm, to collect rationed goods, plus tins of fruit and in particular anything in short supply. Bearing in mind you had to have ration books or permits for practically everything, between this tightly knit group they wanted for nothing. They were not alone, I'm sure this was happening in most towns and cities. There was also a very busy market in clothing coupons between the ordinary people. I remember paying two shillings and sixpence per coupon, but it did add to the cost of everything! To go back to permits, you needed one to purchase wood and even bathroom furniture - even if your home was damaged by bombs.

But manufacturing companies had to, by law, produce goods for the market, otherwise everything would have disappeared and gone under the counter. These goods came under the 'utility' label and were controlled by the Government in both quality and quantity. A good example of this and how it continued after the War was this guy who on becoming Mayor of Portsmouth happened to supply a dustbin to every household in the town free of charge, after the council voted him in to office. He was known at the time as Dustbin Day and he grew richer and richer – although I must admit his wife did good things!

As the big invasion of 1944 approached there was definitely an air of expectancy. We had lived through the news of the countries in Europe falling one after the other, when at long last America joined in the War. There were many in this country who felt that the USA had drained Britain dry before coming in. However, it was great news and soon they were over here and seemed to be everywhere. They completely occupied Hilsea Barracks. They were very popular when running dances for the local girls and passing on goodies which we had not seen in years. The Red Cross was stationed there and very soon they had established a network across the south coast and the officers in charge must have grown very rich as they sold Red Cross supplies to the civilians in this country. I recall on one occasion rushing through the house and stopping short as I saw piles of stockings, sweets, chewing gum of every flavour, electrical goods such as shavers, radios and the like piled high on the big family table. It was truly breathtaking, but trading was established and continued for quite some time.

John, my fiancé and I kept in touch through letters, which we could only hope were delivered as much of the mail was lost through boats being torpedoed. We started numbering our letters to establish continuity. We decided that we would get married on June 7th 1944 which was the day

John had been told he would be arriving back in England from the Mediterranean where his submarine had been on patrol for the past fifteen months. He was not told which port the boat would arrive in but I knew he would 'phone the moment he could. Our parents had gone ahead and made all the arrangements for the wedding with fingers crossed, because nothing was certain. We had just wanted to visit a registry office and disappear – but that was not to be and I eventually gave up organising. By then the country was on full alert, every street was being filled with vehicles, tanks, etc. Travelling was restricted; the country knew an invasion was imminent and I just waited to hear the news. My phone call came on June 6th, John was able to tell me that they had docked in Plymouth, but his Captain had told him that all

travelling had been stopped, so he was unsure if or when he would get home. All the trains came under military control and civilians were not allowed to travel unless they had a pass. However, his Captain came up with an ingenious plan. John was given a travel pass to Portsmouth Dockyard, plus a very important envelope stamped and sealed which he had to deliver there. All his Captain could do then was to wish him luck. John 'phoned me directly he could but said Plymouth had been bombed very badly and he wasn't sure how he would get out of the town. As he was 'phoning me from a temporary 'phone box, enemy planes were strafing the town. Temporary 'phone boxes were erected as soon as possible in areas which were badly bombed. Not many people had their own 'phone so this was considered a priority. John looked up as one fighter plane appeared to be coming straight for him and he remembered quite clearly ducking down and saying "Christ, hurry up" and then the telephone operator saying "Any more of that language and I will cut you off!"

But he did make it and we were married on 7th June. We had a wedding reception in Southsea, our parents having applied for a special licence to buy the food. By then food offices had been established across the country that dealt with any special permits and identity card matters. People had to register changes of address, marital status and new babies had to be registered and issued with their own identity card. I worked in the food office for two or three years, during a period when John had gone to sea again and it was very interesting work.

Coal was also rationed and during one particularly bad winter it was difficult to keep warm. Of all things it snowed heavily on Portsmouth and the authorities piled the snow high on the roadsides. It was 5 – 6 feet high and passages had to be cut through to allow people to cross the road.

Cycling became quite dangerous – after a bombing raid the ARPs organised clearing of roads and streets and the refuse was piled high on the kerbsides until it could be removed. With the blackout strictly imposed at night and cyclists having to cover half of their lights with thick paper it could be a nightmare. I remember once cycling up the side of a huge pile of rubbish until I reached the top and fell off!

The ARP wardens were very strict about the black out and would hammer at people's doors if there was the slightest chink of light.

On the night of the first fire bomb raid it was very frightening. Enemy planes dropped hundreds and hundreds of incendiary bombs all over town. The sirens had sounded early as usual and everyone waited to see what sort of raid it would be. Then we became aware of terrific activity on the streets. Whistles were blowing and there was much shouting and fire engines seemed to be rushing up and down. It was an established practice for the air raid wardens to ensure that buckets of sand were strategically placed around the streets, particularly near public buildings such as churches, halls, air raid shelters, cinemas, etc, which were to be used in emergencies. One spade full of sand would put out an incendiary bomb.

When we ventured outside we were totally amazed. There were so many fires that it seemed like day time. The roof of our flat was alight, so was the roof of the senior school and the church opposite. Our fire was quickly put out, but others still burned and still the enemy planes came over and dropped more bombs. We quickly decided that we should evacuate and head for Southbourne where my grandmother had been moved for safety. We had the use of a small van plus allocated petrol for business use. I remember so clearly driving up Copnor Road towards the hill with fires all around us.

There seemed to be a fair amount of traffic on the road, all I'm sure with the same thought as us! But we realised that most traffic was heading out of town and towards the top of Portsdown Hill. We followed suit, our first thought being to just get out of town. The sight from the top was absolutely amazing, it was just as if the town was bathed in searchlights. You could make out every street and main building. The Guildhall was alight, the dockyard was burning and whole streets appeared to be blazing from end to end. It was truly mesmerising. After a time we decided to head for Southbourne, not sure if we would be allowed through but knowing our parents would be worrying about our safety. We had to make one or two detours, but arrived safely about midnight. Other members of my mother's rather large family were there - she was the eldest daughter in a family of thirteen children - and so we all bunked down anywhere where there was a space.

One particularly sad incident I recall happened on a Saturday afternoon. There used to be a cinema in Lake Road and on this particular day it was full of children enjoying a matinee, when the building received a direct hit from a plane dropping bombs indiscriminately. There were lots of incidents similar to this, where family air raid shelters received direct hits and whole families were killed. The ARP did wonderful work and took great risks when rescuing people. These incidents made the War a very different experience for our troops fighting at home and abroad, because they could never be certain that their families were safe at home. John said he knew of several men who arrived home only to find their families gone, their homes - everything.

When the War was at its peak it was very gloomy at home, we were not doing very well abroad, our ships were being sunk regularly and I felt we were gradually being boxed in. Churchill's wonderful speeches were so uplifting and so necessary to keep us all going. I know he made terrible mistakes but I'm convinced he pulled us through.

During the last year of the War, John was sent to Barrow-in-Furness to stand by a new submarine that was being built there and I joined him as soon as I could. It was one of our 'A class' boats. Early on during the War all submarines were identified by a number. John was on the P31 – when this came to the attention of Mr Churchill, he said this was too impersonal and they should all have a name and so each boat chose its own name and the P31 eventually became the 'Uproar'.

Food was very short for a long time and my mother sent me a sack of potatoes. We were totally amazed. There were so many and they had travelled all the way north with just a label attached to the sack. That would not happen today.

Churchill lost the election after the War because he could not envisage a different country where families could live a more comfortable life and not be enslaved by the rigid class system. There was also the very big question about women's place in the country. Having enjoyed the new found freedom at the workplace with their husbands serving away from home they also yearned for something new. You have to imagine a world where women had no rights, no laws to protect them and men dominated everything; a man could bring another woman into the family home and his wife could do nothing except either accept her or leave. She was not entitled to anything under the law and this was what women's suffrage was all about. The Suffragette Movement was aimed at changing the law right from the start and it was not until the politicians and men in general ignored their requests repeatedly that the women adopted a militant campaign. There is one particular story which I have often told about a man who was able to turn his wife out of the family home with nothing because he paid the rent and all other expenses in the home. He even claimed the dividend his wife had earned through shopping at the Co-op. Even so, I have to admit that there were very few people who were willing to openly question men's dominant position and I was certainly not popular if I broached the subject.

My own family was a perfect example and, when I married, I had to take my husband aside and explain why, regardless of how he felt, I could not accept the status quo and would always challenge anything I felt was against women's equality. At times, I'm sure he felt very uneasy and embarrassed particularly because men inferred he was henpecked! It was the only defence they had, poor things! Over the years people became used to my thinking and so we often had some very interesting conversations and I found many sympathetic friends but very few who were willing to challenge publicly some of the terrible things that were wrong. Women in particular did not want to upset their husbands.

As mentioned earlier, there were no clinics for women and the conditions in hospitals when they gave birth were appalling. At the end of the War I was able to join the Six Point Group which was formed to continue the fight for equality – certainly not popular but we had declared a truce while the War was on. Our policy was the same as the Suffragettes, lobbying members of Parliament and influencing any new legislation. The group had many influential friends and I met many of them personally through lunching at the House and particularly having tea with members of the Suffragette Movement. They were showing their age by then, but were so full of purpose and tenacity after all they had been through – truly amazing.

Maureen Pritchard - *During the War we took everything as it came.*

I realise now that I tried to blank it all out, I was in a kind of daze. It's only now that you've made me think about it that I have started to remember.

None of my relatives served in the War, but we heard so much about what was going to happen. My father was Irish so didn't serve. He was a Customs and Excise officer in a brewery in Bow. In the evening he worked as a volunteer senior fire guard. My mother was at home, my brother was in the Air Force and me at school. My brother went to Canada and was trained to fly there. He came back into Bomber Command. We didn't go out much at weekends. There really wasn't that much to do. Most of my friends were older than me and they had joined up. Most of the boys didn't wait to be called up - they volunteered

When we were first evacuated, a woman took us round. It was as dark as anything. It was Chelmsford and there was another girl with her brother and the women opened the door and said "I don't want girls. I've only got sons I want boys." She was persuaded to take us over night. In the end we got taken out to Maldon and we stayed there. There was little to do. Most of our time was spent drifting about in Maldon, my brother and our friends. Nobody was really interested in you. People were doing what they had to do. You weren't a person you were an evacuee. The person you were going to live with didn't really want you either.

Then my mother got me into boarding school at Launceston - between Dartmoor and Exmoor.

When my parents said there was a place for you in boarding school I could have kissed the ground. The girl who was with me knew my brother at school. Boarding school was mainly for boarders plus a few people like me who wanted to be away from London. I was really happy there, I loved it there. The district nurse used to take us out during the holidays as we stayed there and didn't go home. We had a lovely day out at Bude for example. I can remember sitting there on the sand in my school uniform waiting for hours for her take us home. We went all over north Cornwall. We'd never have gone anywhere if it were not for her.

We never went hungry. If you are hungry you will eat anything. We were in a convent school eating the same food as the nuns so it was OK - canteen sort of food. Occasionally my mother came down and stayed in a hotel and then I was allowed to go to see her. My mother thought she shouldn't leave my father - it was his duty to stay at home rather than come to see me. I came back home in 1941 when I left school at 15.

My uncle worked in the Sun Insurance office and his company was evacuated to Silsoe, half way between Luton and Bedford and he got me a job there. I worked there during the week in the mansion they had taken over and went home at weekends. I knew St Pancras station like the back of my hand. I stayed at Silsoe until the War ended. We were in a mansion with American air fields all around us and, of course, aeroplanes. The enemy bombed during the day and Americans bombed during the night.

When I was away, the American troops were short of girls so used to send in lorries to pick us up and take us to the air base. They had Glen Miller type bands and we spent a few hours there dancing and then we'd get driven home again. We used to get invitations to Thurleigh – Americans – and they used want girls to go dancing every Wednesday. A truck used to turn up and take about 20 of us off to the dances and we really looked forward to them. Wonderful bands and the Americans who were like a different race!!!

During the War we took everything as it came. We didn't moan about it. The job was all right. I liked the people I worked with. I did quite like it.

Thelma Turner - *I took myself off to Cardiff, against my dad's wishes, and got a job*

I was 12 when war began. I was visiting an aunt living just outside Cardiff. My cousin and I were out playing in the fields when my uncle came to tell me the War had started.

The War didn't really hit children, but it hit parents. I went to school quite happily until I got listening to the adults and they said what if… but life didn't change. I'm the second eldest of 4 brothers. They brought the masks round and I had to go into one of these cages and my mother had to use a pump. They showed you how to do it, Mum had to put my youngest brother Herbert in as well and she showed me how to pump. It frightened me because of Herbert.

They built air raid shelters opposite our house but we didn't use them very often as my father put us under the stairs. The first time the air raids happened in Cardiff, one brother turned round and went back to bed. One night everyone was settled when a neighbour came to see if we were OK and we discovered my father had got us up on the 'all clear' in stead of the alarm.

My father kept the Bute (Cardiff Castle) houses in order so was very busy. In that time my grandfather had a car which had to be put away because of the lack of petrol so my father used a hand truck to move his ladders.

When I was in school they used to put cookery lessons on for the adults to make rations go a long way and a friend and I volunteered to do this after school. They would make quiches out of water crust pastry with hardly any fat. They were then filled with tomatoes, onions and powdered egg. If we could get a little bit of cheese they allowed us to sprinkle it on them. It was a very tasty dish. If there was any left over, we, as helpers, were given some, which my brothers loved.

I left school at fourteen and then I stayed at home to look after my younger brother. It was hard for me in school because my younger brother and I have word blindness so it was always assumed I would stay at home. Eventually, aged about fifteen, I took myself off to Cardiff, against my dad's wishes, and got a job as a trainee window dresser and shop assistant – and I then stayed in the retail trade until I was 56!

First, I worked for a shop called England's where I carried the shoes to the supervisor who then sold them to the customer. We couldn't sell shoes until trained. At 18 everyone had to go out of the shop into the factories so my friend and I had to run the shop aged sixteen until we took on youngsters again. A lady was a window dresser and she left to have a baby so we took over window dressing too. There wasn't much stock so we had queues. We had regular customers who would come to ask when we would be having a delivery or to see what stocks we had. You needed ration coupons for shoes – five for a pair of adult's shoes and two and a half for children. We measured and fitted children's shoes.

Opposite the shoe shop where I worked there were two spinster sisters who ran Andrews sweet shop and they liked 'more mature' ladies shoes. We would invite them over to see what we had and in return we got extra sweets for our ration.

During the War everything was delivered by horse and cart. Boxes with the shoes were delivered to Cardiff railway station and then the horse and cart came out to us. Then the draymen would come back a few days later and collect the tea chests that the shoes had been delivered in. These chests were then sent back to Northampton. We then would wait for another delivery. There were lots of shoemakers in the UK at that time – no shoes were imported.

It was a very happy time; everyone was so friendly. People went out of their way to be friendly. The War years were not depressing.

Entertainment meant going to the cinema. We used to save up. It would cost us 9d to get in. We used to go three times a week and on a Saturday used to go to the New Theatre to see live shows. It cost us 6d to sit right up 'in the gods'.

Between 1943 and 1945, every body was keyed up for the D-day and we became really grown up, we had to run things even though we were still in our teens. Everyone was so happy. 1944 was hardest as we were losing so many people, including members of my family. My father was not well enough to go into the Army so he was in the Home Guard. He used to man a firing range at Penarth; he used to cycle over there after a days work and then do a night shift until 8am or 9am the next morning. It was a hard time for anyone. There was not a lot of bombing in Cardiff.

I had a brother who joined the Navy at seventeen. There was a bombing raid whilst he was on leave and he and my dad went out to see if they could dig anyone out. My father was a very kind generous man. If someone's roof had a hole he would go and repair it. That's what you did during the War.

The bread and the milk and vegetables were also delivered by horse and cart. Everyone used 'Camp' coffee unless they were rich. Instant coffee had not been invented.

You could sometimes get dried prunes from someone who lived in Barry. They were always in blue bags, same with sugar. By the time I got home I had eaten half of them.

By 1944 I had started going out in the evening. I had to be in by 10pm whatever and if my father knew I was on the bus he used to be at the stop to meet me even though it was just down the road.

There were lots of Americans around. My friend had met a sailor. She suggested that we skive off work and go out with him and his friend – so we did. My boss rang home to find out why I had not gone back to work in the afternoon. My father didn't say anything to me but after that he waited outside to make sure I went to work. From then on he would watch me like a hawk. He used to cycle 6 miles each way to watch me.

By 1944, when we knew we were winning the War, everything seemed to lighten up. There was no easing of the rationing but people had something to look forward to. The bombing had stopped in Cardiff. Doodlebugs started falling on London.

Coming up to 1945 the excitement of the War finishing was high. It was exciting but we knew it might be dull afterwards. We stood in Queen's Street looking down from the castle waiting for the Welsh flag to go up. Every shop closed. It was a lovely experience. Everyone walking along, sailors, soldiers and civilians all shook hands or hugged each other.

I had wanted to join the Land Army at sixteen but my father was adamant I would not. He was afraid I would move away. When I was eighteen I took the papers home for him to sign and twice he put them on the fire. Eventually my mum sat him down and said "If that's what she wants to do, let her learn the hard way." I loved it. I could lift a sack of potatoes because I had been shown how to do it, but later I developed rheumatism in my back so had to leave. I proved my father wrong though. Then I started back into same shop until 1951.

I married Bill Turner in 1949.

Leslie Harrison - *The thing about the War was it got everybody working together*

I worked for the London, Midland and Southern (LMS) railway in 1936. When the War came they moved us all out - all 4,000 of us - to the Earl of Clarendon's house in Watford in Herts. Watford was where food came in to be sent off elsewhere. The house wasn't big enough and it was very cold - just two fires - one at each end of the room.

All of my family - parents, brother and sister all moved to Watford. Watford was a lovely place for music. All the big halls in London were bombed so we had all the famous singers and musicians coming down to us.

Not many bombs fell in Watford but we occasionally had to go down into the shelters. My sister and brothers worked in London which was much more risky.

My brother was called up and then me. I went to St Albans to be assessed and they found I only had one good eye. At first they thought they would put me in munitions but then decided that the railway was just as important. I didn't really see very much of the War except that the railway line was sometimes bombed and we couldn't get to work

Food was scarce. Everything was rationed. I gave up sugar in tea so that my mother could use it in cooking. When my father was ill he longed for an orange but he wasn't allowed one - only children. One friend gave him hers and he was so thrilled. During the War if we had any raids we had to sleep under the stairs.

There were lots of troops. The local church opened a shop serving food and drink and providing places for table tennis and snooker. I helped out there but at the time I didn't know much about WVS. We kept losing cutlery so we took the troops' caps as a deposit when the soldiers came in. When we got our cutlery back they got their caps back! Then the Americans came with their money, nylons and their own food.

It was very difficult for my mother but she said it was not as bad as WW1 when there were no ration books so you had to queue up, often only to find all the food had gone. My mum hated cooking but wouldn't let us go in the kitchen. She hated housework except dusting. Washing took ages. She had a job helping in a canteen.

I was in the registry at the railway. I had to find the papers quickly for people. We had rail cards. I worked in Euston and then in signals and then supplies. If we went anywhere we had to take our ration book with us, even to friends. I had a friend in Wembley who lived on her own and I did stay with her some times during the bombing. It was a nasty feeling with bombs coming down. One night, the first time it happened, the guns went up to shoot, it was an exciting experience. Then we had the doodlebugs which were horrible – you could hear them overhead but you didn't know where they were going to strike, and then suddenly – crash! She had a Morrison shelter – like a table - and we slept under that.

At home, we had to have four soldiers staying with us as my father was dead by now. We had four Englishmen but didn't see much of them. They only slept there, we didn't feed them.

Then we had two Americans, who had the posh bedroom, and they used to bring us all sorts of things from the canteen. My sister married one of these. She was going to get married at the end of December, Everything was ready and then he didn't turn up. We said "Oh he's American'" but in fact he was involved in a big push in France. In the middle of January he walked in and said "Let's get married tomorrow." They had to wait a couple of days and they were married. After a week's honeymoon, he had to go back to war and she didn't see him again until she went to America about a year later. He'd gone back to America and got himself discharged. My mother was against my sister marrying a yank. It was so far away and probably because he was an American but he was a very kind man. My brother came back from India four days before she went to America but we had gone to Canterbury because my sister wanted to see the cathedral before she left. We didn't know he was coming. He arrived but couldn't get in so left his kit bag in the porch and went to the cinema.

She went to America on the Queen Mary. They called her name out as Mary Johnson, and she didn't come forward. She was always known as Joy. She had to be 'top and tailed' – a medical examination - before being allowed into America. His family were marvellous to her. Her husband was fifteen years older than her. She got a job because she was bored and they said she was brilliant

The thing about the War was it got everybody working together.

Most of my friends, men and women, went into the army. I wish I had, I might not be a spinster now.

Gladys Eadon - *When the War was over we had a big village party on the green.*

I was born in 1914. I had a sister and a brother and my dad was a lock-keeper. Before I married in 1936, I was working in the kitchen at a girls' boarding school in Leamington Spa. I helped with the cooking and general chores. There were about fifty boarders. I lived in and worked from about 6am until 10pm and was paid 8/- a week. When you wanted a pay rise you had to pluck up courage to ask for it – and it was 6d a week if you got it. We had a half day off each week.

I met my husband–to-be at a bonfire night at Napton. I wore a long white satin dress when I got married and I wore a coronet headdress, made of wax. Not many people came to the wedding. We lived in a little cottage which was 3/6d per week at a village near by. It didn't have a sink - we used to wash under the stairs. No bathroom, nothing like that. Yet it was very cosy with coal fires. I didn't get much pay - about £2 off my husband and had to pay for everything out of that. We furnished the home and we never went into to debt. Then we went to another village and lived in a bungalow for a little while and then went into a council house.

I was one of the first women in the village who wore trousers and then shorts. My husband and I also wore plus-fours. We had them made in Leamington. We both liked our clothes. He used to wear a bowler hat, always used to dress smartly. The village used to call us the Duke and Duchess.

My husband never volunteered, nor got called up – may be he was in a protected occupation. He worked in the brickworks until it closed to become an ammunitions factory. It became a brick factory again after the War and he worked there for years afterwards making quarry tiles.

The air raids were awful. The German bombers went over every night at about the same time, accompanied by horrible droning. Then the sirens would go off about 12 miles away in Coventry. One bomb dropped not far from us. Then you could hear our Spitfires going after them - chasing them - and then the battles. It wasn't very nice.

I had evacuees from Coventry. I had a mother and daughter, and mother and son, and girl on her own at first. She was about eight - Connie Young - her parents were Canadian. They used to come every weekend. They were nice. She was with us a long time. She was like a daughter to us as we didn't have a child of our own at that time.

In the village there were two billets so we had to have soldiers to live with us. We had a 3 bedroom council house so had two soldiers at a time. They were quite nice chaps. We had six lots altogether. We had to feed them. They were lively - but my husband got jealous. I gave them one meal a day.

 After the soldiers we had more evacuees. Then we had Mr and Mrs Tointon who were 'bombed out' from Coventry. Mr Tointon was the head one at the brickworks when it re-opened. We kept in touch for many years.

There was not much social life when we had evacuees but, when we had soldiers around, we went to the dances - but the local men didn't like it. I remember one day we had a fancy dress competition in the village, and my daughter had a veil on pretending to be a bride and a boy had a top hat on.

We always did well for food and never went short of anything. My husband kept a pig but when it was killed he had to give half to the Government. We also used to grow vegetables. My father's sister used to live in a bakers shop, so we had cakes and bread. We used to get groceries sent down on a boat. We had a book of clothing coupons but most people had coupons but not the money for clothes. I used to have to cut up scraps of material to make rag rugs.

When the War was over we had a big village party on the green, with church bells ringing

Being evacuated in the UK

When it was obvious that Britain was going to be at war, different people had different ideas about their family. Some people wanted the family to stay together at home. Other people were concerned about their children's safety. Others were concerned for the children and the mothers.

A voluntary evacuation scheme was devised by the Government which meant that children and occasionally, children and mothers, could move to live somewhere that was thought to be safe. In areas where it was thought there would be no bombings, the people of these towns and villages were asked to provide a home for the evacuees, as they became known. These people were paid to look after the children.

The children had to take their gas masks with them in a cardboard box. They also had to take some clothes and were given a parcel of food to give to their new family. Everyone also had to have a label tied on them on which their name was printed.

Many other countries were already at War with Germany and had different ideas as to what was best for the children and families. In France, for example, the families were encouraged to stay together where possible but to move, as a family, to the countryside to avoid the bombings in the cities.[iv]

People who were children during the War knew no different. Their whole lives were affected by what was going on around them and even after the War there was still rationing, as the date on the picture shows. There were also shortages of many goods and war damage to repair. Many people found it hard to settle back into what they now felt were boring lives and jobs.

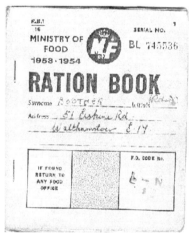

Still some food rationing in 1953-4 as shown by Bob Boother's ration book

Some people also suffered dreadful nightmares about what they had done, under orders. Kennan, quoted in 'Bomber Boys, Fighting Back 1940 – 1945' sums up what many felt:

I felt an unshakeable conviction that no momentary military advantage – even if such could be calculated to exist – could have justified this stupendous, careless destruction of civilian life…least of all could it be justified by the screaming, "They did it to us."

Everyone has a responsibility to try to ensure that such a war should never happen again.

Jean Lawson - *During the War everyone was always smiling, there was always something going on. I wouldn't have missed the experience.*

My father was in the Home Guard as he had a reserved occupation. He was in charge of an office at the civic centre, issuing vehicle licences and petrol coupons.

I was with my parents on holiday in a caravan in Swanage when we were sent a message to say that we were to be evacuated before the War started and that we should come home straight away.

On 1st September 1939 we all met up at school with some clothes in a bag and something to eat. We were given a gas mask and shown how to use it. We then walked to Southampton station to catch a train to Bournemouth, Dorset. The War officially began on 3rd September 1939.

We were taken to East Close School, Bournemouth. Lots of people from round and about came to the school to choose evacuees to take home.

At the back of the cake shop

The house I went to was also a cake shop. There were wasps everywhere on the cakes and all around the bakery. Although I loved cakes, it didn't help me, as I was very homesick. I started crying for my mum all the time; I was only just eight years old and had never been away from home before and had been thoroughly spoilt. It was the same on Saturday, I cried so much they sent a message to my mum and dad. My dad arranged for someone with a car to collect me on Sunday morning, so I got home even before they declared War at 11.00 am!
.

I didn't go to school as there wasn't one left in Southampton. All the schools had been evacuated elsewhere.

In the summer of 1940 the bombing started. The schools which had sort of drifted home were evacuated again. My mother came with me as helper and we went to Bruton in Somerset. My mother worked in the billeting office. The children were distributed about and I was placed at East Brewham.

Jean and Ann at the vicarage

I went to a vicarage there with Ann Kitchen (my mum could cycle to see me as she didn't live far away but I wasn't allowed to live with her). The house was a 14-room vicarage and only two people lived there as they didn't have any children. The dog had its own room and so did the cat. The Reverend Annesley was very smug, 'holier-than-thou'! His wife was a country bumpkin but he was posh. (I learnt later that he became Viscount Annesley as he had important relatives in Ireland).

We were not allowed to eat with them except Sunday lunchtime. The rest of the time we ate in the kitchen. We had to say prayers in the morning, at lunchtime and in the evening. We went to church twice at least on Sunday as the Reverend Annesley was responsible for two churches. There were only about six or seven people in each church including his wife, a young lad who pumped the organ, Ann and me. He spent the whole week writing his sermon for these few people.

We walked along a country lane to the village school, about two miles away. We were told to walk on the other side of the road to the pub, as the Reverend didn't approve of public houses. Our teacher, Miss Morgan, was evacuated to the pub!

It was an eerie old vicarage with owls screeching at night. I still hate anywhere that is dark. Funny thing about this was that my mother used to cycle out to see me and then go and have lunch with Miss Morgan in the pub, but she couldn't tell the Reverend. He never gave her anything, not even a cup of tea.

Very occasionally, my father knew someone with a car, so he gave them petrol coupons to take dad to visit me. The Reverend said to father, "Would you like lunch or tea?" – only him, not to my mother though. She used to take us out for a little walk.

When we were at East Brewham a plane came down at the back of the school – we all went down and grabbed bits of the plane. It was a British pilot who was killed. It was a very near miss so we were really not safe anywhere.

My mum and dad, Mrs Annesley and dad's friend who had a car

My dad wrote to me whilst I was here. He said that he was in the cinema when they started the bombings. The walls of the cinema rocked in and out with the blast, so he got out as fast as he could and started to go home. He couldn't do this because of the bombings, so he went to an underground shelter in the park and stayed there all night. The warden on duty said, "Duck if the bomb comes." My father was worried they might not get out. In the morning, he didn't know where he was because all the roads had been bombed and disappeared. He was completely shell shocked, but when he got to our house he was OK.

My stay at the vicarage ended in September with a letter from dad, because all had gone quiet at home. My father was a lovely letter-writer, he had a very good hand – well known for it and wrote letters for other people. He wrote about bombs here and bombs there and the Gerries. He was in the Home Guard but was terrified of heights and yet they posted him up the Civic Centre tower to spot for planes.

Eventually, school started up again for a while. Mother was in the fire service by now. She wore a uniform and forage cap. Dad was still in the Home Guard. If both of them were on duty together I went to stay at the fire station. Quite funny, my mum didn't go out on fire duty when the bells went. I loved watching all the men sliding down the greasy poles. I thought this was great fun so didn't get much sleep. There was a huge, fat man, called Luker, who snored so much it took four people to turn him over to stop him snoring. When my mother was on duty and dad was not, I used to be taken to the pub by dad and had to make sandwiches at the back of the pub for the customers.

We had an Anderson shelter in the garden and made a gate from our house to next door for the Harrisons – Eddy and Milly – so Milly could come in if her husband, also a fireman, was on duty as she was too scared to sleep in her own shelter by herself. We all slept on one mattress.

In late 1940, the bombing started again. It got dangerous so my aunt, who had a friend called Peggy Payne, who was a schoolteacher at Colden Common, told them about me. She lived at Brambridge in a lodge with her husband, who was a colonel. She said, "Why don't you send Jean here as it is safer?" I went to Mr and Mrs Stevens' house, who lived at Merton on the main road and went to Colden Common School. I used to come home to Southampton on the bus, on a Saturday and often went to the football – mum took sandwiches for our lunch.

Then when I was ten in 1941, I passed the scholarship (11+) so went to Southampton Grammar School for girls. We shared the school with Talbot Heath School in Bournemouth – half day each. We went in the mornings and they went in afternoons. I was billeted out there. After a while the school took over Wentworth College because its pupils had been evacuated to Wales! I came back at the end of 1944.

When at Wentworth College (originally a stately home), there was a lovely garden where we played. We also went over the road to sunbathe on the cliffs. One day we saw these planes come over the sea, so we got up and waved to them. They started to machine-gun us so we dived into the bushes. We all escaped OK but we were not allowed out after that.

I still came home every weekend as the Germans didn't seem to bomb on Saturdays and Sundays. There was not much bombing by 1944, only doodlebugs.

I had a lot of billets at this time. The first was in Lowther Road with three sixth-formers. I didn't like that much. Then I moved to Wyndham Road, Boscombe, near the station. It was a terraced house with Mr and Mrs Cherry. He was a chef at Bobby's store, which is now Debenhams. They had a boy and a girl and we all used to sleep in a tiny room, sleeping top and bottom so our feet were in each other's faces. Audrey (Tibs) Britain slept with me. They were a very kind couple, except Mrs Cherry started having fits (epileptic) so the people who were running the billeting took us away and I went to Mr and Mrs Williams. He was a music teacher, and made me practise the piano for hour after hour and I still can't play a note! They were Welsh. They had one daughter called Valmai who was eventually evacuated to her granny in Wales.

I then went to Kinson and lived with a woman whose husband was an Air Force officer, who was away. She was a beast! She used to give us nothing to eat but bread and jam. She got coupons and money to look after us and it was all spent on her spaniel dog – we were starving.

I never told my parents. I hated going back on a Sunday night as they had enough to worry about with the bombs. Eventually I had malnutrition. I was so ill they thought I had TB. I was sent home and didn't go back. I had to have lots of X-rays – terrible business, rubber things all over you – and then I had to go into a dark room. All I had was inflammation of the lungs, but I was severely malnourished. The doctor used to tell my mother to give me Guinness. We were also given extra food coupons to fatten me up. Then the school came back.

Back again to Southampton where the grammar school was full of American soldiers (waiting for D-day). We had great fun with the American troops who used to get all sorts of supplies, things we had never seen such as chicken and lots of white bread. They used to give it to us. They had a van which used to go down for supplies. They also gave us doughnuts which we hadn't had before. We played baseball with them, and they put ropes in the trees which we used to play on with them – our parents were delighted and we used to bring the soldiers home. They loved having tea with my parents. I was aged about 12 or 13 at this time.

My friend, Pat, who lived in Pirrie Close, had a sister called Doreen who eventually married one of the colonels and went to live in America with him.

We were given clothes coupons but there were not many clothes about. We mainly wore hand-me-downs. Clothes at school you could swap. People made everything. They used a lot of parachute silk from discarded parachutes and made underwear. Some people even made wedding dresses from it. Everyone used to make things and knit things. They unpicked jumpers and knitted them up again a different size.

It seemed as though everyone was on what they called 'the black market'. Many people seemed to get more than their rations. My father was very friendly with Mr Parsons, who had the grocery shop in Wilson Crescent, and he used to give my dad extras – not a lot, but more than many others. I expect my dad gave him petrol coupons, though he never said!

Everyone had corned beef, so there were 50 different ways of cooking corned beef. We also had dried egg – omelettes tasted a bit like leather but were OK in a sandwich. Everyone grew things, 'Dig for Victory' was the slogan – or people kept a few chickens or a couple of rabbits in their garden. People you knew did favours for you and you did favours for them. Everything used to be shared around.

Harry Hobbs, the butcher, used to come and give us sausages on Friday. Lovely sausages, I can taste them now. Sometimes he brought a couple of pork chops. I used to stay with him sometimes at Rownhams. We used to eat like mad out there.

We really had a very healthy diet, lots of vegetables and salads. There was not much fatty stuff to eat as there wasn't much about. People became very clever cooks, they could do things with almost nothing. My favourite was bacon pudding – a few rashers of bacon, onions and suet pudding – delicious. Occasionally my mother used to get enough stuff to make a fruit cake – no fruit, just with caraway seeds.

We had friends in to play cards when the doodle bugs were dropped, so everyone stayed in our air raid shelter. When they went home none of their houses were left so they had to stay with us for quite a long while. My friend's dad was an Olympic swimmer before the War and became manager of the Southampton Swimming Baths, so he gave us as a free pass. I went swimming in the lido come rain or shine. It was a sort of thanks for putting them up – they stayed ages.

During the War everyone was always smiling, there was always something going on. I wouldn't have missed the experience. Everyone seemed more friendly than now; more trusting. You took anyone in who needed a house or just needed a meal. No-one stood on ceremony.

Keith Barnard - *Close to where I was billeted was an ideal place to watch 'dog fights'*

It was February, 1939 - I was eleven. On the newsreels at the local cinemas - there was no television then - we saw the fighting in China and the Spanish Civil War. We saw the bombing, the damage and injuries and deaths that it caused. We also saw the build-up of new aircraft, ships and tanks for the services. Reading the newspaper headlines and articles and hearing adults talking, it came as no surprise when an Anderson air raid shelter was put into a hole in our back garden and later we were issued with gas masks. But things were to get worse.

School finished, and our form master organised a camp for those pupils leaving to go to senior school that year. One evening we were told that our cook had gone - recalled to the Navy. So, next day, we packed everything up and went home. There, I found a letter telling me to report to my new school in Portsmouth at the end of July.

We had some introductory lessons and were then sent home until further notice. On Friday September 1st we had to report to the school with a case with all the clothes on a supplied list, books and things required for school, gas mask and sandwiches for the journey. We hadn't realised we were being evacuated.

We were taken by bus to the town station which was packed with children and people in queues, waiting. Soon we were checked onto a train and were off. Once we left Portsmouth we were unsure as to where we were. but after several stops and starts, we arrived at Winchester City station. Headed by a 6th former carrying a banner, we marched out of the station and up the hill to Peter Symonds School. There, we were given tea and sandwiches and a carrier bag containing a tin of corned beef, a tin of condensed milk, a packet of biscuits and a bar of chocolate. Eventually groups were leaving accompanied by a guide with a list. My name was called and along with fifteen to twenty others we set off in drizzling rain up one road, down another, dropping one or two boys off at different houses on the way. By this time my paper bag had become soft and it was awkward to carry the food. I was a bit fed up. My name was suddenly called and 19, Greenhill Road, was to be my home from home for, little did I know, four years.

There were three of us, Colin Vere, the same age as me and an older boy, John. We were introduced to the landlady, Mrs.Woodland and her lodger, Miss Botham. So – a widow and a spinster to look after three boys! We put our cases in our bedroom, had a cup of tea, something to eat, then wrote home to tell our parents we'd arrived safely.

On Saturday we wandered off to see the city. On Sunday we stayed in to hear the news at 11am on the wireless. We heard we were at war so we would not be going home for a while. Soon after, the air raid warning siren sounded and we went down into the cellar. This was the coal cellar, coal being dropped down a shoot via a hole outside the front door. Down the steps we went with gas masks, chairs to sit on and cushions to sit on or protect our heads. We put our gasmasks on not knowing if German aircraft were overhead dropping bombs or gas already. The all-clear siren sounded and we went back into daylight again.

We started school at Peter Symonds, the existing pupils attended in the mornings and we went in the afternoons. The following is an excerpt from 'History of Peter Symonds', *"A disastrous development was the evacuation to Winchester of the Portsmouth Northern secondary school. Their 450 boys were sent to share the school premises with the immediate result that Symondians could attend for classes only in the mornings. Staff responded by starting lessons earlier and making them shorter and by increasing homework."*

In November our headmaster called the whole school together and said there was an outbreak of stealing from shops, especially Woolworths, which involved some pupils. He said it had to stop. We were visitors in someone else's town and representatives of Portsmouth. This gave the school a bad name. There would be severe punishment for future offenders. I think things improved a little after that.

Soon after the start of the War the blackout came into operation. Street lights were switched off, all traffic had dimmed lights or lights with shades on. Windows were covered with black material or curtains, doors that opened to the outside had double curtains or the light switched off when going in and out. Before we got used to it, there were a lot of shouts from air raid wardens "Put that light out".

By the end of September, everyone was issued with a national identity card and a number. I kept the number until I joined the Navy in 1943, and when I left in 1946 I got my new card and number in Portsmouth.

In the winter evenings we went on a poison gas awareness course at a local school. We learnt about gases and checked our gasmasks in a mobile gas van. Christmas came and home we went by train to celebrate with our families. It was strange being home with my parents again. They had visited me in Winchester three or four times - but to see them and my sister all day for the fortnight was special.

As the year ended we were cheered by the sinking of the pocket battleship 'Graf Spee' by three cruisers, and then the rescue of three-hundred POWs from a German tanker by HMS Cossack, a destroyer.

I joined the public library. Whenever possible we used to make a dash for the side room where the daily papers and some magazines were available for all to read.

The last Sunday in May was a national day of prayer throughout the country for the troops in France. Winchester Cathedral was jam packed and crowds were outside praying. I had never seen so many people in one church before. A week later our prayers were being answered, the troops were brought back from Dunkirk. I don't remember seeing British troops but only Belgian and French looking lost and giving away any small change to children who asked for it. Then they were gone.

The Home Guard was founded and salvage or recycling was being organised. Four or five of us joined the Youth Service Corps, with an arm band to show we were legal. We used to collect books, magazines and papers for salvage or to sort out items for the troops or run book sales to raise money.

Summer came and close to where I was billeted was an ideal place to watch 'dog fights' and the trails of aircraft of both sides in the sky against a background of machine gun fire. The sirens would often sound and when at Peter Symonds school we would slowly walk across 2 football pitches to where the air raid shelters were built, close to the back walls of neighbouring gardens. Sometimes we would stay there for an hour, or the 'all clear' would go almost as soon as we got there. So back we would slowly go to our classrooms being urged on by prefects and masters.

In August, in spite of an air raid on Portsmouth we went home for the holidays. There was one raid while we were home and I cycled around to see the damage.

One thing that used to happen then, that could not happen now, was the delivering of parcels by service bus. While I was billeted my parents had to pay eight shillings per week into the Post Office and my landlady drew out the money to cover my stay. Later Mum provided sheets when mine wore out and clothes. Also she sent the occasional extras such as sugar, home made jam, cake and vegetables.

We only had one wireless in the house and that was in the lodger's front room, downstairs. We were allowed to listen to a comedy show and to Churchill's speeches about the progress of the War. Sometimes we heard 'An American War Correspondent in London'.

There were three cinemas in the city. Later on, my next door neighbour's sister came to live there. She was an usherette/cashier at the Theatre Royal and I often received free tickets for films.

Mrs Woodland had a son who visited her when he was stationed in Winchester in the Military Police. He was married but had no children and used to collect for the Prudential insurance company before the War. His wife, called "Mamselle" by Mrs W., took over his round during the War until he came back. During one of his visits he saw me writing up my diary and said that we should not keep a diary during the War, so I tore it up.

One day the call went out for volunteers, so some of us became dead, badly wounded, walking wounded or just shocked. We were issued with a tie-on label stating what we supposedly were. We stood, slumped or laid round the High Street area of Winchester for a full scale exercise for the Air Raid Services. The police, ambulance, fire and local wardens all took part. I lay down - 'dead! Luckily the weather was fine and, when the wounded were dealt with, I was told to get up and go home.

Another volunteer effort was potato picking. A lorry took us to Micheldever and we spent the day picking up spuds.

My friend Derek Hall had a Sunday job pumping the church organ during the service. When he went home for the weekend he asked me do it for him. After a three mile walk, I stood behind the organ pumping. For this I received sixpence - then had to walk home.

By now I had been allowed to borrow books from the adult library. Suddenly we were banned from the reference room in the library. Somebody had been cutting pictures out of Jane's Ships and Aircraft books as well as others. I don't know if they ever found out the culprit but we took the blame as we were evacuees.

Winchester had many air raid warnings - caused by planes raiding the ports or flying over to other parts of the country - but no raid as rumour said that Hitler was going to be crowned at Winchester when England was beaten!

Soon after Christmas the blitz on Portsmouth and Southampton increased. Letters would arrive later than expected. Rumours flew around the school, this place had been bombed, that road damaged. Then letters arrived and told me that the family was safe.

In March, Mum told me they had moved to a new address. Bombs had blown out the back of our house, so they moved to dad's boss's bungalow which was empty as he had moved away. At Easter or just after, I went to Portchester to see our new home.

Back at school the Air Training Corps (ATC) had been formed for fifteen year olds plus. The juniors were very put out that there was nothing similar that we could join. In 1942 the Army Cadet Force formed a company at the school. We had uniforms and boots and paraded, marched and did manoeuvres on the golf course with old Ross rifles.

In 1942 there was a large Commando raid with the Canadians on the French coast at Dieppe. After their return they were stationed next door to the school for a while. In March 1943 we marched to the Royal Green Jackets' Barracks to be assessed for our War Certificate A, which involved marching to the orders of the regimental sergeant major (RSM) of the Gloucestershire Regiment, stationed there at the time. Happily he was well satisfied with us. We also used to take part in inter-company shooting.

During the War there were many special days or weeks of exhortation to "Save for a Warship, Aircraft, or Tank." A saying from National Savings was 'Lend to Defend the Right to be Free'. 'Is Your Journey Really Necessary?' was around early in the War, but in 1942 they organised a 'Holidays at Home' summer to cut down on travel. In Winchester events were held in the Guildhall and at the North Walls recreation ground. Some of the London Scottish Band, stationed there then, marched and counter marched in the afternoons and the dance band section played in the evening.

Margaret, my sister, by then back from a short evacuation to Wiltshire, was by the sweet/tobacconist shop on the corner of Queens Road and Copnor Road, when the bomb landed on the church and the blast blew her to the ground and the glass from the shop window shattered over her but she was unhurt!.

In 1943 I sat for the combined Dockyard Apprentices and Naval Artificers Apprentices Examinations and passed. Dad came up to Winchester and we talked over which to choose. The War was still on and looked as though it would last for a few more years yet, so I decided to join the Navy as an apprentice in the Fleet Air Arm for 5 years and then serve for twelve years after the age of eighteen in war and peace.

I left Winchester and school in July and joined H.M.S. Daedalus, Lee on Solent on 4th August 1943.

Being evacuated overseas – Fred Steele, Alan Corbishley, Beryl Harris, John Cole and Dorothy Pelosi/Harry Hargreaves tell their stories

Before the War was declared parents across the country worried as to what would happen to them, but especially they were worried for their children. Some families decided that at all costs the family would stay together. In other families, the father was called up or volunteered to fight, which left the mother and her children on their own. When the Government introduced a system of evacuating children overseas, to America, Canada, South Africa, New Zealand or Australia, some families jumped at the idea in the hope of sending their children somewhere safe. Other families couldn't bear to think of their children going so far away so agreed that they could be evacuated in the UK. Some mothers went with their children when they were evacuated but most stayed at home and sent the children away for their safety.

When the Government asked in June 1940 for volunteer children to go overseas, 211,448 child applications were made by July. The Government was overwhelmed by the response. Only a few could be chosen. Everyone who applied had to know, or be related, to someone in the new country.

Some children who did not get chosen to be part of the Government's scheme were still sent abroad but went as private evacuees.

When parents received this letter they were pleased. They thought their children were going to a place of safety!

The following, tell in the words of some of the evacuees, what happened to just a few of them:

SDL/16

CHILDREN'S OVERSEAS RECEPTION BOARD
45, Berkeley Street,
W.1.

Telephone:
Mayfair 8400

CONFIDENTIAL.

Dear Sir (or Madam),

    I am writing this personal letter on the instructions of Mr. Geoffrey Shakespeare who is the Minister responsible for the administration of the Children's Overseas Reception Scheme. Mr. Shakespeare is sure that you will appreciate its reassuring nature.

    You may have heard over the wireless, or have read in the Press, that the Government cannot take responsibil for sending children overseas under the scheme without adequa naval protection.

    In the accompanying letter you are notified

~~You have already been notified~~

that your child (or children) has (or have) been accepted for evacuation overseas. You can rest assured that arrangemen will be made for naval convoy. You can also rest assured that we shall not let your child (or children) go overseas if at the last moment we find that the situation has changed and that no convoy can be provided.

    In the interest of the safety of your child (or children), and others who will accompany them, we ask you to regard this information as confidential - that is to say, you should not discuss the matter even with your neighbours, and you should ask your child (or children) also not to talk about it. We know we can rely upon you in this matter.

Yours faithfully,

Fred Steele – SS City of Benares – of 90 children on board, 83 were lost, only seven children survived.

I came from Hull in 1939 and when the overseas evacuation scheme was brought forward, I wanted to go. I had a brother in Canada, in the mounted police in Montreal. We left home under supervision of a school master. When we reached Liverpool we had to go into a housing complex until the ship was ready.

The ship was like a palace. It had an Indian crew – anything we wanted we could have. Of all days to sail it was Friday 13th. We should have sailed a day earlier but something cropped up. We joined up with a convoy of 16 ships. We were the biggest ship which meant we led the convoy. We had two Navy escorts but once we got out of the 600 miles limit they thought we would be safe. We were told 'U' boats didn't work out that far – but little did they know!

The ship's escorts had just left us. It was 17th September 1940. I was in my bunk. There were four bunks in our cabin. There was no one above me, but two of my mates were in other bunks. There was a terrific crash. Warning bells started going off. The next thing I knew the top bunk came through on top of me. The water mains had burst. I managed to get out and woke Paul. The young boy below couldn't find his glasses, so was crying. We had a quick look round but he wouldn't come, so we lost him.

A torpedo had come in under us, so there was a big hole in the ship which we climbed over. We got up on the deck. A huge seaman grabbed me by the neck and threw me into the lifeboat; a few more people followed including someone called Mary Cornish. She wasn't meant to be in our lifeboat. She was a teacher from London, as an escort for other girls, but she looked after us in the lifeboat.

The 'U' boat was a U48. There was a lot of screaming as the ship went down. About 40 people including six children were on our lifeboat. The crew laid us down in the life boat as there was quite a storm going on. We were thrown around. We watched people and ships crash around us. It was dreadful. We drifted out and that was the last time we were seen for eight days. In fact, we learnt later that we had been reported as dead.

We tried to make for Ireland. We rode out three massive storms. One day when the weather was quiet we thought there was a submarine nearby but luckily it turned out to be a school of whales.

CANADA.

CHILDREN'S OVERSEAS RECEPTION BOARD,

45, Berkeley Street,
LONDON, W.1.

The following is a suggested outfit for each child undertaking the journey:-

BOYS.

Gas Mask
1 overcoat and mackintosh if possible.
1 suit.
1 pullover.
1 hat or school cap.
2 shirts (coloured).
2 pairs stockings.
2 undervests
2 pairs pants.
2 pairs pyjamas.
1 pair boots or shoes.
1 pair plimsolls.
6 handkerchiefs
1 comb.
1 toothbrush and paste.
1 face flannel.
1 towel.
x 1 suitcase - about 26" x 18".
Stationery and pencil.
Ration card.
Identity card.
Birth Certificate (if possible)
Bible or New Testament.

GIRLS.

Gas Mask.
1 warm coat and mackintosh if possible.
1 cardigan or woollen jumper.
1 hat or beret.
1 pair warm gloves.
1 warm dress or skirt and jumper.
2 pairs stockings.
1 change of underclothing, including vests, knickers, etc.
1 pair strong boots or shoes.
1 pair plimsolls.
2 cotton dresses or overalls with knickers.
2 pairs pyjamas.
1 towel.
3 handkerchiefs.
1 hairbrush and comb.
1 toothbrush and paste
1 face flannel or sponge.
Sanitary towels.
1 linen bag.
x 1 suitcase - about 26" x 18".
1 attache case or haversack.
Sewing outfit.
Stationery and pencil.
Ration card.
Identity card.
Birth Certificate (if possible).
Bible or New Testament.

x No trunk will be permitted.

All clothing should be clearly marked in indelible ink with the child's name and the Children's Overseas Reception Board Registration number.

No Passport will be required.

Each child should carry a sufficient supply of food and thirst quenching fruit to last 24 hours. It is particularly requested that no bottles should be carried. The following are suitable and can easily be packed:-

Sandwiches, egg and cheese.
Packets of nuts and seedless raisins.
Dry biscuits and packets of cheese.
Barley sugar (not chocolate).
Apples, bananas, oranges.

This was a very long list for some families – many children were used to sharing with their brothers and sisters

We were some way out when on the Sunday, we spotted a merchant ship. We were sure she saw us. She slowed down and we were waving and shouting, but for no reason at all, she put her foot down and left us. We were so disappointed.

We learnt later that this ship may have been HMS Ascania. This was an old Cunarder converted to an armed merchant cruiser, returning to her base in Halifax after handing over to a local escort off the Irish coast. One of her lookouts reported seeing a lifeboat with children aboard, but nothing else was seen and he was told he must have imagined it. The Ascania then steamed on to Halifax.

We were eventually spotted by a Sunderland flying boat with an Australian crew. They circled us and dropped a few supplies and signalled that they would be back with more supplies. They said a destroyer was on the way.   A second plane came back and dropped food and also a smoke flare.

It was 3 o'clock in the afternoon when we were finally picked up by HMS Anthony. This was another lucky streak as she wasn't looking for us but was diverted from something else. She took us to Greenock in Scotland.

My dad came and brought me home. On the way back, near London, they had to stop the train and reverse back because the enemy was machine-gunning the line.

I couldn't walk for the best part of a month as I had frost bite. My friend, Paul, had two toes amputated. Two of our survivors both lost their five-year old brothers who were on the same ship. After the War I met the captain of the 'U' boat who said he had no idea that children were on the ship as he wouldn't have hit us.

Alan Corbishley – SS Volendam – all 320 children on board survived

My parents were worried about the bombing, so applied to the Government in June 1940 for me to be part of the overseas evacuation scheme. The only criterion was that you had to have someone to stay with. Living near my parents were Mr and Mrs Graham and their daughter, Eunice. He was a bus driver with the Hants and Dorset Bus Company. One of his rural journeys, and one of his stopping points, was Minstead post office in the New Forest. The postmistress had a

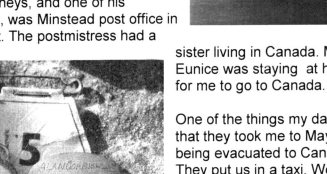

sister living in Canada. Mr and Mrs Graham decided Eunice was staying at home so my parents applied for me to go to Canada.

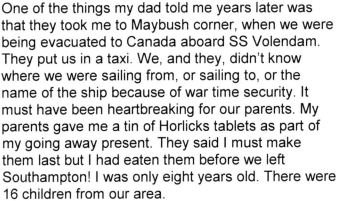

One of the things my dad told me years later was that they took me to Maybush corner, when we were being evacuated to Canada aboard SS Volendam. They put us in a taxi. We, and they, didn't know where we were sailing from, or sailing to, or the name of the ship because of war time security. It must have been heartbreaking for our parents. My parents gave me a tin of Horlicks tablets as part of my going away present. They said I must make them last but I had eaten them before we left Southampton! I was only eight years old. There were 16 children from our area.

We all had a wrist bracelet and an identity disk around our neck. It's strange but there was a different number on my bracelet from that on the necklace. When we got back my necklace was all chewed, it must have been nerves.

Soon after our naval escort left, we were torpedoed by a U-boat. All I can remember is sitting on the floor in the lifeboat. Our lifeboat was picked up by a banana boat – and I was hoisted aboard in a basket usually used for carrying bananas.

I can't remember getting back to Glasgow. I must have blanked off. I got everything back including my suitcase but I lost my teddy bear. We stayed overnight in Glasgow, then came back to London by train and then travelled home. We had our group photograph taken and met the mayor. One girl chicken pox, so she couldn't come back immediately.

After the War the German U-boat commander presented a plaque to the local submarine museum, Gosport. The U-boat crews are world-wide friends now.

Beryl Harris, née Pinnick – SS Volendam – of 320 children on board 320 survived

In 1939, my sister and I were evacuated to Ringwood in Hampshire to stay with an aunt, but we didn't get on with her, so came home. Then mother decided that as we had cousins in Canada, we should go to Canada, so she applied and filled in a form. We were all going to stay there together.

My diary notes: *August 24th 1940 went to Liverpool, there was an air raid, enjoyed train journey. 25th, went to church, Sunday afternoon played games with some other girls. 26th, played rounders, pm went shopping.*

Eventually we sailed on 28th August. I enjoyed the whole experience of going on the boat – the sailors gave me a souvenir of the buttons off their coat. The Dutch sailors were wonderfully kind and we all enjoyed ourselves. It was a luxury liner. We were well fed and watered in the dining room. Pam (my younger sister) and I had our own cabin with a washbasin but no lavatory. This was way down in the depths of the ship.

What I did notice in the afternoon before we were torpedoed was that we were in a huge convoy and the only means of contact then was Morse code.

There was a lot of that going on and the convoy closed in on us. There were battle ships, oil tankers, all huge. Why didn't they sink the battleship? I often wonder about that.

When the alarm went off at about 11 pm we were divided into groups of approximately ten children and were looked after by a Church of England deaconess still wearing her robes. She was very kind. She knocked on all our doors when the alarm went off and we put our life jackets on. We had previously had a drill but this time we had to get into a lifeboat for real in our nightclothes. I put tremendous trust in adults. I can't honestly say that I was petrified. We were in the lifeboat for two and a half hours. I was very sick. We were picked up by an oil tanker.

I can remember as they were rowing in the lifeboat, someone shouted, "Get away from the bloody boat." This was the first time I had ever heard swearing in public! The ship was listing and they were afraid it was going to come down on us. By then I was being seasick. We were lying on the floor under the boards where the men were rowing and we were all over each other.

What I didn't realise, at the time we were picked up, was the danger we must have been in. There were very strong winds and very rough seas. We were told to jump from the lifeboat to the oil tanker which was low in the water. We were told to jump as the lifeboat came up to the same level as the oil tanker. It was amazing that we all got from the lifeboat to the tanker. Someone just said, "Jump." And we did as we were told.

All the children were very sick on the oil tanker. The captain gave up his cabin for us. We all piled in and ate ship's biscuits because that was all there was to eat.

We were taken to Scotland and were the first off the rescue ship. When we came ashore, clothes were brought to us. They must have asked local people. I had long boy's socks. People rallied round. The Scottish people were all wonderful to us.

Eventually we went home and were met by the mayor, still in these clothes.

Another person I know had a slightly different experience – John Roberts was tied to a rope around his waist and hauled up the side of his rescue ship.

One child and some dogs were left on board the Volendam. Despite being badly damaged the boat didn't sink and a skeleton crew was sent back on board to rescue the ship. A tug was sent out from Liverpool to tow it back.

Arriving in Scotland

I didn't talk about what happened for years, I shrugged it off. I just got on with living. In this day and age I most probably would have had counselling. The doctor said, "Keep her off for a few days," but my mother sent me back to school straight away. It was a normal time. The bombing was far more horrendous than this experience.

It was an amazing experience, but, at the time, I didn't realise it.

John Cole – a private evacuation overseas

I started my second year of school just as war was declared. The first thing that seemed serious to me was when we were issued with gas masks. They smelled strongly of rubber and the visor misted so they were very unpleasant to wear. We were told that we had to carry them at all times. One day I set off to visit my grandparents. When I was less than half way there the air raid siren sounded. It didn't worry me but the fact that I had forgotten my gas mask did bother me and I began to cry. A woman who lived in the area saw me took me into her air raid shelter and consoled me. The "all clear" sounded not too long after and I continued my journey.

Unbeknown to my sister Christine and me, auntie Gwen, my father's older sister and uncle Len, whom we had never met, had cabled my parents at the outbreak of war, offering to have us in Canada 'for the duration'. We confidently expected this to be months. Unbeknown to us was that my parents had been trying all autumn and winter to get us a passage on a neutral ship. Eventually, in June 1940, with the capitulation of France imminent my parents decided to send us on the Dutch ship, the SS Volendam sailing from Southampton. Our departure from England could not be announced because of wartime security. A cable was sent wishing my aunt a happy birthday, a pre-arranged signal to say that we had sailed.

Christine was four years old. I was nearly eight. We were put in the charge of a Dutch stewardess who spoke only a few words of English but we were told that we were going to live with auntie Gwen and uncle Len and that "everything will be alright". We had a large bound wooden steamer trunk and Christine had her treasured little basket containing her hair brush and the keys to the trunk. My parents didn't indulge in histrionics and, as far as I remember we were not homesick. The stewardess was ever present and firm but kind. She ensured that we conformed to the ships routine. The weather turned progressively warmer and it seems that it was about a fortnight before we entered port, New York. Some kind people took charge of us. The next day we were taken to the railway station. We were handed over to the conductor. The day dragged on with frequent visits from the conductor.

At last he announced that we were due at a place called Buffalo. We were to stay put while our carriage was shunted to connect to another engine which would take us to Toronto where our auntie and uncle would meet us. In mid evening we arrived and went into the arms of my aunt whom I could barely remember and an uncle whom I had never seen before. Think what it must have been like for Christine, not yet five.

We were shown our bedroom with bunk beds which uncle Len had made. In today's world the counsellers and psychologists would say that we must have been traumatised and be in need of special treatment. What we got was straight forward loving absorption into family and I don't recall any homesickness. We were introduced to the neighbours and friends in a matter of fact way and some of Gwen and Len's closer friends were designated as aunts and uncles. After a few days, a reporter from the local newspaper came to talk to us. We were the first evacuees to arrive in the city. We were dubbed 'War Guests'. The newspaper cutting was put in the scrapbook which Gwen assembled over the next six years - medical history and school reports mainly. The reporter asked me what I thought of Hitler and I replied 'He is an evil old man'.

We didn't think about it at the time but it must have been a great upheaval in their lives. Gwen and Len were still making their way as immigrants and there were no subsidies or benefits to cushion the costs of our arrival. A kind manufacturer of toys provided me with a box of about two dozen push along cars. Birthday and Christmas presents, especially from our honorary aunts and uncles, tended to be useful dressing gowns and new trousers. However, we had all the essential winter clothing. I was given a pair of ice skates at Christmas. We had a sledge which we could use to tow each other in the garden or along the footpath. Later we would be given skis and a toboggan. So we never went without. I started school in September. The teachers were all female; Most were 'Miss', probably because the men of their generation had died in the first war. Gwen had arranged for the daughter of a friend to take us to Sunday school. She was in my class at school and was very kind.

I caught endless heavy colds that winter. Doctors were expensive and Gwen applied her family remedies, all without success so I had to have my tonsils removed. A Dr Rundle operated on me in his surgery. Dr Rundle never sent the bill. Dr Langmaid was the dentist and he discounted the bills quite heavily.

Len had two weeks summer holiday each year and we always went to Floral Park on Lake Couchouching, just north of Lake Simcoe. Floral Park didn't have any flowers as such; it was a working farm. with simple wooden cabins set amongst the trees. Our holidays at Floral farm were action packed. A number of Gwen and Len's friends had summer cottages. We were invited for the occasional weekend. Of course, not all was sweetness and light. I was forgetful and at times disobedient.

I wasn't aware that Christine had any trouble settling in Canada. She got the attention that a sweet little girl of her age would attract anywhere. It was a year before she started at school. She soon had friends of her own age. A brother was born in October 1940, about four months after we had left. We received letters and occasionally snapshot from home. By now the Canadians had began to collect salvage - aluminum foil, scrap metal, newspapers, even animal fat which apparently was used in the manufacture of explosives.

The little airfield north of Oshawa became a hive of activity. Numerous old biplanes, Tiger Moths began flying. It was an Empire Training school with mainly British pilots sent to safety to learn to fly. During the winter months the planes operated with skis.

Food was never rationed but there were shortages of a few things. I was aware of the general trend of the War. We were vaguely aware that some mail was 'going missing' without the details of the considerable loss of shipping in mid Atlantic. Later, after the Normandy invasion I became aware that the allies were beginning to win. VE (Victory in Europe) Day was celebrated but no mention was made of our return to England. I was due to start my first year at the high school in the September.

The celebrations on VE-Day had been joyous because so many Canadians were involved in Europe but the news that Japan had capitulated brought crowds into the parks. Bonfires were lit and there were scenes of jubilation late into the night. People were crying and laughing, dancing and hugging. Motor cyclists altered the timing of the engine so that it backfired - a substitute for fireworks. Although the War was over, nothing really changed for us. There were no places for civilians on trains. The passenger ships were all troopships. Presumably they were occupied returning partly trained servicemen to Britain and sending relief workers to the ravaged continent. So I started at the high school

Then I was going home. There were 'goodbyes' from school friends and the many people that Gwen and Len knew including my honorary aunts and uncles. I was booked on a troopship, the SS Georgic but it was not deemed suitable for a ten year old girl to travel with me in such spartan conditions. There was a boat train from Montreal to Halifax. Friends of Gwen and Len would accommodate me overnight in Montreal and put me on the train. The brown steamer trunk which had conveyed all the worldly goods of both Christine and me on the westward journey was full of my possessions now. The send off from Oshawa was sombre. Once on the boat train however, it all seemed so definite. The reality of going 'home' was not accompanied by the reassurances of all the kind people who looked after us in 1940. Now, I realised what I was leaving, but I didn't know what to expect when I arrived 'home'.

I was very miserable and I wept. The eastward journey across the Atlantic must have taken six days but I have no recollection of it. The Georgic arrived in Liverpool on a dull day. The ship's public address system gave details of who could disembark and my turn was not for some time. I scanned the waiting crowd and as it began to clear I could see two women who seemed to be waving tentatively in my direction. I decided that one definitely resembled my mother from the photographs which had come during the War. Eventually it was my turn to disembark. I politely shook hands with my mother and my aunt who had accompanied her. It retrospect it must have been very upsetting to have such a cold response from a near fourteen year old when you had seen off a near eight year old. Although I had always known that I would go 'home', the reality was that I was going to the unknown.

We went to a hotel for the night and caught a train for Southampton the next morning. The train was small, crowded, smelly and dirty compared with the Canadian ones. If you opened the window for more ventilation, your eyes were filled with gritty smuts from the smoke of the engine. The hotel had provided a packed lunch of dried up sandwiches with wafer thin dried up tinned meat. No sooner had the train worked up a bit of speed than it pulled into another station where it seemed to loiter needlessly before chugging for another few miles. We eventually arrived at Southampton in the late afternoon.

My parents had been able to buy a three bedroomed semi-detached house in Shirley, in Southampton which had escaped almost all the German bombing. I was introduced to my 'new' brother, David Ross. It was probably a bigger shock to have me imposed upon him. Mr and Mrs Appleton with whom my parents had been billeted at Compton were an elderly childless couple and David had had their sole attention as well as that of my parents. This underpinned all future relationships. My father tried not to get drawn to take sides. He was tired from years of overwork during the War and was working equally hard to re-establish a peacetime business in war weary and war torn Southampton. I was taken to my father's old school, to take some test papers so that I could be put into a class at the most appropriate level. I was kitted out with school uniform, all on the limited clothing coupons with which I had been allocated at the time. I soon discovered that the Canadian curriculum did not tie in with the teaching here. I was behind in some things and ahead in others. My classmates, along with everyone else, noticed my Canadian accent but this disappeared within a few months without any conscious effort by me.

Dorothy Pelosi and Harry Hargreaves (brother and sister) - another private, overseas evacuation

We lived near shipyards and our parents were frightened of the Germans, especially after the fall of France. They arranged a private evacuation for me, my brother and four cousins. As part of her war effort, my aunt sponsored six of us to go to America. We stayed with my aunt Dorothy and her friend in New Jersey and then in New York. The two ladies were both unmarried and had no experience of having children. Eventually, the four younger children went to boarding school and I stayed with the ladies.

I realised enough was enough so it was decided I would go home. I had been too young to appreciate the experience of being in America and too young to be separated from our parents.

We travelled by train to Texas. I boarded a Dutch ship, SS Jagersfontein, which left from Galveston. In June, 480 miles off the coast of Bermuda, we were torpedoed. For four days and four nights we were in lifeboats.

When we were in the lifeboat, a submarine surfaced and two men jumped into the water to get the name of the ship which was floating in the sea.

I had a passport when going out to America but not one coming back, as it had gone down with the ship. I needed a guardian so they gave me a Mrs Jenkins.

We were rescued by a Swiss ship, the St Cyr. The worst bit was climbing up a rope ladder. We were later put down in Gibraltar where I stayed for three weeks. We were then brought to Greenock by one of the Union Castle Line ships.

I sent a telegram to my mother so she knew I was still alive.

"After an exciting experience"

was all I could say, as it was censored.

Harry and cousin James Hargreaves later returned to the UK. They were aboard a Royal Naval Aircraft Carrier, HMS Khedive. It was mainly crewed by a British crew but most of the fleet air arm crew were Canadians. The chairs were tied together with rope because of the dreadful weather in the North Atlantic. They arrived in the UK on November 19th, 1943 with about 20 other young boys. The Canadian crew was brilliant. The boys arrived in Liverpool and stayed for two days before eventually going to Glasgow to be met by my mother.

I couldn't watch the Titanic film for years. I still believe that my experience was similar, but as a child I had no fear.

PS – a message from Harry in Canada - *I hope some day to go to Greenwich and check out the log of HMS Khedive. A photograph was taken of the children on board during a meal. When given the picture we were told not to talk to anyone about the weather conditions on the voyage. I believe that the Navy was trying out a new convoy route. The photograph we were given stated on the back "not for transmission to the press". It is lost. I remember this – and much more – vividly. But some things I would rather not talk about.*

Some thoughts about child evacuation

It is hard to imagine what it must have been like for the parents of the children. They sent their children abroad in the hope of keeping them safe. Instead, many children perished at sea. Others had horrifying experiences when the ships they were on were torpedoed and sunk and other children came home almost as strangers.
It is even harder to imagine what the parents must have felt not knowing, in many cases, what was going on or where the children were.

"NIGHT OF HORROR WHEN 83 CHILDREN DIED IN TORPEDOED LINER" October 4th 1940, War Illustrated

Newspapers made headlines about the sinking of the ships, but the parents had no idea until much later whether their own children were safe and well. They had to wait for a telegram or letter to give them the news.

A welcome telegram to the parents

CHILDREN'S OVERSEAS RECEPTION BOARD,
45, Berkeley Street,
London, W.1.

Mayfair 8400
Ref.

1st September 1940

Dear Sir or Madam,

In confirmation of our telegram, I am glad to tell you that although the ship on which your child/~~children~~ was travelling has received some damage, we have heard that your child/~~children~~ are safe, and there is therefore no cause for anxiety. As soon as we have further information regarding your child/~~children~~ we will communicate with you at once.

Yours faithfully,

Marjorie Maxse

Letters to worried parents giving hardly any
information about their children

Many children did get safely to their chosen countries. However, when they came home, many years later, they found life very difficult. Rationing was still in place, they hardly knew their parents and the way of life was very different.

Megan Paxman - *Eventually she (my mother) thought cami knickers were rather rude so she bought me knickers to go under the camis*

I was thirteen on the Sunday that WW2 broke out. My mother burst into tears but I thought it was rather exciting. She said dad is too old but Richard (my brother) will have to fight and he might be killed.

He was doing A levels at school and having passed them he went to the London School of Economics (LSE). Before he went to university he was a member of the LDU (Local Defence Unit). He had a horrid smelling khaki uniform and huge boots.

Daddy was appointed as chief ARP warden and had to go to the station. He had a special gas mask. We lived in Rochdale. In the cellar dad had made bunks for us as somewhere to go if there was an emergency. If there was an air raid warning we were allowed to go to school 1 hour later - which we liked.

My brother was evacuated to Phwellii in N Wales. After a year there he was old enough to sign up and he joined the Fleet Air Arm. I don't remember any planes at that time. If there was a warning at school we had to go to these horrible bunkers. We were all scrunched up together. During that time we were deprived of some things, of course. My father said "Go and buy me some chocolate." I said "What about the coupons?" My father knew nothing of them. My mother managed everything in the house and often used to barter with the butcher for example.

Later we had a considerable number of air aids over Manchester. My mother's teeth used to chatter with fear which was worse than the noise of the planes! Often, after the siren went off, the raid didn't happen so we went on with life.

Shop assistants used to wear long dresses. When you went shopping you got dressed up, My mother wore a hat and a fox fur, even during the War.

There was much more community spirit during the War. All the shops were separate, there was a pork butcher and a beef butcher. Dogs would put their paws on the counter. Our butcher had a piano in his shop and you had to queue to spend your coupons. He said, "You must sing a song or do a dance before you get your meat."

My mother was a great hoarder. We had tinned ham and all sorts of food stored in a cellar at home. She used to buy clothing coupons – "They want the money and I want the coupons." It was jolly wrong looking back.

Whilst still living at home during the War my mother took me to see 'Gone with the Wind'. The cinema had an organ that came up through the floor to play music. Before we went to the cinema I went to Woolworths to buy a lipstick. My mother and father didn't approve of make-up. I put it on in the cloakroom and after the film I had to wipe it off before I went home. It made me feel grown up though I don't suppose anyone noticed. My mother and I were sitting in the stalls and I sat next to a complete stranger. He was so carried away by the film he hit me on the knee and said "The bitch" when Vivien Leigh was being difficult.

My mother said "If you have camiknickers, it is four coupons but if you have slip and pants it is six." Eventually she thought cami knickers were rather rude so bought me knickers to go under the camis. We were walking one day and we could hear clicking, I didn't know where the noise came from - it was the large buttons I had sewed on to the flaps of the knickers!

School continued and then I went to college in London, St Katherine's for Christian students. I was doing an advanced PE course. I desperately wanted to join the wrens because I liked the uniform. My father said no not until you finish your education.   I said why, and he said "The WRACS were very loose women during WW1 and we had to appoint other soldiers to guard them!"

The college was evacuated to Babbacombe. We lived in four hostels as students. It was a very pleasant life. There was a ten mile ban from the coast inland for people unless they had a reason to be there. Nearly all trainee pilots were billeted there – ACRC air receiving station. They had white flashes on their caps, meaning to us that they were intelligent people! It was lovely for us because we had all sorts of dances. We had to be back in the hostel by 9.20pm. If you were late you lost one of your Saturday privileges (in at 10pm.).

We used to go to the local dance hall and leave our coats at the door, because we knew it would take us five minutes to get back. There was always someone there to check up on us. We were there for two years. Life was great. We had no problems, no air raids, then the Americans came and they were billeted nearby. They brought out a white piano every night and played beautiful music. We leaned out of our windows to listen. My friend and I met two Americans and one of them bought me a box of chocolates which I hadn't seen since the War began. I didn't want to open them.

We had a Scottish cook in Babbacombe. We never got butter – that went to staff – we only had margarine. My friend used to put on a Scottish voice to the cook and tell her we were hungry. We always got something.

We had to learn how to use a stirrup pump to put out fires. My friend said "You pump and I'll hold it", but she held it to her face to see if it worked and the water went all over her.

Pilots used to drop supplies to POW people who were so hungry they came to get the food even though they were told not to so they were killed. They were so hungry they couldn't wait.

When in Torquay, on Sundays you were allowed to go to St Mary's church or the one at the college. One night we went to the college as the principle was giving the lesson. We heard the sound of an aeroplane going round and round, then a bomb dropped on St Mary's church. It killed 28 of our pupils plus quite a few of the local people. It was a stray bomb. There was a memorial plaque erected after the end of the War.

During that time, we got very annoyed with the Americans because we used to buy sandwiches for 4d but they went up to 8d as soon as the Americans came so we couldn't afford them. The food at college was awful. We shared a room, three of us, me, Margaret Jewell and Isabel Rebecca Leinster who came from the north. My parents used to send food parcels which I shared, but when Isabel had hers she would hide them under the bed. One day we were so hungry, I said you hold her down and I'll get the tin. There was a huge cake so we helped ourselves to a slice each.

All the time we were learning how to 'jitterbug'. We had pleated skirts which swung out. We were doing this at lunchtime when the Bishop came in. Miss Ottley, our tutor, was a very clever person but not much good as a disciplinarian. She was not pleased to see us dancing.

In Babbacombe, the chemist used to get a monthly quota of make up and we used to queue up to buy some. We used to flirt with him so we got more; he told us to come round the side.

An officer from the RAF came and asked for someone to be on the stage and just say a few lines. I was chosen. We went to the theatre in Babbacombe. I only had one line to say and I used to practise it. They sent Maxfactor to do the makeup. I had to wear a long evening dress. In the play a man had been accused of murder. In those days you had cami knickers which did up with buttons. Mine came down when I was on stage and I couldn't move. I stepped out of them and kicked them away and they went into the face of the prompt! For ages afterwards my friends teased me, "Megan, have you left anything behind?" We had a late night extension because of the play. Maxfactor had given us wonderful make-up and then we had to report back to Miss Otley. She said "Aren't you wearing a lot of paint on your face?" She was horrified and said we must wash it off immediately.

Everything went on very peacefully until just before D-Day. We knew something was happening but didn't know what it was. There were parcels on the docks, plus many ships. Then Torquay was bombed and we had to go down to the town to give blood. It went straight from me to the person who needed it - who was lying on the bed next to me. The next day we knew that D-Day had happened.

My brother had been trained as a pilot and he had been in America for three years. Because he was allowed home I was given permission to go to see him. I can remember my friend, Margaret, seeing me off from Torquay at 3pm in the afternoon. I was to go to Manchester where he was meant to meet me. The train was full of troops. It was so crowded they had to sit on kit bags in the corridors. There were no lights on the train, all the station numbers were blacked out. I can remember sitting and the two soldiers on either side of me both fell asleep and had their heads on my shoulders, they were so tired.

We got as far as Crewe as there had been bombing in Manchester. It took fourteen hours to get there. My brother was there in his uniform and as he escorted me to where he had left his car there were water pipes which we had to step over. It was dark so we couldn't find our way. There were many black people. My brother pushed them away. I said "Why did you do that?" He said "That's what we do in America." I told him it was appalling.

When my brother went to America, he got boils because the food was too rich. He was 'adopted' by the DuPont family where he was billeted so he was really spoiled. They insisted on paying for all his meals and they loaned him their car. When he came back from the States he brought make-up and a bikini. It was white like satin. I thought it was very smart until I dived into a pool and it slid off! We used to plaster all the Maxfactor on our faces. We put so much on we thought the sun would melt it!

I completed my teaching certificate. You couldn't choose your job. You were appointed. I went to Rochester in Kent. I remember being told 'how very lucky we were because we were getting the first Burnham scale increase. We got £17 a month instead of £13. I lived in the YWCA hostel for £5.50 a week - for that we had bed, breakfast and an evening meal. The school had three floors. Boys were on the top floor, eleven years and over in the middle and the bottom floor was for the infants. The man on the top used to throw something out of a window and everyone rushed down stairs to try to catch it.

I had to teach seventy five-year olds because of a flu epidemic and the teachers were ill. I had never taught little ones, I was only qualified to teach teenagers. In my own class there were forty-eight pupils.

I remember D-Day. We went on a boat trip from Rochester to Sheerness. Despite the dreadful things that happened around us, we were rather cushioned from the worst.

Freda Davis - "...........Certainly not, if I had anyone it certainly wouldn't be a teacher"

I qualified as a teacher in 1935 after two years training. Then I had to do a year's supply teaching. Soon after that the powers that be decided that this was wrong for a new teacher. My first teaching job was in Church Street, Portsmouth. We shared one ruler which we kept under the door. As for discipline, a sharp rap on the table did a lot of good!

When war broke out I was at Court Lane school in Cosham. It was a very old school, and wasn't at all nice. The head was Miss Craddock. I was on holiday in Ireland when the news broke. We heard rumours about war and didn't know whether we would get back in time. When I got back Miss Craddock had been bothering my mother who said she didn't know when I would back. At school we had been making lists in triplicate all through the year. The children and teachers were given a 'yes' or 'no' card to fill in, saying whether or not they wanted to be evacuated. My head teacher kept getting on to me about bringing my card back so eventually someone came round to the house so I had to make a decision and decided to go with the children. We had been a whole year writing lists in triplicate People kept changing their minds about what was going to happen.

My mother was very upset. We talked about the horrors of war. We thought the bombing was going to come straight away. I remember my mother and I going up to Winter Road to a material shop and buying some light brown and white striped material. We spent the evening sewing to make a dress that I would take with me. We thought we were going away the next morning.

We had been given a list of what we had to take. I used a knapsack so my clothes were very screwed up. We had to report in the school playground at 9am and our names were ticked off on the list. Corporation double-decker buses were ready and the mothers were trying not to cry as they waved the children goodbye. Parents were not allowed in the playground. We really thought the Germans would be in Portsmouth the next day. That was the attitude.

Miss Craddock brought her sister as a 'helper' as a way of organising the evacuation. Most helpers didn't do much. It was convenient - a way of getting out of doing other jobs back at home - especially if their men were in the forces.

When we arrived in Wilton, Miss Craddock expected to be the head but she wasn't. She didn't like that.

Next to the school there was a donkey in a paddock. All the children – and the parents – were staring at it as they had not seen one before.

I went to the rectory with twelve girls. Mrs Bancroft had two girls and one boy, very blond. The girl's mother had said to the girl she should look after him. So when they were boarding the bus she had the boy hidden under her coat. Miss Craddock didn't like it when she found out.

We spent the first week settling the children down. We had a little church hall to use as a school and made a class at each end of the room. One half of the children went for a walk in the morning and the other half in the afternoon. The lessons took place as if there was a wall. We also had lessons in the rectory.

Materials were in short supply so we used the margins of the newspapers to write on.

The weather was good mostly as otherwise I'm not sure what we would have done. Local senior girls organised games for the younger children. Also, to fill in the time we were taken around Wilton House and Salisbury Cathedral.

Teachers were effectively on duty twenty four hours a day. No one told us what to teach, we just got on and taught what we wanted. Miss Craddock was still our head but we didn't have respect for her. If you saw her in the street you didn't acknowledge her. There was no check on the children's progress or on the teacher's. Several girls took the 11+ from there and they all passed so we must have done something right. The teachers were not informed even though one of the girls came second and another ninth in all of Portsmouth.

The pupils were made aware of different things. There was a map right across the board and the teacher went through where troops were stationed, where bombings were happening - so it became really interesting.
Back at home, my father, who was sixty-three at the time, had cancer but it was kept under control because he had regular visits to hospital where he had radium treatment on his face. It

got better and he was not in bad health really, but when war broke out his treatment stopped. This obviously hastened his death.

After I went off, both my brothers were called up and my elder brother was sent up to Leeds in a clerical job. He became very ill and then when he got better he was given quite a good pension. My mother, who was a very honest person, said "I think Geoffrey would have had that illness whether he was called up or not." My younger brother, Roy, had heard, before the War, about Warsash, where you could learn to fly as a hobby. He loved it so much. He was a schoolboy at the time and, prior to him starting flying lessons, the school used to send for my mother so say that he wasn't working hard enough. When war broke out he was called up because of his flying training. He was not killed in action, but in a plane crash on take-off. My dear mother was at home with my ailing father and had a telegram to ask where they wanted him buried even though she hadn't been told that he was dead. I was back home from Wilton for the weekend.

My mother was living at home alone and keeping things going. She was out walking the dog one day when she saw a WVS notice saying they wanted people to darn socks. She was good at needlework so she thought it a good idea. They wanted her to come in but she hoped to work from home because of the dog. The WVS changed her life completely.

The first Christmas we were at Wilton volunteers were called back to teach PE in Portsmouth so I went back. I was home for a week or so for enrolment and then I got into school proper but then I was evacuated back to Wilton. I thought I was going to go into my nice little billet but the Americans were there with their wives and Wilton had been made the Southern Command. There were soldiers everywhere and where I had stayed before was full. Mrs Aston was very worried and knew I had intended to go back but knew if she took an officer's wife she would get a lot more money so went round knocking on doors, trying to find me a place to stay. "Certainly not, if I had anyone it certainly wouldn't be a teacher" was the usual reply. Then a lady stopped me and said "I wonder if you would consider staying with me because I don't want to have Americans." From that day I was very happy and stayed for about three years. By that time I had my bicycle with me. The fare back to Portsmouth was 10/0d so I used to cycle back. The man I was going to marry was located close by so we went together.

I'd met Fred through the Girl Guides in about 1936. Fred was now working on Salisbury plain in a reserved occupation. Often there were dog-fights overhead as we cycled back so we got off our bikes and rolled into a ditch. Eventually, we decided not to cycle. Soon afterwards he was called up. He went to Assissi. He was put into the medical core and moved up through Italy where he brought the casualties back to be treated. He was not trained but worked in a helping capacity. At that time, most of the fighting men came home on leave every couple of years but he didn't get any leave here until the War had stopped. He went on leave in Italy. We communicated through letters which were censored. It was a printed form which you ticked – 'Are you well?' etc. There was no real information in it.

I came back to Portsmouth before the War ended in time to be included in fire watching on a three week cycle. I went to Highland Road school with my colleague, Miss Rook, who worked for the council. We slept in the school whilst on fire duty. We didn't get undressed in case of an emergency. I was getting quite tense as I hadn't been called out once. The fact was that the bombing was at an end.

Once we married I couldn't be a teacher. It was the same in the civil service – once you got married they froze your remuneration. I was a guide captain, so had to give that up too. Some girls went guiding all the way through the War but I had to just drop it. There was no provision made for the guides that were left.

Being A Bevin boy

Harold Goodwin - *When I only had a month to serve, the overseer approached me and asked if I would like to train as a deputy. I said, "NO THANK YOU!"*

I was born in December 1926 and we lived in Manchester. My father died in February 1939 so my mother had to bring up four children. When War started in September both my younger sister and I were evacuated. My sister went to Charlesworth, Derbyshire, and I was sent to Fairhaven which is between Lytham and Lytham St Anne's. It was not very pleasant as the family was all separated.

I went with a friend from next door of similar age, yet we were parted. We were in this community hall with labels on us and elderly people came along to choose - it was like a cattle market. I stayed with two sisters and a brother who were not married and were not used to having children about the house. There was another evacuee there, who I didn't know. They were out at work during the day so we were not allowed in the house.

They left a packed lunch for us in the shed. I learnt to play cards at Fairhaven, particularly a game called Conncan which is a bit like rummy.

After about three months I went to the house of a wonderful lady who was a widow. There were six of us. She fed us and looked after us really well even if we were naughty. She had a fire that burnt blocks of peat. We used to go the peat fields and bring back a stockpile for her.

Fortunately, being evacuated didn't last very long, it was totally unsuccessful for us as a family and within six months we were back in Manchester with our mother. When I was evacuated I had just started high school. When I returned to the school, we were not able to start any lessons until September so we spent about a month learning to play chess with our Latin master. He was in the ARP and in the middle of the chess lessons, he jumped up on the desk and showed us how to fall off a desk without injuring yourself.

We lived about a mile from the school, so I used to walk or cycle there. On another occasion, this master said that when I go up the hill on my bike I should go diagonally – it was possible to do this as there was so little traffic about.

We also learnt map reading, so we were able to help the Army when we were on the A483 to Oswestry. The large convoy was lost because all the road signs had been removed, supposedly to confuse the Germans! The officer in charge asked us if we could show them where they were on the map. We were very pleased to be able to help.

In 1940, Manchester was blitzed (23rd and 24th December at 6 pm). It didn't finish until 6 am the following morning. The next day it started again at 6.30 pm and finished at 1.30 am. Manchester was burning – apparently it could be seen 30 miles away. My mother was born in Middlewich, Cheshire and had a younger sister and older brother still living there. She said I should go to let them know we were still alive - there were no telephones, faxes or e mails then.

I was just 14 at the time but I cycled 24 miles on Christmas Day. To me, it was exciting and I was able to tell my mother's brother and family that we were OK. They had been worried because they could see the red sky in Manchester as the city burned. I had a lovely Christmas lunch and cycled back.

When I was 13, I took a newspaper round to help get some money for my mother. I did morning, evening and weekend rounds. As a boy the War was exciting, we didn't think about the dangers. We used to go on the rounds looking for shrapnel and swap it with other children. If you found part of a landmine parachute that was the best swap.

During the blitz, in December, we were in an Anderson shelter – it only saved you from shrapnel, not a direct hit. My brother who was six years older than me was in the Territorial Army and then called up to join the Royal Engineers. We were all in the shelter - my family, the cat and the family up the road, so we were packed like sardines.

On the first night of the blitz, we felt the shelter raise slightly from the ground which was the effect of the landmine hitting the houses about 150 yards away. The explosion was so great all the windows in our house were blown out and the place was full of soot.

Then there was another blitz, in February 1941,that lasted for about six hours and again did terrible damage, a lot of it due to the incendiary bombs.

All industrial cities had fumes from the factories as well as the smoke and dust from the bombing. This caused really thick smog – we called them 'pea-soupers'. The air was so thick you couldn't see ahead of you even in broad daylight. On one occasion after going to the cinema with two cousins, we came out to such a smog. No road traffic was running but then a number 13 tram came along. At the front was the guard who was following the lines of the trams. The tram was full but behind it were about 200 people all walking, following the tram. We joined them for about three miles, to a point not too far from home.

I obtained my school certificate when I was 16 and had to go to work to help with the finances. I started work in a firm of chartered accountants and in the evening studied bookkeeping. I was also in the Boy Scouts then the Rover Scouts. I became very fond of camping, particularly Rover Scout functions. I also did a lot of cycling, including taking our bikes on the train.

In 1944 when I was 17, early in the year, I mentioned to my brother who was on leave at the time, that it wasn't possible to go into the forces without volunteering. He said, "Don't be a damn fool, don't volunteer, wait until you are called up."

In December, I received a letter from the War Office, Minister of Labour, Ernest Bevin, saying that my national service number had been drawn as someone who had to go down the coal mines, instead of joining the forces. The reason for this was because the Government allowed thousands of miners to volunteer for service midway through the War. Most of these young miners realised that this was the only way they would get away from the mines. Unfortunately, this left a shortage of miners.

The Government realised they needed as much coal and tin as possible – hence the *Bevin Boys* scheme began. If 'your number came up', then you went down the mines instead of joining the armed forces.

'Your number's up' became a term for many years, meaning you were very unlucky or, that things couldn't get much worse for you.

If 'your number was up' you couldn't get out of it. If you refused to go down the mines then you had to serve three months in prison. Some got out on medical grounds, if they suffered from asthma or similar illnesses, but if you were A1 (in good health) then you had to go down the mines. A cousin of my friend, he refused to go down because he was claustrophobic. He served three months in prison and then had to sign up for 12 years in the Army or face another period in jail. He was put in the Black Watch regiment and ended up in Korea.

Where we lived, most of the Bevin Boys - as we became known - went to one of two training areas. I went to Durham and lived at an ex Army camp near Catterick for about a month. There were over 100 of us, no-one knew anybody. We came from all walks of life. We were given a helmet, a battery, headlamp and waterproof boots with metal toecaps.
I always remember waking up one morning in the Nissan huts we were in. There was a severe gale, and there was snow on my pillow.

We received basic training at Horden colliery. It was more or less how to look after yourself and how to stop the small truck which carried 30 cwt (1524kg) coal. We were taught how to lift it back on track, or how to stop it if it was going too fast, as that might lead to an accident. You used a chock, a heavy metal bar with a ring where you put your hand in. You had to judge the speed of the truck and thrust the chock into the spokes, thereby bringing the truck to a halt. The training worked, as I had to do it in real life, on more than one occasion!

After training, I was sent to a mine. I had to stay down the mines even when the War was over. The mine was Easington colliery, part of which went under the sea. It was an old mine, owned by Lampton, Herreton and Joycey collieries. You went down in a cage, which took about 20 miners at a time, a drop of about 600 feet. We were able to walk upright in the mine for about quarter of a mile and then we had to walk almost bent double. There were about ten Bevin Boys there.

I was trained to operate a hoist, which consisted of two drums and two levers. On the drums you had a wire rope attached to big scrapers. If you operated the levers one way they went along the face and then scraped the coal the other way. In front of the hoist was a bridge, where the forward scraper would be drawn onto the bridge beneath, which was the truck where the coal was loaded.

We were told always to remember the regulation was that the hoist must be secured in position. The position was changed on a daily basis as the excavation moved forward. The miners were meant to put six wooden props into position to prevent the hoist from falling over onto the bridge. Unfortunately, the miners were paid on piece work – how much coal they mined - so they took short cuts, which were sometimes dangerous.

There was a problem for me on one occasion, so I said, "It won't happen to me again." Next time, I checked to see that there were six pit props in place but there were only four, so I said I was not operating until the regulation number was there.

You just had to accept the conditions.

I tried to make the most of it. You came out each day absolutely black and there were no showers at the first mine. I had to get clean at the house where I was staying. We took food with us, as we had to walk just over a mile to the coal mine, then we walked again in the mine. We also had to paddle, occasionally, through water to get to the new coal face.

I found out, through a friend of a friend who knew a Bevin Boy, who he was in a coal mine in Lancashire. He had also trained at Horton colliery so I asked for a transfer. I obtained one and went to Crompton colliery, between St Helens and Knotty Ash in Liverpool. You could walk fully upright in Crompton, the seams of coal were deeper and there were more Bevin Boys at this mine, probably about 100.

In Durham, I lived with a lady whose husband and son were in the forces and then when I went to Crompton I lived with my aunt who lived in Knotty Ash. I was in coal mines for three years and two months until February 1948.

When I only had a month to serve, the overseer approached me and asked if I would like to train as a deputy. I said, "NO THANK YOU!"

The Easington pit had ten ponies underground that pulled the carts. These ponies worked all the time underground except for one week a year when they were brought up and allowed in a field. The ponies had stables underground and worked a shift system similar to the miners.

When you finished your shift you either came up in the cage or you could walk up the 657 steps. The teenagers often raced each other up. We made our own fun. We played cards at night with local lads - brag, poker, pontoon.

When I saw my brother some four years later, I reminded him of the very BAD piece of advice he had given me!

Warwick Taylor - *We didn't want to be Bevin boys*

We were all listening to the radio when they announced that we were at War. I was attending Watford grammar school. Guess who my classmate was? Terry Scott, the comedian. His real name was Owen. He got all the best parts in Shakespeare.

At that age you think war is exciting. You could see the glow of the bombing persistently at night; then going out to pick up pieces of shrapnel in the morning. At school there were lots of air raid warnings. We didn't have shelters but re-inforced cellars and wire mesh against the windows. We spent a lot of time down there playing cards.

I joined the Air Training Corp (ATC) and remained in after I left school because I wanted to go into the RAF. I learned a lot about radio. It involved one week night training and all weekends. We also went on visits to air fields and occasionally made a flight. We did many drills – a good thing because it taught us discipline .

I left school and took a job in exporting and importing as a junior clerk at a salary of £78 per year for a five and a half day week. The job involved one week in the office doing ledgers, one week on the switchboard and one week travelling to London. Lots of companies took over old houses in the country. I lived in North Harrow.

There were about six junior clerks. We all wanted to go in the RAF. Eventually, four got in. I was really jealous. One chap was not fit enough. I went to register for national service in August of 1944. The chap behind the counter said "We have a lottery. Every fortnight a number is drawn from 'Evans' bowler hat." My number came up. In my case there were no grounds for appeal "It's the coal mines for you." they said. Next I was called for a medical examination held in a Territorial Army hall. It was a farce, breathe in, breathe out, A1 fit. I remember my mother saying he's not going but if I refused I would have been summoned and spent three months in prison - and I still would have had to go when I was released.

The day came, about a month after I received my direction order and railway warrant. You could be sent to anyone of thirteen Government training collieries. I went to Wales. I had to go to Oakdale, which was the training centre for South Wales. I set off from Paddington. When I got off the train at Newbridge there were many other lads. There was also a person from the Ministry of Labour. His job was to get us accommodation. We went to the National Services Corporation Hostel. There were forty-four of them in UK, all built like army camps with a warden on site living in a bungalow close by.

The training session lasted for four weeks after which we were re-located to another colliery in that area, then two weeks training. However, when I arrived it was thick snow so we had to use shovels to get the snow off the railway tracks. On the second day we got kitted out, helmet, black boots, coupons, overalls, plus PE kit which we had to give back after training. The training consisted of classroom work and physical training by PT instructors, and the remaining 50% underground.

The initiation drop was 985 yards, with a regulation speed of 30ft per second but we were allowed to be dropped at 70ft per second. It caused nosebleeds and problems with our ears. At the end of the third week of training I had a very nasty cold, one morning. I felt so ill I couldn't get up. The warden told me to get up but I collapsed on the floor and they put me in the sick bay for five days. I had a high temperature so they sent me to hospital by taxi, still in my pyjamas with a blanket around me. The taxi driver said we have got to collect someone else. A lady came out and she was in the final stages of labour.

I was in and out of consciousness. I came round in bed with a consultant leaning over me. He said I had double pneumonia. They said I wouldn't live through the night. Penicillin had just come out and they gave it to me every eight hours. Next day my temperature was back to normal. I couldn't get up and was in hospital for six weeks surrounded by very injured men who had been to Dunkirk. They were about the same age group as me and I realised it could have been me. I kept making them laugh and got told off. The penicillin made my hair fall out but it recovered in six months.

I was called up before the medical board and they said I was A1 fit. But for the first three months I was to be sent to a Ministry of Works gun site to work as an assistant electrician. They were building huge guns at Mill Hill but then I was called again for a medical and sent to the coalmines where I had to be retrained even though the War was finished. I remained at that pit. We didn't want to be Bevin boys. The locals thought we had come to take jobs from their own boys but we couldn't get away from there quickly enough.

I kept appealing and appealing and they got fed up with me. I was sent to the RAF. I stayed for two years to complete my period of national service. The ironic part was that on my RAF documents it said I couldn't get into the air crew because War was finished, so I went into motor transport and learned to drive a five ton lorry. It also said 'This airman has done exceptionally well and can be highly recommended to go back to his job in the coalmines.'

By then my mother had divorced my father and gone off to Canada with a new man. I couldn't get a job so I came back and went into digs. I got a job and then went as a traffic clerk at BOAC. I did thirty-two years there.

Being in the forces

Doreen Embling - The CO said, *"I am not going to say 'welcome' because I didn't want any wrens on my ship.*

When I was 17, I volunteered for the WRNS (Women's Royal Naval Service) and they sent me my papers. I had to go to Mill Hill in London for brief training and then you were drafted elsewhere.

On my way to Mill Hill I got lost on the underground. A Canadian soldier started talking to me and helped me find my way. I eventually got to Mill Hill and got off the train. The streets were completely dark because of the blackout. The Canadian had to go back so I started walking on my own. Somehow or other I got inside a barrier and fell into a hole, which I found out later was a bomb crater.

I shouted and shouted and a man came along. He hauled me out and took me to a TocH welfare club, founded by Tubby Clayton,[v] where they gave me a cup of tea and cleaned me up. Then, this man took me to the naval draft centre which was a partially-built hospital before the Navy took it over.

It was very cold. The building was all stone with concrete steps. It was horrible. We had to get up at 5.00 am. A huge alarm went off. I was on the top bunk, I fell off straight onto my case. Mill Hill was awful. I was there about four or five days. We had to drill in a road each morning for about half an hour.

I went to HMS Northney at Hayling Island in 1942 and was drafted to HMS Dryad, at Southwick, in 1944. These are both land bases which were given ship's names. I had billets at Hayling Island, Southwick and Southsea.

My first draft was HMS Northney, a repair base for Combined Operations. We repaired landing craft. At Havant station I met up with several other girls also on their way there.

On the first day, we were lined up on the parade ground to be greeted by the commanding officer (CO). The CO said, "I am not going to say 'welcome' because I didn't want any wrens on my ship. Don't think you are going to be treated like goddesses. You're supposed to be replacing seamen and that is how you will be treated. Now go to stores and get a sweeping brush and come back and sweep the tide off the parade ground!"

On Hayling Island, we lived in Westfield Meadows. A whole house had been turned into cabins, four of us in this little cabin. We had double bunks, five or six shared one hand basin. There was one bath in the house. Everyone tried to get back first as there were 30 people in the house.

I was assigned to work with a motor mechanic, grinding valves on a V8 engine. I was bored to death and used to pop across to the boat shed to talk to Jack the Rigger. He was an elderly gentleman who had spent all his time in the Navy when "*Sailors were seamen, not like those bloody ragtime lot!*". When the War broke out he had volunteered his services.

He wore an old sailcloth coat and his old Navy cap. I could sit and listen to his stories of the China seas and sea shanties for hours. He asked me if I would like to work for him. I was delighted, so he fixed it up with the CO and I became his mate. He taught me to splice rope and twine and make every nautical knot there was. I was once hauled up to the top of the rig to splice on a new rope.

Jack and I spent a lot of time putting lifelines along the sides of the landing craft and renewing steering.

Before D-day we had terrible gales, I was the boson's mate. The CO came into the boat shed and said, "Get your wren to tie those boats down that are up the creek. The gale is coming up." I had the lines on my shoulders and started tying them up. It was bitterly cold. My hands were frozen. The boson had a 'Davey Jones' locker and delved into it. He brought out a bottle of rum and said, "Have a swig." Every time I went back in from heaving the lines I had another swig. The truck came to take us back to quarters and I was swooning along!

During the War, if you met someone who came from the same place as you, he became your 'townie' and he looked out for you. Ginger was my 'townie', he came back and found me. By now I was drunk. He got the tailboard of the truck down, he kept trying to help me to get on board. Eventually I said, "I'll take a running jump." He grabbed me and got me onto the truck.

What I didn't know was the CO was watching from the wardroom. I didn't go for supper as I was feeling so rotten. I went straight to my quarters and flopped onto my bunk. One of my friends came in. "Dot, (my nickname) you are on the notice board, the first officer wants to see you." I was feeling too ill and couldn't go until the next day so I was in double trouble.

I was later billeted to Southsea. I was often in trouble. My punishment was usually spud-bashing (peeling potatoes) or gardening.

The girls who worked on the repair base were in separate quarters. We often went down the fire escape to go swimming. The sister's room was below us. We were just going back up when she saw us. "Bowdler, what are you doing there?" I don't know how she knew it was me, she could only see my legs, but she reported me to the first officer.

The first officer felt a bit sorry for me so decided to give me another chance. She said "You can dig the garden." It was so rough and hard work. Another wren, Betty, didn't get caught as she was already on the roof ladder. I said she had to help me with the digging. As we dug it we found lots of onions and dug them up. We put them on the compost heap.

A few days later, we were in our cabin which was on the roof. We heard sister (Queen's Alexandra's nurse) and an ordinary nurse talking, "Yes, it should be very pretty. I put in a lovely lot of tulip bulbs. We should have a lovely show come April." "We will have to go out at midnight and get those onions (tulip bulbs) and put them back in," I said to Betty. Needless to say, they didn't come up as sister expected – she had put them in a pattern!

Another time, I was in the dining room with petty officer (PO) Cook, known as Cookie. She didn't like me at all. "Bowdler," she said, "I've put out the sack of potatoes for you, make sure you get them all done properly." I said, "But we have a table tennis match tonight." She said, "I am going to do you a favour then and let you use this new-fangled machine for doing the potatoes."

That night, we started the table tennis tournament. I had put the potatoes in the machine and switched it on. Suddenly, I said to a marine commando, "Oh, the potatoes, quick come and help me." We dashed into the galley. There were masses of peel everywhere and the spuds were like marbles. I said, "She'll kill me." The commando asked where the potatoes were kept. He broke into the store, got another bag of potatoes out which we peeled properly. We cleaned up, collected the peelings and the tiny potatoes. He took them back and got rid of them later in his truck. No-one was any the wiser.

On another occasion, we were going into an inter-ship drill competition. We had a marine sergeant who picked out the best of us and started training us. Marine sergeants are far worse than sergeant majors. He took us to a quiet residential road, near the sea and sand dunes.

We had been marching when a despatch driver came and started to talk to the MS. He said he had told me to take over as marker, but I hadn't heard him. "Where are we going?" everyone asked. I said, "Keep going, we are not allowed to stop." In the end we were just about in the wet sand when he came running down shouting "Halt, you idiots."

Some of our friends and work mates

We all had to use the same, shared bath. In service you were only allowed three inches of water. There was a line drawn around the bath AND you were only allowed a bath once a week.

Whale Island officers were the toughest, they were the worst. You had to go at the double on Whale Island. It was the gunnery training base.
On everyone's hat band during the War there was no name of the ship, only HMS so we couldn't be traced if anything happened.

I was always late for the truck that came to collect us. I used to slide down the banister and leave a cushion at the bottom so I didn't hurt myself. One day, 'wow', it really hurt. Sister had taken my cushion away. "In future, you will walk down the stairs like all the other girls," she said.

I'd had to have a tooth out at the front, so had one on a plate which I put in a mug at night. There was one hand basin for all of us. I used to leave my mug with the tooth in on the windowsill. We had a gale one night and some idiot had left the window open. My tooth was blown onto the gable roof as the mug had fallen down. "I am not going without it," I said. "You hold my legs and push me down the roof until I can reach it," I said to the others. I had my bell-bottoms on (wide legged Navy issue trousers). The others were holding my legs and then they gave me a stick. It took about half an hour to get it. I looked after it better after that.

I switched to radar division and went to Dryad. We didn't have any leave for ten months before D-day.
-day was postponed because of the weather. All hands had to re-camouflage the boats, because the sea was grey, not the blue and white they had expected. It was all hands to the paint pots. A 'chippie' wren didn't know what to do. I told her to stick the brush in the pot and paint the deck. She managed to paint all around herself so she couldn't get off the boat! "What am I going to do?" she cried. The CO who was passing said "Just stay there till the paint dries".

The funny thing was that evening. I was a bit late getting back to base. It was a lovely drive up to these old houses. There was a whining sound and 'rat-a-tat-tat.' We were being shot at. All the girls were under the table of the house. That was my scariest moment. The War was real by now. I was just 18.

The horrible thing was the boys (who had manned the landing crafts) who came back after D-day. They left as young, carefree boys and seemed old men when they came back. The experience of seeing people shot, killed or blown up had affected them badly.

When the boats came back, that was horrible, we had to clean up the landing crafts from the effects of the battle. It was August and hot, it was horrid. There were only us girls doing the cleaning. One girl was sick and refused to go back.

Pat Caine - *...so I was made a lieutenant, then captain then major - only days from lieutenant to captain!*

I was the eldest of five children and my father and grandfather were both regular soldiers so the Army was nothing new to me. I lived my early life in many places including the Channel Islands where my father was a master gunner. He had to inspect guns at various places.

I was nineteen when war began. I was studying at university, BSc Engineering. Everyone's life was turned over. I had started an apprenticeship at the Royal Arsenal at Woolwich which I was due to finish at age twenty-one. I managed to continue some of my apprenticeship combining with my studies at the university. However, the War took me into the army via the Territorial Army.

At university I was taken into the Army Officers' Emergency Reserve. I was then contacted by a regular officer, Colonel Douglas Henchley. At university he took me under his wing and he supported me in what he thought I could do best for the services - which was Intelligence.

In June 1941 I obtained my degree and joined Lord Hankey's 'War Office' scheme for civilian officers to set up and maintain the new AJA Radar units just coming from the factories. We attended an eight week course at the Royal Naval College, Greenwich and then an equipment course at the Army Radar School, Petersham for ten weeks. We were then sent out to anti-aircraft sites in Bristol, Dorset (including Portland Bill) and in Devon and Cornwall. We had a large van, filled with electronic equipment that was manned by a sergeant and two craftsmen/drivers.

On 21st March 1942 I was on a site on Mount Edgcombe and the Battery Commander sent for me and told me I was now a second lieutenant in the RAOC (OME Branch). I was sent to be kitted out in uniform. On the formation of REME on 1st October 1942, I was promoted war substantive lieutenant REME and posted to GHQ Home Forces at St Pauls School, Hammersmith for duty with the Combined Intelligence Secretariat in Norfolk House in Piccadilly. Our task was to look into all possible landing sites in Northern Europe, especially in Normandy, for the future invasion (later code-named OPERATION OVERLORD). We made the decision it was to be Normandy about two years before the operation. We had to have the crafts made.

Lord Hankey arranged living quarters for me plus an office in St Paul's school, Hammersmith. We received intelligence and sent out questions about things which we wanted to know. This arrangement worked very well. We had an office in the War Office as well. I was working with Colonel Henchley all this time. We had a number of contacts in France. The mechanism I don't know, but I said what we wanted to know and the information came back. I turned the details into something useful for the Army. Sometimes it took a week, sometimes a little longer. I don't remember a time when we didn't get the information we wanted. It was a very secure system.

The North African landings intelligence for US General, Mark Clark had just been completed. This was a very interesting posting for me and quite out of the blue. We studied the coastlines and hinter lands from stereo photos supplied by the RAF and called for information from agents in France. We asked for holiday snaps and any other information people had. We also liaised with the other agencies such as the Ministry of Economic Warfare at Berkeley Square, (Berkeley Hotel), and we supplied secondary targets for the RAF. The hours were long but one or two of us used to walk from Hammersmith to Piccadilly daily almost all the way through the London parks for exercise. This was until 1st August 1943 when General Montgomery took over command and formed the 21st Army Group to replace GHQ HF. His first act was to order all officers to do physical exercises on the sports field every morning.

On 30th August, I joined 158 Infantry Workshop REME (53rd Welsh Division) near Faversham in Kent where we were almost always on field exercises, sleeping under the vehicles, and with officers using motorcycles. On 21st December, I was promoted to acting captain and posted to HQ 1st Corps, where we prepared orders aimed at organising the units under command ready for the Normandy invasion.

On 6 February 1944, the Colonel for whom I worked was transferred to HQ Lines of Communication and he transferred me with him. Our task was to prepare the REME units for the beach-heads in Normandy, arranging training in recovery on the beaches and setting up areas for repair just off the beaches so that the fighting troops could pass through quickly and be supplied with their stores and repair needs. Promotion to temporary captain followed on 21st March. I had no training for this.

Obviously people didn't like being under the Germans so were willing to help at their own risk. They gave us the information we needed about landing sites, beaches, what sort of crafts would be best. The troops needed to practise how to land so we used beaches in England to get them to practise. This practice also had to include how to get on and off, how best to land without letting anyone know about our intentions. We were doing this about a year before the Normandy landings.

I was just one of the hacks in the War Office doing planning. There were about six of us. It was a very small team, very secure. I used to worry when I walked across the park thinking that if I was mugged I had far too much information in my head. When the landing was taking place I was still in the Home Office. They changed the date for the invasion but this was a higher command decision.

When you look back, you realise that some amazing things happened during the War. For about a year I knew as much as anyone about what was going. I was a civilian all this time in the Territorial Army, then one day they said you had better be conscripted so I was made a lieutenant, then captain then major within a very short time - only days from lieutenant to captain! They wanted to regularise it. Some people were still civilians though. We all worked together with the Navy, Army and RAF personnel.

The other intelligence I worked on was related to running a war - all the bombings. Where we should bomb and why, getting information from France about the best place to bomb in France which was acted upon. We collected the information then decided what we should do with it, who wanted it. My work was entirely secret. I didn't discuss it with anyone. We knew so much but we didn't know what the troops were told.

I enjoyed all of it. I was young with no responsibilities. It was exciting. I just treated life as normal. I never fired a gun in anger but I was given a revolver which I had to have with me all the time – I was not happy about that.

The impression I had was that the landings went exactly as planned. We had planned it to the utmost degree. We knew everything that was going on. We planned how casualties would be treated ie how rescuers would arrive, how the ship would empty and how the casualties would be put in and taken back to England.

For me, planning, studying of maps, working out and looking at other landings, how they got on, how we could improve, was a great experience.

Rationing affected everyone. There was only a very limited type of food, nothing special, very straight forward simple food. At St Paul's school there was a central canteen. I walked six miles each way with another officer so ate at the War Office. We received no special treatment as no one knew what we were doing.

There was very little social life because there was so much to do. I did go to dances but usually ones organised by the Army. I met my wife during the War.

The good part was having studied the beaches during the War I visited Normandy after the War and remembered everything. I don't remember any bad parts.

Do Lemm - *You have no sense of fear when you are young.*

It was 1939 I was thinking about getting a job, possibly going to London to train as a nurse. I lived with my mother who was widowed when I was seven. After about six months the War was well started and I wished to join up. I came from a military family. My mother was not happy about this but my elder sister persuaded her to let me join.

I joined The WAAF. I trained as a radio telephone operator, taking over from the men. I had nearly four years as a corporal in the WAAF, where I met many interesting people - I once spoke to Winston Churchill when he came to Dover to the combined headquarters. I had a wonderful time - the camaraderie and everything and the excitement. Often I had to give bearings to rescuers, based on information we had, so that they could put a fix on people in order to rescue them. Life was very 'here today gone tomorrow'. Friends you danced with the night before were gone the next day.

Once I went back to see my mother. She thought I wasn't fed but we had wonderful food. I was stationed at RAF Debden in Saffron Walden. I left home to go back to London to meet my watch but no-one was there because of the bombings. Then the air training officer (ATO), who was liaising between forces, spoke to me. He told me there was a late train to Saffron Walden. It was full of soldiers, half of them merry. I got out of the station at Audley End because Saffron Walden was a Quaker station so no trains stopped there on Sundays. I had to go three miles with a case full of goodies my mother had given me. It was now after 1am in the morning. Three men got off the train and I thought, "I hope they won't speak." Then they asked "Where are you off to?" and I said "I am stationed in Saffron Walden in private digs." "Do you know what time it is? It is 2 o'clock" this guy said. "I wouldn't want my sister alone" so he came with me for the remainder of the journey. The rest of my watch had got

back earlier. It was a cold winter's night when I said good bye to him. I never saw him again. I was really frightened but he was so kind. That was my best experience of the War.

Whilst dancing in London in the Albert Hall, I met a Jewish girl whose boyfriend was prisoner of war (POW). She and her parents kept a beautiful pub in St John's Wood, The Princess Royal. I went to stay there. They were so kind to me. They used to ask who Rita's latest boyfriend was and I used to say: "It's OK, he's Jewish" because if you married out of your faith you were despised. She was my friend for two years until she was sent to Scotland and I was sent to Dover. Dover was all fortified - you can go to see it now. We were about sixty feet under ground – under the castle. The place had been dug out by the 'un-fit for duty' men. There was a complete Navy, Army and RAF force under the cliff. I was in the Connaught barracks. The old barracks had been bombed but some had been renovated so there was a section for WAAF and a section for ATS. On a clear day, using binoculars, we could see the patrols of Germans in France.

When we were being shelled everyone had to take shelter. I sheltered under Shakespeare cliffs many times. My claustrophobia was terrible and I wished to be outside.

From Dover I was posted to Tangmere in Sussex. I worked in the operations (Ops) room. The Ops room was at Bishop Otter College – it had to be separated in case it was bombed.

Then from there I was sent to guard the pylons and transmitters, where we took over from the men who were needed for other things. We worked at night, on watch.

I used to speak to the pilots – ground to air. I was always talking to the pilots over the channel. You could speak to them as long as there was no barrier in the air or on the ground. We had to log everything and the book was taken after raids as they had to check what was said. During the dawn patrol the pilots would get bored so they would call us. We would use our code name and they would say nonsense things such as 'Get the breakfast on, bacon and eggs' or 'See you tonight' - but we didn't log these things.

I was on duty with one of my friends who had married a Canadian. There was a May Day call. He went down.

You have no sense of fear when you are young. Sometimes in the barracks we would get the warning and put our great coats over our pyjamas to go to Fort Burgoyne. There were three groups of people - those who took pillows as if they were going to sleep; those who were going to make tea or coffee, and me and the card players. I loved playing cards. You would usually be there two or three hours. After the last shell you waited half an hour before the 'all clear' but then sometimes there would be another warning so you had to stay longer.

I can remember dancing in London with an American. He was boasting and bragging. He was very funny and very kind. We were dancing in the Hammersmith Palais. In war time you saw no civilians. There was every nationality, loads of Americans, then, suddenly, the military police walked in. Half of these Americans shouldn't have been there. Suddenly they disappeared – marched off by the military. That would happen quite frequently. There were lots of Navy, RAF and Army men in London who shouldn't have been there, but the poor lads knew they may have been shot and killed the next day.

The Americans were completely self-sufficient - they had everything in their canteen. I was with this American and I told him that we had no coupons but in the military we had everything provided. I said I was short of soap. The next day he brought me a huge box of soap which I shared out.

I kept my sister in vests and bras as she was short of coupons. We were allowed 'one on, one off and one in the wash' so I used to ask for more. I was told to go to the kit parade and say 'lost in the laundry'. All our clothes said 'air women for the use of'. Our knickers were 'blackouts' and 'twilights'. Blackouts had elastic and were thick. The others were silky ones for the summer. Half the time you spent climbing up ladders so blackouts were best. When I first joined I took my own underwear with me. The first time I washed it and hung it up I never saw it again. It had been stolen.

The trains were always full of forces, but no-one said anything about your camp because 'walls have ears'. You said nothing about where you were stationed or what you did, nothing.

Our pillows were long bolsters full of straw. Every time you went on leave you handed in your bedding and your pillows and then when you came back you got clean and fresh ones. We had striped flannelette pyjamas and the men said you have pinched all our nightwear so we have to sleep in nothing.

I used to hitch to and from Cambridge where we did our initial training. When hitching it was mainly military personnel who picked us up but on one occasion two civilians picked us up. There were three of us. I never hitched alone. They called us Faith, Hope and Charity! Once we hitched to London and stayed with a friend at The Princess Royal. We went dancing all the time. One night we were asked if we would like to be on 'In Town Tonight', a radio programme but we couldn't because we had to be back on watch. We mostly hitched, but, if it was dark, we would take a train back.

My pay when I joined was twenty-two shillings per fortnight. There was an initial spell of 'square bashing' for three weeks and then onto three months training. I had to have a basic knowledge of physics and then I was sent to the signals section of the air force.

I didn't get promoted until later on. I was going to be a sergeant but found I was pregnant. I was going to take the commissioning examinations but I enjoyed being in the ranks. There were one or two WAAF officers in the welfare squad and I thought "What a miserable life." I didn't want their miserable existence. I was aircraft woman first class and then corporal. By the time I came out I was earning thirty-five shillings per week which was all spending money. During the War you were also allowed to have your hair done, teeth done plus uniforms, food and lodgings.

During this time the shops didn't stock large amounts in case of fire so although we were given extra money we couldn't spend it. I banked mine. We were allowed £2 extra per week so when I left the air force I received two cheques worth about £50 each. I also had £45 gratuity. My husband was a Naval reserve and he had £45. He was offered a commission to stay on but he chose not to. He had been on minesweepers.

I met my husband, Percy, when I was fourteen. He was sixteen years older than me. He came to the house to pick up my sister to take her to a dance. I was I was doing my homework. I was a proper straight Jane. I used to think "I hate that man." I like blond hair and blue eyes. I hate tall dark men – he was 6' 2" tall. Then the War came along and I never saw Percy again. My sister didn't marry him but he was always a friend of the family. When I came home on leave I went to the Unicorn pub in Chichester where all the forces people used to meet. I went in that night, my second leave home. I guessed I would soon see people I knew. This farmer chap, Reg, was there and he gave me a hug and said "This is my friend Percy Lemm." I knew Percy didn't recognise me. I never wore civy clothes as you always got better looked after in uniform. We were dancing and he said "How long are you home for? Perhaps we could go out for meal or to the flicks." I played it cool, I said "I must get home." He slipped his card in my pocket without me knowing. I was broke by now. So I thought "Why not?" So I said "If you meant what you said I'm free." So we went and that was it.

When I got married I wore a black suit, a pretty frilly white blouse and a black and white hat with ribbons. I was married in the Register Office in Chichester because I was a Catholic and he a Protestant. It was 7th March 1945. We had the reception at the Bosham Country Club – six of us and then Percy had to go back to the Navy. I stayed home for a while and then went back but then I had to leave just after VE -Day because I was pregnant .

During the War I had wonderful times I will never forget them. The intense camaraderie was my most endearing memory. You would sit on the train and in no time everyone was chatting - that doesn't happen any more!

Betty Thompson - *It didn't bother us what people's background was.*

I remember the day war broke out. I was going for a walk with two boys. We went into a sweet shop and we could hear the radio. The shopkeeper said "That's it, we are at war." I remember thinking "What does that mean?" I was thirteen

Some of our children and teachers were evacuated.

My father was out of work a lot so he became a full time ARP warden. We knew everything that we had to do. We were told about bells and whistles. When the sirens sounded, we were to sit on the steps. We always took the dog. We heard the all clear so thought everything was OK. Then we heard bells. We went back into the cellar and wrapped a towel around the dog's head. My father came back in and said "What are you doing?" We'd got it the wrong way round!

We went to a dance at the parish hall. We heard aeroplanes. Something was happening and we could hear footsteps on the gravel drive. We thought it was a German. We all stood still. Keith, my friend, went to the door only to find it was my father who had come to pick me up.

We were at school until we were fourteen. At that stage many lads that we knew were going in the forces. Everyone wrote to each other. On one occasion, we went for a walk near a reservoir. There was a soldier on guard. This lad said "I'll see if he says 'who goes there'. " He did, but we got a rollicking.

Leeds was not bombed but only got the left-overs from the bombings elsewhere. I think we had the bomb that dropped on the museum and an unexploded bomb. We all went to see what it was.

My mother worked as a nurse during the War. She coped very well. I never went hungry. She didn't queue for food as she was working. The main arguments in the family were about money. We had club checks, a sort of chit that took you into certain shops, and then you had to pay the money off. I think I was a bit common in those days. When I got to sixteen I started thinking about going into the forces. My mother was against it.

I joined the ATS at seventeen. I thought I was going to be a truck driver. I knew a girl who was one and she wore trousers, leather spats and gloves – I really fancied that. They did all the tests and stuck me in an office as I wasn't mechanically minded.

I went to Pontefract barracks where we had six weeks of training. There were forty-four of us in a dormitory and only three of us didn't get nits! We used to comb each others hair at night. We did various tests and I was put in the Pay Corps and went to Radcliffe in Manchester. The office was in an old cotton mill. While we were there, the War ended. Very gradually we were getting people who had been in the War coming to work for us - but they were useless. They were fine to fight but useless in an office so we gave them simple jobs to do. We had some Scottish lads; they could hardly speak English let alone write it. They used to go out and get drunk. One day they broke into a shoe shop but of course only stole only one foot of each shoe! They didn't know what to do with them so they put them on the roof of our offices – these lads ended up in jail.

Whilst in the ATS we were in civy billets. Our landlady was in her thirties and she had a little girl. Her husband was in the Royal Engineers. The landlady had been with a Canadian soldier and the baby was his but her husband never worked it out! His sister was a prostitute in Bury. She used to tell us about the men she had been with. The landlady used to let us have parties. She used to say "Bring the lads round, but bring me a man."

We didn't have ration books in the forces. We could eat in the canteen but it wasn't much. I don't ever remember going hungry. The landlady used to make us Lancashire hotpot if we had a party. The only thing was fruit. I remember John the sailor, coming in from Liverpool. He had a big rucksack and tipped it on the floor and it was full of oranges. The landlady's daughter just stared - she had never seen oranges before.

In both the houses I was in, we slept in the same bed, Joan and I. The first thing Joan did was light a cigarette – almost before she opened her eyes.

Then we went to Radcliffe. We went to a chicken farm in a place called Unsworth. Out walking, one day, a voice said: "Halt who goes there?" It was an American and he was 7-3" tall. He said come down to meet the lads. They gave us all sorts of things, butter, canned ham, pineapple chunks. We got very friendly with these lads, but they then had to move on.

One of the girls got very friendly with an American and he used to fly her home in a bomber to Blackpool for a weekend. We used to call her the cotton wool blond. She used to bleach her hair with peroxide. Bits of her hair used to drop off as the bleach she used was so strong.

The Americans were military policemen. They were really good and they never took advantage of us. I was in a blue dress and this guy was asleep. Someone woke him up and he said 'Oh I've gone to heaven'.

Everyone wrote to everyone else. We were getting letters from all over the world. I only knew two boys who died, they were both in the RAF. Some of my friends went into action, firing guns somewhere in Wales. John, one of my friends, saw some action. He was on a merchant ship bringing food in.

I had known Gordon (my husband) since I was fifteen. We danced well together. He asked me to wait for him and I said "No way, you are a great flirt. Wait until you come home." He went away and we agreed to write. We courted by letter. I had loads of boyfriends, especially a Canadian. I loved him in a way but he didn't really do anything for me. I wrote and told him that Gordon was coming home and he said "I was going to ask you come out to Canada." This business with the boys in the forces, you went out with anyone and everybody. We had plenty of boy friends.

83

Gordon was involved in the D-Day landings but he doesn't talk about that - he talks about the laughs he had.

I came out of the ATS in 1946.

It wasn't a bad war as far as I was concerned. A lot of it was a big laugh. All the people we met. I met people I would never have met in normal life. My mother would have been horrified. It didn't bother us what people's background was. If they were nice people so be it.

Kath Graham - *I saw signing on as my chance to get away*

When the War started I was in service getting 10/3d per week. I'd been there for six and half years but couldn't save a penny. I could have got exempt from joining the Armed Forces as my employer was an invalid, but I saw signing on as my chance to get away. I looked forward to getting on a bus or train, something I had only done twice in my life before. The neighbours thought I was mad but it was the happiest day of my life when I left. I had to leave at 6.30 am. Half of the village came up to see me off. I saw a girl at Portsmouth station crying her eyes out so we travelled together and stayed together throughout the War. We had to get to Melksham. I signed up as a cook as it was the only thing I could do well, or so I thought then.

Then I went to Morecombe on a training course and passed out OK. We had to do all this training – I had learnt it in the Guides – I had led parades. Then we went on this cookery course and I passed out with flying colours as some girls hardly knew anything. For the first time in my life I had some money because the uniform was free and our food was provided. Only six of us passed. The chap who was running the exams was married to a girl in Hambledon. I noticed that he was having a love affair with another girl. I was made LACW – I am sure it was only because of that!

Then I went to 53 Squadron. It was jolly hard work but I had the time of my life. All the girls were together in billets. Before I joined up I was on my own and only allowed out a few times a week.

The RAF was better than the Army, especially for food, it was wonderful. There was loads of food. I worked in the airmen's mess, then sergeant's mess, then the officer's mess and then I volunteered for catering. I had to put rations up for families – that was a doddle. I didn't want to be promoted, I enjoyed the fun too much. I didn't want to be a corporal and stay in the guard room.

All the airmen were out for bit of a spree. You were never short of a boy friend if you were a cook as they expected double helpings. If it was two knocks on the door it was for me and three knocks was for my friend

It was a wonderful carefree life. We had bombs falling - but when you are young you don't think about the danger. There was always loads of entertainment, and dances. The NAAFI was a godsend.

Charles Richard Underwood - *We learnt later that we had rescued the U-Boat secret code.*

I was in the Navy in Portsmouth and was sent to Scapa Flow Naval Base as a steward. I spent eighteen months there and was promoted to petty officer. I went back to Portsmouth barracks and then was drafted to HMS Wrestler which was operating from Freetown, Sierra Leone (now Ghana). I was there until 1942 when I came home and was drafted to HMS Petard. I was in charge of the ward room. Most of the ship's company were younger than me. We commissioned the ship and after extensive trials we went straight to the Mediterranean Sea. We were based at Port Said.

On October 30th 1942, in the early morning, a signal was received from one of our aircraft saying that a U-Boat had been sighted a hundred miles away. Three destroyers were sent to track it. The U-Boat was depth charged and at 10.30pm, HMS Petard got a final hit and the U-Boat surfaced. The German crew all jumped into the sea and we rescued them.

In the meantime the first lieutenant, Tony Fasson, swam to the U-Boat. He got on board and got all the important information. We were sworn to secrecy though we did not know how important the information was. We learnt later that we had rescued the U-Boat secret code.

It was about 11.30pm when I took charge of the captive crew. They were put in a small compartment at the stern of the ship.

The information we had saved went to Bletchley Park. Alan Turin was a brilliant Cambridgeshire mathematician and he cracked the code. From then on every U-Boat in the Mediterranean and Atlantic seas could be tracked. During the War, the Germans never realised we had cracked the code. As soon as a U-Boat was brought to the surface, the first thing the captain should have done was throw the code overboard – it was on special paper which disintegrates.

Everything had to be kept secret for years. It was only years later that we found out what we had captured. The Petard got a medal because it sunk German, Italian and Japanese submarines. I should have been awarded the Victoria Cross but because of the secrecy I couldn't get it so received the George Medal instead.

About fifty years after rescuing the code breaker, a Naval officer, Lieutenant DePass discovered that he still had films in his camera. When they were developed at the Imperial War Museum they were clear images of the event. He gave a copy of them to the twenty of us who were still alive.

On HMS Petard we were always at sea and saw a lot of action. We didn't have much time for anything else except when we went in dry dock for repairs. The Mediterranean was known as the destroyer's graveyard as six destroyers had been sunk before we got there.

At odd times, petty officers were allowed on the quarter deck for two hours with the officers. The food was pretty basic for troops. I was responsible for ordering the food for everyone and was given an allowance for this.

I had one leave of seventeen days in Alexander when the Petard was in dry dock whilst the boiler was being repaired. Six petty officers were selected to go to a houseboat used by millionaires which was moored on the Nile. It was great, it was very plush. There used to be a dance on the other side of the Nile on a hospital boat. All the women were Egyptians or Arabs so we were not allowed to fraternize with them.

I was on the Petard for eighteen months. There were destroyers and battleship waiting for the Italians to come out. I then got instructions to come back. We moored in midstream at Malta. The first lieutenant said "I want you to go ashore. There will be transport for you." They took me to a big house which was the headquarters for the Army, Navy and Air Force.

I was told I was to accompany Eisenhower for three days and give him the best of everything. Eisenhower then came on board during darkness. He was in my care. He was such an easy going man. He stayed a few days. He wanted to view the Sicilian landing from the seawater side so he could make his plans accordingly.

We were in Malta and I got a draft sheet and was sent to St Angelo transit camp and then went to a landing ship with lots of secret equipment on board. The landing ship could detect enemy planes coming in. We stayed there for ages until we nearly went round the twist so we went to sea for a bit of peace. Unfortunately we got sunk by a U-Boat. There was a naval patrol vessel in the area and it came alongside. The ship didn't go down until early the next morning.

I met my wife in Portsmouth barracks. I was up on the first floor and I could hear a shrill voice. This was in 1941. She became a petty officer wren. I married her when I came home after being sunk in April 1944. I had no uniform - I had to wait three months for another uniform so I got married in battledress. Letters to my wife were hit and miss. She used to write regularly. I sent her a telegram when I was rescued to say I was safe. Later she had to leave the Navy when she got pregnant.

Bill Turner - *There were a lot of casualties. There was a young girl who didn't have a stitch of clothing on so I gave her my overcoat.*

In 1939 I was fourteen in November, a couple of months after war broke out. If there was an air raid on, they organised us into groups. We acted as messengers trying to avoid any break down in communication. Quite often we would know there were troop ships going down to the docks as we lived near the railway. I was a messenger until I entered the forces. I did other jobs such as on a building site, and at a garage but the garage got bombed. The Labour exchange detailed you to work. You couldn't just work where you wished. I started in the cadets at sixteen.

My mother kept chickens all through the War. People used to come around from the farms with one day old chicks. Right until after the War we always had eggs. Most of the gardens were turned over to vegetables.

My father was out at the back of the house when they dropped a couple of bombs a mile away and within seconds he was at the front to make sure my mother and I were OK.

Once they dropped incendiaries and we went round with dustbins to cover them up because dustbins contained dust from fires which put out incendiaries.

They were working on a power station. We were watching enemy aircraft and there was a big explosion two hundred yards away. Everyone ran for cover but quite a few people who worked there were injured. Right next to this station there was a first aid station. It was the first time I saw dead people.

I volunteered when I was seventeen years old. You had to have a signed permission from your father. I forged mine. What I didn't know was that there was a slight mix up with my RAF number and I was called up anyway. During my first six months in the RAF I learnt to fly a Tiger Moth plane but there were so many would-be pilots we had to take a series of tests and they found out I would make a better flight engineer so I was transferred.

We were right on the point of being sent to squadrons when the War ended – the Japanese War. So instead of flying I was maintaining planes. The last eighteen months of my service was spent in Egypt. They wanted volunteers to act as baggage masters in transport aircrafts. We used to fly to Cyprus, Malta, Italy, and Tripoli and back. We didn't see much of the countries. The officers had quarters but we mainly slept in the aircraft. We enjoyed ourselves because the crews would invite us up to the cockpit and let us have a turn flying.

I was in London for a couple of months during a lot of the bombing but because we were at a training school we weren't called on to do much. We were stationed in Putney and I remember we were walking along the High Street when a bomb hit a nearby dance hall. There were a lot of casualties. There was a young girl who didn't have a stitch of clothing on so I gave her my overcoat. Later her dad bought it back. We helped the ARP with the recovery.

On another night there was smoke coming from a building and the front door was open. We went upstairs and found someone still in bed asleep even though an incendiary bomb was burning in the corner. He hadn't heard a thing. It had come through the roof and through the ceiling. The shock on his face when he woke up was a sight to see!

Before I left the air force I contracted Malaria so was redeployed as a clerk.

My dad was in the fire service during the War.

Grace Kattenhorn - *There were men on camp but we weren't allowed to fraternise!*

In 1939 I had just started work in a factory making war clothing. I can't remember much about the factory. There was some hand work and some machine work. When the sirens went you went down into the shelter - it was chaotic. Mum stayed at home, there was nothing much she could do, she was too old for war work.

In 1939 my dad worked in a factory which went over to war work - munitions. He was exempt from call-up because of this.

My dad did his turn as an ARP volunteer. When he was doing that he got no sleep that day. His job was to make sure no-one had any lights on, and to warn people to take cover when raids were starting. There were no street lights. As soon as the siren went you went down into the shelter. Sometimes you came up to get a bit of fresh air and then went back down. My brother was at school. He was called up at nineteen. He wanted to get married and had to get my mother's permission as he was under age. He went to sea. His wife was a couple of year's older than him.

When war broke out, I got called up for the forces. I could have gone in the ATS, the Land Army, or the Air Force or worked in a factory making ammunitions. My father said 'Don't go in ammunitions', so I went into the Army. I was just 19 when I joined up. I had my 21st birthday in the Army. I was stationed just outside Nottingham in Chilwell. I was there for nearly 2 years. All the officers were women. There were men on camp but we weren't allowed to fraternise!

Occasionally we saw drivers, but that was all. I liked being a soldier. We were restricted so we couldn't come to London because of the bombing. We had an American camp up the road and exchanged dances either at their place or ours. You could go from one camp to another in an Army lorry. We went to dances in uniform.

When the bombing was quiet we were allowed home. I got friendly with a girl in Sheffield, named Nelly. When we couldn't come to London and we had forty-eight hours leave, she said come home with me as it's not far away. Off we went. She had three strapping brothers who worked in the mine. They came in all black covered in soot. They used to bath in front of the fireplace. They all shared a bed in one room downstairs. I slept upstairs.

One day we had a roast dinner. Every one had a Yorkshire pudding the size of a dessert plate. I was wondering when everything else was coming. We ate the Yorkshire pudding. Then the main course came afterwards. I mentioned it to Nelly later and she said that it fills you up so you don't want much else. Another time we had a suet pudding then dinner. I kept in touch with Nelly for quite a while after the War.

I did a bit of everything in the Army, including cooking, gardening and in between we had different military exercises. There was little marching. Being in an Army camp, we were under surveillance, so not much went on outside. I didn't want promotion - too much responsibility.

After eighteen months I got married while still in the Army. When I got married, I wore all borrowed clothes as everything was on coupons. In the forces we didn't get coupons. Just a few people came to the wedding – seven, plus me and my husband. After the wedding we went back to my mother's house, she had done a buffet. When the War ended, being married, I had to leave the forces.

My husband was still in the Army. We lived with my mother, for a couple of years, then we had the option of a flat and went there for a good while. Then I lived for fifty years in the same house. My sister-in-law lived upstairs and we lived down stairs. There wasn't much to do there. I got a job in a pencil factory when I came out of the Army. My husband came out a couple of years later and went into the family greengrocery business. Then I went to work there as well. The greengrocers had been closed down during the War as everyone was called up. Unless you had something wrong with you, you just got called up.

Where we lived we saw ack ack guns and barrage balloons as they were working on the downs near us. There was not a lot of bombing there. The railway had many near misses. The west end of London got it mainly

We used to go to the pictures but eventually cinemas closed down and the theatres too.

When I married my husband, I had eight brothers-in-law and two sisters-in-law. I am the only one left now. My brother has gone too.

One funny story I remember was when I went to meet my husband's family. You had to be taken home, rather formally in those days. His brothers knew I worked as a cook in the services so they asked me to make a pudding for them which I did. Afterwards I went out into the kitchen and the four boys were all lined out on the floor clutching their stomachs saying it must be the pudding that had upset them. Not being used to male humour I thought they were serious!

Maud Beaman - *I never saw a gun or any fighting throughout the War.*

I was in service in 1939 but I was bored. I joined the Army when I was 17 though I said I was 18. I did my training at Durham and was then posted to Lincoln as a cook.

It was hard work; I had to do night work. We had a lot of overseas drafts. We cooked for about six hundred people at a time. Food was rationed. When they went on marches we had to give them set rations. It was mostly men in the cookhouse, the girls used to do the waiting on the table – orderly girls, the men used to do spud bashing and washing the tins. I helped with the cooking. We had a sergeant cook in charge.

I did a course at York for six weeks, and a six week NCO course at Newark. I then got posted to Skegness for a week and joined the 3rd battalion service corps, then moved to Sutton Veany in Warminster. We used to go to Bath every Saturday on a special troop train – sixpence. I didn't like it there. If you wanted to go to the pictures you had to book and there wasn't much else to do there. At Warminster there was a big school of infantry.

It was a good life. There were dances to go to and troops around the aerodrome used send invitations for girls to go which included transport. We went to the American base. The Americans had all the sweets and chocolates on show and you could help yourself. We used to go to the assembly rooms. We knew about twelve RAF men, and we used to take them to our barracks. We used to wear sphinx badges - Lincolnshire regiment – and used to pretend we were from Egypt.

We didn't cater for special diets in those days. We did all the kitchen jobs – even boned the bacon.

I got on so well in the kitchen, the sergeant put me in for a stripe and I was surprised that I got two. I was made a corporal. This gave me more money and more privileges, Privates had to be in bed by 10pm, corporals by 11pm plus we had two late nights a week. An orderly sergeant checked girls in and out.

I was on duty one night; a private Lacey was confined to barracks. She came and said she was going to have a bath - is that OK she said. Then someone came in and said private Lacey was in the pub. I reported her.

I was caught in Harrogate once with no hat on and I was on a charge and told off. I just didn't want to spoil my hair.

We had to go out in uniform, we were not allowed civies. I remember once my friend, Peggy and I had been to the pictures then went to the fish and chip shop. It was blackout. We were queuing up. Some Americans asked if we had any stripes. We said no as we didn't want to put them off, then when we got in the shop they said you told a lie, you have stripes. They said corporal is the best rank in the army – you pass all the problems on to the sergeant, they take the rap!

I met my husband in 1942 in Lincoln; he was going to the Middle East. I wrote to him for 4 years. I used to visit his mother when I was on leave. He was a sergeant in the Royal Fusiliers. He went on one of the Commando raids to France/Germany.

I got demobbed from the army in February 1946 and went to London and stayed with his mother. I got married in September 1946.

I never saw a gun or any fighting throughout the War.

Christine Cooke - *I spent the whole war and didn't see any bombing*

I was 16 when war broke out. I was living at home with my parents. I had 2 sisters and a brother. My brother was in the Royal Navy. At that time I was too young to be called up so I went away from home to a domestic science college at Shrewsbury for 2 years. I wasn't very clever at school and my parents thought that would be the answer. It was.

There was no shortage of food there! We had drills in case of raids but we were not affected.

When I was 19 I volunteered to join the Navy. My parents were very much against it.

I had to do training and they sent me to Mill Hill in London learning how to cook for officers in a particular way. After 6 weeks they sent me to Plymouth. I had lived a sheltered life. They put me on a train on my own. I felt completely lost. However, they eventually took me out to Tamerton Folio where there was an enormous camp. It looked very bleak. They said you are only staying one night and then you are going to Falmouth. The next day I was taken to the station and then to Falmouth. It was April 1943. It was beautiful weather and the quarters, a converted hotel, had been taken over for the wrens. The views in Falmouth were lovely. I used to cook for a group of officers who were there. There were only 2 of us - one on watch and one off.

I was then moved to Bristol. The barracks in Bristol were Nissan huts. They were huge and very primitive. We just had a bed and a locker. We slept in double bunks. The girl above me was a character, she worked in the mail office. Bristol was very bleak. The girls were from all parts of the country which took a bit getting to know as I couldn't always understand them.

In Bristol we had a huge galley. I was one of the 2 cooks for the officers' food and we had stewards to serve. The rest of the kitchen staff was for the sailors and the wounded patients who had been sent there. This chap called 'Chief' was very strict and you had to do as he said. We had our own larder for the officers' food. We had 20 officers to cook for and some officers wanted particular things. A wren officer was in charge of the wrens.

The morning shift was 7 am and we worked right through until after lunch and then the later shift came on at 4 pm and they did teas and evening meals until about 9 or 10 pm - a lot of work without a break for just one person.

I had my bicycle there and used to ride around on my days off.

I met my husband on a blind date when I was in Falmouth. This Edna suggested we should go out for an evening. She said "I've got a chap who's got a friend called Cookie". I said I was game for anything. So we set off. We had to walk into Falmouth. As we saw them she said "The tall one's mine and the other one's yours." Cookie was about my height. I thought he seemed all right. "My name's Cookie, my real name's Ronald" he said. After that we started going out on our own. No proper introduction or anything!

The wren officer was not popular with either the wrens or the officers. My husband had quite a few run-ins with her particularly after we were married. He was a sub-lieutenant. I remember once he was on leave. If you were married you automatically got leave with your husband. The wren officer said no. My husband insisted and eventually after threatening to complain she agreed. I left the forces soon afterwards anyway.

I know we hadn't long been married and I had my 21st birthday. I remember my husband taking me to a pub which was quite an eye opener as I had never smoked or had anything to drink. I had gin and orange and one of the girls in the wrens was there with me and she got me to smoke. That was the first and last time I smoked.

I spent the whole the War and didn't see any bombing. We heard the planes. After I left Falmouth a whole lot of wrens were killed as the hotel barracks we had been in had a direct hit.

My eldest son was due on May 8th 1945 which was VE day but he came 4 days later. I can remember seeing the beacons all around – no parties for me! My cousin who was in the wrens was going to the celebration even though she was getting married soon. I was living back at home at this time but mother wouldn't let me go. My mother said "You can't possibly go like that!"

We had 4 bedrooms at home. I was the youngest with only me living there. After I went my mother was approached by the local council and she had to take someone. She had an American soldier called Joe and he was our best man when we were married. Before we got married by husband said "I haven't got a best man" and I said "Why don't you ask Joe." Joe had never been in a church in his life but he was very nice. They were sitting in the pew waiting for me and he turned to my husband and said '"Here's the gaffer?" – meaning the vicar. When I was expecting the baby Joe had gone back to America and he sent over food parcels to my mother. He also sent baby clothes. With rationing we were limited at home. We kept in touch for a while. As the years went on we were living in Devon and I had a telephone call one day from my brother who had taken over the family home. They had a telephone call from Joe. He asked for my mother, who was dead, so he asked for my number. He got in touch with us from America. It was as if all those years had gone by without us noticing.

I can remember when I was expecting Brian it was difficult to get fruit. You'd get a message that bananas were in and you went and queued for hours just to get one or two. I never had chocolates or sweets. Even though I was a cook my mother did the cooking when I went back to live at home until my husband was demobbed.

I ended up as a leading wren. I met some lovely people. I never really found any hardship as far as food was concerned. They were some happy times.

Mary Grant - *In the wrens you were in it together but outside the forces it was quite different, especially for women.*

I joined the wrens and took part in the D-Day operation.

I left school at the age of seventeen and at that age you weren't allowed to join up. I went to work for the London County Council (LCC) but joined the wrens in 1943 initially because the wrens were quite a small service. I went to the central depot at Mill Hill where you are assessed as to what you should do.

After the assessment they said I should be a radio mechanic. I went for training to a civilian technical college in Essex. Our billet was at Woodford Green. We had to do basic radio training there. Afterwards you went on to particular Navy equipment which was at HMS Aerial in Warrington in Lancashire. After that if you passed you exams, you were allocated as part of the service. I went to the Fleet Air Arm but then because D-day was being planned they pulled out about twelve wrens and sailors to go to Fort Southwick. We then trained on the equipment that they were going to use for the operations.

From there we were sent in twos or threes to various sites along the south coast where there was a possibility that the troops would land. I was sent to Swanage. When we got sent there in March 1943 the wireless had been constructed. I was a petty officer (PO) in charge of ratings.

We only had one commissioned officer who came from time to time to see how things were going.

I tried not to make it too complicated whilst I was at Swanage - wireless mechanics and radio mechanics 'nixt the twain shall meet'. I was given some training to be a wireless mechanic. We had personnel from the Marines, the RAF and American sailors. This made for a great spirit of comradeship. Visitors were allowed so we had a whale of a time off duty with parties on the beach etc.!

The wrens were billeted in a guest house to an elderly couple. I shared a bedroom with a PO who was running red watch.

As D-Day approached, my watch - green watch - was on duty. We had all the communications from Southwick channelled through the wireless station, but it was all scrambled - we couldn't understand it! We were really there to maintain the equipment. We stayed there I suppose for about five months and then I was sent back to the Fleet Air Arm. I went to Yeovilton to maintain radio equipment used in aircraft. It was a simple operation because we knew exactly what we were doing. It was just a routine maintenance job.

We were sworn to secrecy – on the night that they landed in Normandy, you came down on duty in the morning. Mr Blitz came down and said "I don't suppose you have heard the news - they have landed." – so we obviously had kept it secret.

I remember a chap in the RAF organised a barrel of beer and put it in the woods at Studland. I was very sick afterwards! I drank cider and it was years before I could drink cider again.

Gradually, the War came to an end. I left the wrens in May 1945. I was in the wrens for three years. My career, like many others, got really messed up by the War. At school I took matriculation so normally I would have gone to university or to a trade. I had started training as an architect for two years before I volunteered for the wrens.

When I was sent to a scientific establishment in Surrey on a course I met my husband, who worked there. He was an electronics engineer. We became engaged to be married so when I left the Navy I couldn't return to the LCC because they took no married women.

I certainly found in the wrens you were in it together but outside the forces it was quite different, especially for women.

Sam Lipfriend - *Life was too short to worry!*

I was born 1st April 1925, I am the sixth child of Israel and Sarah Lipfriend who came over from Poland in 1898. One of my brothers became a judge of Her Majesty's Judiciary.

When war was declared they said "As the Germans have not retreated from Poland we are today at war". This was at 11am on 3rd September 1939.

During the early years of the War we had the appalling situation at Dunkirk where lots of our boys were killed and this made a great impression on my mind. I was indignant that a man from a foreign country wanted to come over to our country, take it over, and run it according to his way of life. I understand this feeling of being indignant was not just peculiar to me. It occurred to numerous other servicemen who volunteered for the forces as early as they could.

I joined the ATC and spent two years learning various subject matters relating to the RAF. This stood me in good stead when I volunteered for aircrew in early 1943 before I was eighteen. After an interview at St John's Wood, I applied to become a flight engineer. This was because if I had chosen to be a pilot I would have had to wait 18 months, a navigator 15 months, a bomb aimer a year and flight engineer six months. It suited me as I wanted to go to war and fight off Hitler.

Having been called to report for duty in August 1943, I spent 4 weeks training - physical drill, aircraft recognition, maths and a period of social acclimatisation with people from all over the country and of different educational and intelligence abilities.

From the Aircrew Receiving Centre we went to initial training wing at Torquay for a period of eight weeks and then we were posted to St Athens near Barry in South Wales. We stayed there for six months learning all about the aircraft and how it operated.

In May 1944 I successfully passed out and became a sergeant. After leave I was sent to 1667 Heavy Conversion unit where the pilot, navigator, bomb aimer and wireless operator met up with the flight engineer and two gunners, making seven men in a Lancaster and Halifax bomber crew. Selection was very casual, sort of hit and miss, saying "Would you like to join me?" Within

my first crew they were all English. From the Heavy Conversion Unit we went to No 1 Lancaster flying school at Hemswell, where we did circuits and bumps in the plane which meant, take off, flying round and landing continuously. From Hemswell we were posted to Ludford Magna in north Lincolnshire - 101 Squadron - where on our last training cross country from Hemswell we were asked to return early because there was mist coming in off the North Sea.

We were subsequently sent westwards across England to try to land – we had tried eight aerodromes and then at the ninth - RAF Litchfield, near Wolverhampton - we crashed, possibly because we ran out of fuel. We were busy trying to follow the perimeter lights to get in through funnels to the runway. When I awoke lying on my back, I heard someone calling so I joined in calling. Eventually I was found by a member of the fire rescue team. The next thing I knew I was lying on a stretcher in sick quarters. The padre came round. I asked about the other members of the crew and he told me they were OK. He did not tell me then that three of the boys had been killed - although I was eventually told.

I was taken to a hospital at Shifnall and the following day we were visited by two RAF officers from Cosford who had agreed that we would be taken to Cosford the following day. I stayed there for four weeks and although I asked every day, "Will I be able to fly?" I was only told on the last day that I would be able to fly again. After three weeks sick leave, I went back to the squadron.

After two weeks I was posted to 100 Squadron, at Waltham near Grimsby as a flight engineer. The previous guy had resigned unable to cope. Pilot officer Edlund had already done four operations when I arrived. With them I did four operations on Cologne and Dusseldorf. Then I was posted to 550 Squadron at north Killingholme alongside Immingham. There I did twenty-eight more operations over Germany the last four with different crews as my original crew had already done their quota.

On Freiburg I saw the cathedrals on fire. On Karlsruhe I saw a German fighter pass from the opposite direction three hundred yards up. This was at night. On Merzberg we had ice on the perspex and wings and on another trip we lost an engine.

On one occasion when we were sent to another aerodrome for ditching practice, we were sat in the body of the Lancaster which was placed on the water. After the required two thumps we scrambled out through the escape hatch in the roof of the plane onto the wing. Two of the boys went to the dinghy which had been placed on the water. It was upside down so they had to turn it over. One guy, Eddy then mentioned he couldn't swim so we had to pull and push him on board the dinghy – he had been three years in the Merchant Navy!

We had many near misses and many people were very superstitious. I always carried a rabbit's foot with me that someone had given me and some men even peed on the rear wheel of the plane.

We all unwound in different ways - going out with girls, getting drunk, smoking and swearing. Life was too short to worry!

You did not mope about the loss of one the crew. You drank to their good health! You had to be like that to survive. If you got upset, you went downwards.

I didn't come out of the RAF until April 1947. I did a flight mechanics course and then I was just wasting time. They couldn't let us all out together, otherwise too many would have been on the job market in one go! When I came out I joined my brother who was a tailor and learnt about tailoring. I then had a ladies outer garment factory for twenty years. I then bought some property and later became an estate agent after selling a factory.

Olive Robinson - *I remember the date (I was called up) - it was so important - my freedom.*

I was fifteen when war broke out. I was still at school living in Norwood Green in Middlesex. It was a very nice area. I was living with my mother and step-father. My father died in 1931 – flu - when I was five and my sister three and we went back to live with my grandmother for a while.

My mother then met Mr Clements and married him. We moved around a lot and I went to so many different schools. I won a scholarship and went to Balham High School but I was only there for one year because the family moved again to Southall Middy in 1937.

In 1939 the War started - I was fifteen - and I remember very well the sirens sounding on that very first day and all the apprehension. Whilst I was still living in Southall we had quite a few raids. There was one really bad raid when the planes came over and dropped a stick of bombs. They did a lot of damage but luckily they were either side of us and we were safe. We had an air raid shelter in the cellar – it was only a table high.

I belonged to the Girl Guides part of St Mary Church. I am still part of the Guides today. I went to weekly meetings and we were linked with the Scouts and did various things such as collecting newspapers and clothes which were passed to those who needed them.

I was never evacuated. I left school when I was fifteen and I got a job with the Great Western Railway (GWR) in London. I was in the telephone enquiry office at Paddington station. I went up by train. We had to do shift work, the earliest was 8am and the latest was 4pm – 10pm. We had a few problems with the raids but luckily I was not personally involved and was always able to go to work. I had done a little shorthand and typing so occasionally I did letters for Miss Davenport who was the office supervisor. Otherwise it was the telephone all the time.

We did not know how long the War was going to last and I wanted to go into the wrens, partly because my grandfather and an uncle had both been involved with the Merchant Navy. To do this I had to volunteer before I was eighteen otherwise I would not be allowed as working for GWR was classified as a reserved occupation. So I volunteered and was called up on March 3rd 1943 – I remember the date - it was so important - my freedom.

I had to report to the main place at Mill Hill with all the other volunteers. We were interviewed and one of the things on offer was to be a torpedo wren which I thought sounded exciting. They desperately needed us as we only stayed one week at Mill Hill. I was a Victory wren. When you joined the Navy you were allocated a situation and you stayed that way despite being posted to different bases.

Twelve of us were sent to Brighton where they taught us how to be a torpedo wren – we did electronics. We were issued with a uniform and I lived with the other eleven in a very nice horseshoe shaped house in Marine Parade, right opposite the beach. We had to go out on the parade on the sea front and do exercises. We had to work very hard learning about electronics and torpedoes. I am very good with electrical things even to this day.

We spent six weeks there also learning about depth charges, mines and how to change plugs etc. and we were then posted along with others to Glasgow where I was attached to the DEMS (Defensively Equipped Merchant Ships) gunnery school. The reason I was there was to go on board and check and clean and put back together the Paravanes (anti-submarine weapons). These are wires coming from the ship's bow out into the sea on a long line – the idea is that when the ship goes through a minefield the mines are on wires. The wires with teeth from the ship's Paravanes go down and cut the wires of the mines. The mines then come to the surface and the sailors can then deal with them.

I did this when the ship was in dock. I needed to be quite athletic to get up on them. I was in Glasgow for nine very interesting months. Paravanes are not stored in the same way on all ships or in the same place so I had to go on board and check them. Sometimes I had to climb on them to check the teeth, or I had a hand pump to force air in to get the right pressure to maintain a certain depth.

The office I worked from was in the docks and on one occasion I was in there and I could smell gas. I thought that's funny and went into the kitchen, opened the door and the gas blew me across the room. I ended up in hospital. They attended to me but it had singed my hair and eyebrows. People thought I was a 'war wounded'. Another time I caught German measles so was put in hospital – in a children's ward.

I enjoyed my time in Glasgow. I was there over Christmas and went to the pantomime but couldn't understand the accents. I was then sent back to Brighton to do a LTO (leading torpedo operator) course. Another six weeks and this time we were based at Rodean school – the pupils were evacuated elsewhere. I wasn't allowed to go back to London for any time out but my grandmother and relatives lived in Eastbourne so I would cycle to Eastbourne to see them. Rodean was a beautiful place to be, right next to St Dunstan's which was also used by the Navy.

I was then posted to Newcastle-on-Tyne where I was attached to HMS Calliope under Commander Bembo. He was a little fat man who wasn't very popular with us. Our wrennery was fantastic. It was right on the sea front at Tynemouth in the Grand Hotel. Different sized ships came into Newcastle. One of the jobs I had to do was to install telephones on ships once they were tied up. If it was a big ship we put a telephone in the captain's cabin. For a small ship we put it in an office. When the ships were due to go out I had to go back on board and disconnect the phones and bring them ashore. On one occasion whilst on a big ship, they had already taken the gangway away so I couldn't get ashore. A crane came over; I put my foot in the hook with the telephone under my arm and was winched ashore!

On another occasion a girl was standing on the jetty - she was not a torpedo wren. I don't know what she was doing there but one of the lines holding the ship gave way and it curled round and wrapped round her leg. It twisted her leg badly and she was in hospital for ages.

The reason I didn't like Commander Bembo was because the wrens who worked in Newcastle would sometimes be given a day out in one of the big ships but, if there was a telephone to be installed, Bembo wouldn't let us go. I used to think 'I wish you were seasick!

The most dangerous thing I ever had to do was in Newcastle. The chief came to me just after I got back from the LTO course. He told me there was a problem and as I'd just done my course I was best placed to deal with it. He told me we had to deal with some gelatine that had come over from Ireland with its detonators in. We had to remove them. We had a car so he brought the tools and we were driven into a field to this pile of gelatine. We had to sit there and carefully take out the detonators – not sure how many - but we worked for at least three hours. I do think carefully now when I think about those Army people who have to defuse mines. I survived thank goodness.

I was on leave in London when the Japanese capitulated. There were great celebrations. I got back to Newcastle and I remember being down in the dock where there were more celebrations. I had the opportunity of staying in the wrens but once Japan had capitulated they didn't need torpedo wrens any more. I could either be a writer, or a steward but I said "I can't do that, I'm a trouser wren not a skirt wren." So I decided to be demobbed. Because I thought I had no real skills for civy street I thought it would be a good idea to get on the job market before everyone else was demobbed. I left the wrens in December 1945. I worked in one of the London offices in Queen's Gate in the small ships section which was trying to link up all the people and vessels that were used for the D-Day landing – I was there for about four months.

When I was in the torpedo section I was not allowed to go abroad because white women don't get their hands dirty! After I was demobbed I found out in my papers that I had been recommended for PO but I had already left the services by then.

When I came out I went back to Southall and met up with my girl friend. I worked for Garner Motors Ltd as a secretary and became the managing director's secretary. I stayed there for another five years. I didn't go back home. Instead I lived with an aunt in Harrow for a while. Then I moved to be nearer the job and lived in a small room with a family in Ealing.

Then I met my future husband. He was ex-Navy. He was a student. Like me he didn't have any qualifications. He was two years younger than me. He was trained in the Navy as a telegraphist. When he was demobbed he wasn't sure what he ought to do and went to speak to his old headmaster. The headmaster arranged for him to be interviewed at the Hammersmith school of building. He was a student there for several years learning to be a structural engineer.

I used to love eating condensed milk so became very fat. I just got on with life, I still do!

Joining the Land Army

Jean Batchelor - *The first time I wore trousers was when I went on the farm.*

In 1941 I was 18. and worked in a local office in the small town where I lived. When I was called up, I was given a choice of Army or Land Army. I chose Land Army, probably because I was more a country person and there was more of a chance of staying in the area.

I had to go to the west of Scotland, agriculture college – Auchencruive - near Ayr for a month's training. After that I went to an army hostel in Barassie, near Troon, a famous golfing area. I worked for two or three months from the hostel at various farms. The only things I can remember were hoeing turnips and the worst job - lifting bales of straw. I had never done anything like it before, it was quite a shock. About twelve of us lived in the hostel and were looked after by a warden/housekeeper. We split up to where we were needed each day.

Later I got a job in my home town, about four miles out of town. My friend and I cycled to this big estate. We worked 8am – 5pm all week and 1 pm on Saturdays in all weathers. I was working on the home farm on the big estate and my friend worked in the gardens. There was a third girl who was shared out as needed. She lived in the big house, we lived at home.

We were there for 6 years.

We had uniforms – dungarees and boots with corded trousers for best. The first time I wore trousers was when I went on the farm.

There was a herd of cows and we looked after them. There were chickens, guinea fowls and turkeys. The farmer looked after the horses and ploughing and we all helped when corn threshing time came. Hoards of people were needed then as there were no combine harvesters.

You were given a permit to buy a thermos flask for hot drinks – no extra food allowances and no perks in the way of food from the farm.

I had no feeling of being inferior in any way. The people on the big estate were very nice to work for. A lot of girls were unhappy with some of the farms they worked for. I worked for the farmer and his wife and they were very good to me, no problems.

The ploughman was just married. There was one young daughter of the owner and she went to school riding her horse there and back. All sections of the estate were more or less self-contained. The farmer had two children, one in the Army and one at school. Sadly, his eldest boy was killed at Pautaleria. It was very sad seeing the telegram being delivered. Weekends we did a lot of excursions on the Clyde steamers and visited various ports on the Clyde. Saturdays we went shopping. We also went to the cinema but did not go dancing very often.

Clydebank and Greenoch were bombed and there was a great loss of life. We heard it and saw the sky lit up. That was the only bombing we experienced. Paisley was also bombed. We had a friend who was the ARP warden – she was killed.

We were really not affected by the War.

We had an ammunition factory to the south of us but that didn't get blown up.

We were all rationed. I remember my poor mother going down to the town each day. The queues were terrible. This went on until I was twenty–one when I married. I met Bob in1942 in Largs. Bob was part of the Scottish command and stationed in Largs. We met at a church social – the church ran a canteen. Courting entailed walking. A lot of my life revolved around the church. I did a lot of voluntary work.

We had a church wedding and a small reception at a local hotel. No white dress – but a pale blue suit with lovely fancy hat. Nice wedding except that it was VE day and the photographer was booked from Glasgow but he was so drunk he didn't turn up but we had a few people with cameras. We went to Callender on honeymoon and then lived with Bob's parents until we bought a house in Southampton. Bob came out of the army in 1946.

Following a good deal of campaigning by many people, the Land Army were given recognition by the Government of their services to their country during WW2. We were given both a certificate and a badge.

Betty Parker - *"I don't think you will last very long."*

My family home was blitzed so we left Portsmouth and was evacuated to Waterlooville in Hampshire. I was going to be a hairdresser. I had done about a year's training. A Land Army lady came to have her hair done. She said, "One of you will have to be called up as there are two of you and you are 17." I said I would join the Land Army. They put me in touch with Tom Parker at Hambledon. My friend Joan and I got a bus to the Green Man pub there and then walked a very long way. I was wearing wedge heel shoes, nail varnish and had a posh hair cut.

We arrived at a very small bungalow. We met a George Dorey, who looked at both of us and said "I don't think you will last very long." But the farms were desperate for workers so we joined. We had to do everything from picking sprouts, planting potatoes, hoeing and harvesting. We also had to put sheaves up into stooks - this scratched your arms.

The highlight of all of this was a nice young man I met who was one year older than me. He was called Tom and was the son of the owner of the farms we worked on.

98

We were billeted in Hambledon where the food was diabolical. We complained to the Land Army representative. She arranged for us to go for an interview with a Mrs Chillingworth near-by. She was a lovely lady, very tiny, very well educated. She said yes she would take us providing we didn't have a lot of young men calling or a lot of telephone calls. The house is still there, called High Bank Cottage. We lived there and worked on the different farms. We didn't work with any of the animals though there were many herds of cows.

The family weren't very keen on my romance with Tom. He was only 18 in 1942. His father wouldn't let him go to war saying he was in a reserved occupation. During the War food was very scarce so when we met Tom brought his sandwiches for me to eat. He used to ride his horse from Charity farm and we met in the barn.

I had to walk everywhere so I bought a bike and rode to the different farms where I was sent though I had never ridden a bike before.

The different farms owned by Tom Parker senior, employed a lot of people. They had milk floats

which were driven by the girls. The girls also bottled the milk and drove around collecting milk from the farms. Some girls milked cows. They also lead cart horses, drove tractors and looked after chickens.

There was this place for prisoners of war and they came to work on the land as relief workers. There were also quite a lot of men on the farm, some didn't want to go to war. One Land Army girl married one of the men on the farm and they emigrated to Canada.

Encouraged by the Government, people made pies called Lord Horton pies. We could buy them in the village shop. One day I was eating this pie when something was very chewy. When I looked it was a piece of elastoplast! Things weren't very hygienic then. We always had dirty hands as there was nowhere to wash when we were working. We also went to the loo under the trees.

There were dances in the village hall, then the Americans came all along. They swept the girls off their feet but I remained faithful to Tom. The yanks had jolly fast motor bikes. Girls got stockings and sweets from them.

There was a limited amount of petrol so Tom didn't always use the car. We used the bus and walked quite a lot. We went to young farmers' dances, socials and clubs. When you went to the cinema you hoped you would not be bombed. There were air raids all through that period and bombs were dropped close by - sometimes they were enemy bombs and sometimes RAF bombs being unloaded.

I was demobbed in 1945. I thought I would go back into hairdressing. I did it for about 8 months then I was supported by my young man. We got married in September 1947.

I learnt to drive a car and for years I drove to Stoke Wood and did my mother in law's hair every Friday. As I left George Dorey would come out and I would wave and say "You said it would never last!" but it did. We were married for many years until he died.

Audrey's Story - as told by her niece - A happy ending

Audrey joined the Land Army in 1944. She really enjoyed the experience. One Saturday she went out with the other girls from the farm. Unfortunately she got very drunk – she had never tasted alcohol before and was unaware of the dangers. Two months later she realised she was pregnant aged nineteen. She was devastated. Today we would most probably call it rape. Every effort was said to have been made to find the person concerned. However, in 1944 he was not found.

Audrey was cast out by her family as she had had brought shame on them. Audrey did not touch a drop of alcohol ever again. The Land Army people were very good and supportive and put her in touch with the Seaman's Mission where she was to have the baby.

When she was eight months pregnant Audrey's father died. She went back to her parent's home to go to the funeral but was unwelcome. Her mother was furious and made her go into the back room of the house until after everyone had left. Audrey then went back to the Seaman's Mission until she had her baby girl.

In those days, the girls kept their child for six weeks before giving up the child for adoption. By now Audrey had met Tom, the man she would eventually marry. He was willing to marry Audrey straight away and bring up the child as his own, but her mother would not allow this to happen. Twenty-one was the age of consent in those days and many parents kept to this rule very strictly.

Audrey did eventually marry Tom and they had three children - a boy and two girls. When her son was born she treated him as though he was the daughter she had given up. Despite protestations from her sister she sometimes put him in dresses. Tom died and then her son died of AIDS at quite an early age but her two daughters are still alive today. Audrey lives in Sunderland where she has lived all her life and is now in a nursing home.

On a recent outing with her aunt, Audrey's daughter told the aunt that she had received a letter from Audrey's adopted first child, now sixty-four years old, who wanted to make contact with them. The aunt and daughter went to see Audrey and told her. Audrey sobbed inconsolably for over 45 minutes. She then started to tell them her story.

Audrey always thought that no-one knew of her plight. In fact her sister knew all along and had told her two daughters who were sworn to secrecy.

This story does have a happy ending. Her daughters organised an eighty-fifth birthday party for Audrey. Unbeknown to her, Audrey's first-born child was invited. The whole family are now reconciled. Audrey is happy because she feels that her daughter has forgiven her for not making contact before. She has also acquired extra grandchildren too.

Being in a Protected Occupation

Norah Hull - *Farmers did get plenty of food but they earned it!*

The War started two years after I was married. I was a farmer's wife. We were very poor so, for our first harvest, my husband and I did all the work and didn't employ anyone. I had two children. Later we could afford to employ a man. The only official thing I have ever done was when we had a group working together making men's pyjamas for wounded soldiers. I used to cut them out – the ladies taught me how to use scissors.

We were at one farm for several years. I looked after chickens and pigs. I had one lot of evacuees from London. A mother and two children came - the youngest was still being breast fed. They didn't last long. They were dreadful. Their bedding had to be burnt when they left. They were so messy. I hardly saw them. After that we always seemed to be having relatives come to stay as they were getting out of London. My uncle Joe came to stay from London. He was a German, he had been in England for years and years, been accepted but when the War broke out he was no longer accepted so he decided to get out of London. He stayed with us for quite a while.

During the harvest, we had school boys from Reading – they were very good. We had corn, potatoes and one cow. My husband used to take the cow and take a bucket, then stoop down and milk the cow wherever the cow was.

My husband was in the Home Guard and our house was the headquarters so we had sandbags in front of the house.

The farm was called Pound farm because, when cattle got loose, they were rounded up and put into a small field called a pound, until they were claimed.

Our house had four bay windows, lovely old beams, low ceilings plus several out buildings. We were near Benson aerodrome so quite often an aeroplane came in on fire, which was dramatic,

In 1942, we moved to Rogate, beyond Petersfield, to a much bigger house with a dairy. We were encouraged by the Government to grow sugar beet and potatoes. There, we employed several regular men plus a girl in the house. The house had cottages for workers.

My job was in the house, looking after the children and fetching things for my husband. We had students plus relations. Everyone thought it was a safe spot. We often had ten people for a meal. I made everything I could.

We had milk from the dairy and killed a pig once a year. The butcher would come and kill it and hang it and then when hung over night and its nose touched the ground the butcher came to remove the entrails. We then cleaned it before it was cut into joints. We salted some. We had a back kitchen which had salt pans. We put the meat in and turned it every few days. Eventually it was left to hang up to dry – this gave us bacon all year round.

The chickens ran all over the buildings. When my children's friends came they went to look for eggs. I went to Sparsholt College where I learned about poultry. When a chicken needed to be killed – I did it – and plucked it. I could deal with rabbits too.

Deer went through the farm – there was a wood through the middle. Deer were considered a pest because they ate the beetroot. There was a shoot once a year at the farm. We would be given some of deer in payment. There were other shoots - pheasants, partridges – again we had a share of the spoils.

There was an area just beyond the buildings and farmyard and I decided to make it into a garden. One of the men on the farm did the first digging. I did the rest.

I belonged to the Women's Institute. We made jam of course, and at the vicarage they had a canning machine so we used to take the fruit there – plums, apples and pears. We had a very active WI anything that arose, we helped out. I represented the WI at the Albert Hall one year.

Every year we had a harvest supper. It was really something. The farmers entertained their men. The wives produced the food. There were always apple tarts, it was a big affair. At

harvest time we had harvest rations to be dealt with. For some reason or other the Government granted extra food – cheese, margarine, bacon and meat pies. It would come in huge blocks and I had to ration it out. The pies were a joke!

I did have one job - I collected paper. I was given a badge from the Government - as though it was important.

I had surplus cream and 'sold' it to friends and locals and did the same with eggs. I had a bowl that held a gallon of milk. I went to the dairy, filled it, brought it in, then left it over night so the cream rose to the top. Next day I put it on the stove until there was a real crust, then let it get cold before I skimmed it off. This made clotted cream. The skimmed milk was loved by children.

We had a car. Most of the time the children were able to get to school but I had to take them occasionally.

In the beginning we rented the farm but eventually we bought it. Any sensible tenant farmer says yes because we got it at a better rate than on the open market. Later we sold it and moved to a bigger farm with the proceeds.

One day I had about six children playing on the lawn and a bomb landed on the lawn and made a basin about six feet wide. It covered the children with sand, and broke the telephone wire but that was all – no explosion - oh that was lucky. It was one of ours!

We heard bombers going over, German and English. When the paratroopers went over in their gliders, it went on and on and on.

In the village, there was one big house used by the Government, where Monty met Eisenhower. There was a fair number of naval people in the village. They were somewhat pompous but the War broke down barriers and everybody joined in. We were always doing things in aid of someone or other. I was able to get away from the house to go to the village but not very often. Apart from that I was not really aware very much of the War.

At one time we had Italian prisoners to lift potatoes. There were quite a few of them. One did some carving for me. They were fetched and carried. Later, just before D-Day, we had the Calgary Highlanders (Canadian) who camped on the farm because the area was crammed full of soldiers and lorries hidden in woods. One day, in mid-winter, they gave me a sack of Canadian flour which is drier and better for making pastry - but it also meant I made an awful lot of mince pies. I never finished the sack as it had mice in by the end!

As a farmers wife you are always like a little queen. You keep an eye on the farm workers. One couple were having marital trouble, so I helped sort that out. There were five cottages - people in all of them. The three-hundred acre farm was labour intensive. Some of the wives would come to help with the potato picking. We grew quite a few potatoes and would send a tractor and trailer up to the village and all the women would come on the tractor to help. They seemed to love it

Farmers did get plenty of food but they earned it!

Dennis Pink - *I wouldn't ask anyone to do a job I wouldn't do myself*

I was seventeen during the War and my father, myself and one other man, plus two Land girls were farming in pigs, poultry and horticulture. My papers came through for call up and my father said I'd be more use on the land than going to war and made an application for deferment, which was granted on a six-month basis. This happened three times. On the third time there was a letter enclosed which said I would not be called up as I was more useful on the land.

We were at Cranbury Park in Otterborne on the Chamberlain estate. At the height of the War they had the Canadian GHQ there. Their work was mainly operations planning. Some of the D-Day operations were planned there. We had Canadians all round our area. I was interviewed and was given a pass that enabled me to go anywhere, including the docks. I could go where police couldn't go! The wrens were wonderful people, particularly those in the sergeants' mess. We got to know them quite well. There were many sad stories of the ones who didn't come back. They were super people.

The American officers used to visit Cranbury Park. There were troops all round the mansion, and it was guarded by guys walking around with automatic guns. It was in a very big park, well off the beaten track. There were only two entrances, one at the top of Otterborne Hill and the other came in from the Hursley Road. We lived in what used to be the old garden house – a cottage. We were the only tenants there, except for the dairy farm which was rented out. We kept many pigs and a lot of poultry. We used to grow flowers too.

We used to rear and take all the mismarked and unwanted saddleback pigs from Mr Marks at Brasefield – he was a renowned breeder and only wanted perfect markings. The looks didn't matter to us. All we were doing was fattening them up for meat which we sold directly to the bacon company. I did everything appertaining to pig farming. We also used to collect the waste food from the camps around as food for the pigs – my pass came in useful.

I had very little leisure time. On a Saturday I would have a bath and change of clothes to go into Winchester. I would cycle down and leave my bike at the lodge, then catch the bus and go to the pictures. Once, when I was all dressed up in clean clothes, my father said, will you go up and have a look at that gilt (young sow). I went up and told him she was unwell so he made me get out of my good clothes and help out. That was my weekend scuppered.

We used to go to the Conservative club in Winchester, just above the market. It was the main club of Winchester. We got to know a many people there. I could go from the bottom of the High Street up to the top and I knew all the owners of the shops. We used to trade quite a lot with the horticultural stuff. There was a bartering system in place for almost everything - a couple of dozen eggs worked wonders! Probably someone who was a bit jealous might report someone but generally there were no problems. We were issued with coupons, but we never had time to go out to places. Once you got vehicles you looked after them to try to make them last. We were never short of petrol because we were doing a job and classed as essential users. The chickens we had were for eggs which we sold to local shops. We didn't really know there was a rationing system going on. We had everything we wanted because we were so well known.

There were very few rules and regulations. Health & Safety today is going to be the ruination of many farmers.

Land girls were local. One lived near Eastleigh. She worked for my dad for many years, even after the War. She was trained by father, she was a wonderful girl. The Land Army did a lot of good work during the War. The other girl only came in for a couple of years she was also very good. One was married. There was a section of Land Army who did forestry work.

My father was originally running a large pig farm in the Wiltshire area but he wanted to cut down in size so he swapped over. My father found out that one worker was a conscientious objector and Dad didn't approve so he got rid of him. Dad had no trouble with women. Dad was a very good governor. Some women were better than others of course. My mother was a hard worker.

Coach loads of women and children were sometimes brought out from Southampton or Portsmouth to Holcombe Road, just to give them a break from the bombing.

I've always been lucky with staff. My oldest employee worked with me for forty-eight years. I was trained by very good workmen, I wouldn't ask anyone to do a job I wouldn't do myself and my dad was the same.

Being a nurse

Alex Stockwell - *Life was very hard but a lot of fun*

I was 16 at the beginning of the War. I had wanted to be a nurse all my life. I found a cottage hospital called Henry Brock hospital. It was a mansion turned into a thirty bedded small surgery unit with one sister, one matron and the rest young girls wanting to be a nurse. I had a very happy 2 years there, meeting up with a few soldiers who were in barracks in Loch Lomond.

The first of the War I can remember was when Clyde Bank was bombed and we got a lot of the patients who were injured. The injured were more or less all from the Gorbles area. We had to de-lice a lot of the women and clean them up.

Then my father died so, to be nearer home, I went to Dundee Royal hospital. I had one day a month off and worked a ten hour day solid. Our only relief was going to the Palais de Dance and meeting up with the Yanks. I was pushed over the wall of the hospital by Yanks as we were meant to be in by 10 pm. We would creep up the backstairs then climb up a drainpipe as our room was 3 floors up. Everyone talked about attempted burglary but it was us! It was a very hard life but we made our own fun.

The other place I can remember there being a bomb was at St Andrews. My mother had brought my sisters, who were nine years younger than me, to St Andrews and I managed to get across for my two days off after night duty. I was playing in the sand with them, there were three fleet air arms officers, making tunnels towards us. That evening I accepted their invitation to go to a dance, they were nice, I shook hands with one who took me home.

My mother was up one night chasing a mouse when suddenly a plane came over and dropped a bomb just near us. That was very scary.

The Yanks reputation was that they were over sexed and over paid. I kept company with a sergeant, named Hank. He didn't lay a hand on me. Another was an officer called Bill and he was nice company. I said cheerio to him on the train and when I got back upstairs my room was full of yellow chrysanths from him. Going out with the Americans was a bit of relief from our hard work

On another occasion my friend, Joan Bruce and I were in a café and some Yanks were making eyes at us and we ended up going to the pictures with them. They paid for us. They then wanted to go for a stroll in the park. I was not happy with that so we took to our heels and ran off with them chasing us. We managed to just outrun them and we got to our boarding house.

We did four months night duty at a time and got four days off at the end. At 8 pm we had a meal and then worked until 8 am. There were 50 patients in a ward with only two nurses.

Towards the end of the War in Britain I did my midwifery course. I went to Perth to be near my mother. I did six months instead of a year – part practice. After that I joined the QA nursing service as a sister and landed up in York in a field hospital for six months. I was involved in a lot of brain surgery in York and from there we were shipped out to Italy, Udine for about six months and then transferred to the HCCS hospital in Trieste where I met my husband. We quickly got engaged and eventually married.

There was an RAF officers mess in Trieste and they invited us to a party. That was the first time I had experienced any drinking. I wasn't used to it. I drunk gin which I didn't like much and then we had cherry brandy. I threw the lot up in the toilet so didn't drink either again!

We had a nice swimming pool. As a nursing sister you were ranked as a lieutenant so we had all the facilities. We were often collected by a jeep. A RAF chap bought us to the swimming pool in the jeep. When he went to take us back the jeep had been stolen. This often happened or sometimes the wheels were taken off.

All the nurses in Italy were Italian. The male orderlies were very good but you had to show them how to work. They would do it if you did it, but you had to do it with them. In the maternity ward there were nursing sisters and Italian midwives. I could practice midwifery and there was no problem because there were other doctors with you.

Italy was still occupied. The army had not wound up. We worked in a military hospital mostly treating British patients, some still injured from the War, some serious accidents. I remember a really bad accident. I was the only sister on duty, the rest were orderlies. A soldier rang me and told me about an accident. At the time I was in the maternity theatre looking after a 'lady' in labour. I remember leaving her with a well experienced Italian midwife while I went down to deal with the accident. Next day, I was brought in front of the matron and questioned about having left the woman in the middle of her labour with an Italian midwife. I was really on the carpet about this and eventually the matron, a Miss Davis, took me in front of the colonel. I said I felt it was more important for me to go to sort out the accident when the lady was in the care of a well qualified midwife. Eventually I went back to the labour ward where the 'lady' produced a baby boy when I was there. The colonel was very pleased but didn't show it - he was pleased I attended to the lads. He didn't give me a dressing down, took no action in fact. Matron was very small and I think she didn't like me as I was tall. We were given mess money to buy food and she always bought things I didn't like.

I had loads of boy friends, but they were just friends. One particular boy thought I was serious but I wasn't. One married guy took me out and I thought I was safe! Victor Sylvester, the famous bandleader, was a captain in the army and he ran the entertainment for the troops. People sent him requests. One of the requests was "There was I waiting at the church". This was meant to be for me to have a laugh at because I preferred to go out with this married man. Then there was another one "Oh you beautiful doll", this was from the orderlies and patients from one of my wards. Life was very hard but a lot of fun.

In Dundee I earned £7.50 a month, in the army it was £21 pounds, of which I sent home £3 to my mum. We went on duty at 8 am and off duty at 6 pm

We were invited to lots of cocktail parties on ships that came into port. Four of us always put our names down. Miss Davies wanted us to let someone else go but there were no others so we ignored her and went anyway. That is how I met my husband. I had gone on board with a marine captain. Later, we all went off the ship to drink and dance at the Otto Club, which was an

officers club. I was dancing away and I was tapped on the shoulder by someone. I was a little tipsy, so didn't take much notice of who I was dancing with. The next day my friend said that someone would like to have a date. I said I can't remember who it was but I went out with him to dinner then to the officers club and had a dance.

He took me out every day after that. On the Wednesday we went to the officers club for tea. He had brought all his family photos with him. I wondered what was going on. He said they were sailing on the Sunday. He asked me to marry him on the Saturday. I said yes, as I had fallen completely in love. We didn't see each other for another three months, until the ship came in again. I took a week's leave and we went to Venice on a bus. We stayed in the Danielle hotel, it was an officers' hotel and we paid 9d per day for which we were also fed. Now it is the best hotel in Venice. We had separate rooms with 4 poster beds. We went out to Harry's bar in the evening. We only met one other officer.

At that time the borders were closed between Yugoslavia and Italy. During our stay in Venice we had to get back to Trieste. There was a border control so soldiers asked for our pass. We didn't have any but showed them our meal tickets, they obviously couldn't read English so let us through.

PS. This photograph is of the orderlies dressed as fairies but prior to the performance they all became very drunk. I found an officer and asked his advice as to how to sober them up as they couldn't perform. He gave them all an injection but wouldn't tell me what it was - but it worked!

Evelyn Gray - *we treated him just in time*

Before the War had started my friend and I had both joined the Red Cross. We did all our exams – home nursing etc, then spent many hours in St Mary's hospital in Portsmouth. We went every Wednesday afternoon and all day Sunday. Matron said we could stay for lunch. It was all voluntary

When War started matron asked me to go full time so I gave up the grocery trade. Then she wanted us to take our training, but I didn't wanted to be trained. I still liked the Red Cross so became a nursing auxiliary – VAD (voluntary aid detachment).

You could be sent any where. The farthest I got sent was to the Isle of White because there were so many cases of influenza. When I got there, there were more nurses than patients so I thought this was unfair so came home to St Mary's.

We lived near Copnor Bridge at the time so it was easy to cycle to work. Shearer Road was badly bombed. Every time I could hear it was getting close, I put a pillow over my head.

I did day duty for about six months, then three months nights. Often other nurses couldn't get in so often I did extra nights. The sister didn't like Red Cross nurses. She put me on an observation ward – all babies with infectious illnesses. The observation ward nurses thought

there was something wrong with one child but couldn't pin point it. We told the staff nurse but she said nothing, then we told the sister. We then worked out that the child had meningitis – we treated him just in time.

On day duty I went to a children's ward dealing with skin diseases. We put patients in baths and covered them in some special liquid. We also dealt with a lot of people who had lice. Sometimes we put a plaster on their heads to cut out the air supply and kill the lice

There was a patient, an old man, called up for the War. He said to me "Hear that noise - that man's choking." I got some cold water. We then put this towelling with water round his head then massaged his head and he got better. Later on I was on a ward on my own, I did the same thing to another patient and he suddenly opened his eyes. The patient in the next bed said I'd saved the man's life.

Another night when there was only me and a male nurse on duty, a patient was wheeled in by the police. He looked like a waif and stray. He had collapsed. We washed and cleaned him but his legs were full of maggots on his ulcers and in his feet and toes. We told him he wasn't going to get anything to eat or drink before he got cleaned up. We got rid of the maggots. The only food available was bread and butter, milk and sugar. We made him a slop plus a cup of tea. He went to sleep. About a month later I walked onto this ward and a very tall distinguished man greeted me and said he was pleased to see me again. It was him, I hadn't recognised him

One Thursday night the sister asked me to swap with another nurse. Usually it was my night off and I went dancing at Clarence Pier. So I swapped. That night Clarence Pier was bombed!

Often, when on our way to the Clarence Pier Pavilion, we had to crouch and creep through the ack ack guns firing on Southsea Common.

One night there was a funny noise in the sky, but we couldn't understand what it was. Mr Norris, one of the patients who couldn't sleep because of his asthma, and I went out on the balcony to look. We were blown across the ward – it was the first doodlebug. I got myself up and went back to make sure flames were not coming towards the hospital. That day, the ward was laid out ready for casualties so we couldn't give our patients any breakfast but we got them ready and washed. Most casualties had eyes and faces that were burned. We had to decide where to put people in different places according to their condition. Some were taken straight away to different specialist hospitals.

Towards the end of the War, I was on the ward when a young naval chap was sent from Hazlar hospital in Gosport to St Mary's. He said he was on a very good drug for a prostate problem. I asked a male nurse to get the doctor and we got the drug for him. Some time later, I was with my mum in Lake Road, and we went to one of the kitchens. This same guy was the engineer there. He shouted "Nurse I'm still going - still passing water through my penis." My mum said "Oh you must not say that word". I said: "Mum, that's what you call it."

I enjoyed all of it. I enjoyed going to work and meeting different nurses, and different patients. Nursing is altogether different now. Today, you throw everything away. We kept all dressings and washed them and hung them up to dry, then rolled them up ready to use them again. You didn't waste anything. I always saw that the patients were all right.

The most frightening experience was when I was on night duty on the old ward and a patient died. I ran and told sister and she came with her book. She said this patient is cold you must have fallen asleep. I objected - I was annoyed. I wasn't going to be a scapegoat so I pulled the emergency cord that would bring a doctor. When I pulled it the patient sat up. She lived about another five or six days afterwards. It was very scary.

Every night after working at the hospital I had to count the tokens for the cheese, butter and sugar from my parents' grocery shop. They then had to be taken to Mayfield Road school which had been taken over as offices in order to get vouchers to get more produce. I married in 1943 but carried on nursing. Our first child was born in 1948.

Friendships

Doreen Emblem - *Bunty was my bosom friend. She was loving and loyal with a gift for laughter and a sense of the ridiculous.*

During the War, people met others from different parts of the country, from different walks of life in unexpected circumstances. Friendships were made that lasted forever. Doreen was asked by Bunty's husband to write something about her best friend, after she died. The following is her story.

I was sitting with a number of other wrens in a large high-ceilinged room in the Royal Naval Barracks, Portsmouth. It was a bleak November day, the room was freezing cold. The wren sitting next to me had a bad cold – she was shivering violently. She was a very attractive girl, with dark, wavy hair, and beautiful brown eyes, which a friend of mine was later to remark, 'would fetch a duck off a pond'. An officer had taken our details - the usual name, rank, number and previous establishment, and then gone off. I exchanged names, hometown, and various naval experiences with my shivering neighbour, for whom I was beginning to feel very sorry. The fire was made up in the grate, but when I suggested we light it, the general feeling was that we dare not break the rule that 'no fires are to be lit until after 5.00pm'. "Well, I'm going to light it," I announced, "my friend here is not well, and if anything is said we all take the blame, OK?" It wasn't with quite a few of them, but I lit it anyway, and before long my friend was feeling much better – she was almost sitting on it! When the officer returned, she asked, "Who lit that fire?" Near silence, but several glances came my way. "All right," she said "if no one is going to own up, a report will be sent to the CO of your new establishment, and you will all be punished in due course." I could feel that I was going to be most unpopular in my new establishment so decided to own up. "I'm sorry, ma'am, but my friend Hughes has a very bad cold and couldn't stop shivering, so I lit it." "And you are?" she demanded in a steely voice, "44746 D Bowdler, ma'am." "A report will go with your draft, Bowdler, and your new CO will punish you accordingly," she smirked. My new friend was most upset and wanted to take the blame instead, but I told her not to worry. We now knew we were both going to the same ship, so I should insist she shared the spud-bashing, or confinement to quarters or whatever punishment I was given. As it happened we never heard another word about it and could only assume the CO thought it too trivial to warrant his attention.

Later that day a Navy truck took us to HMS Dryad in the village of Southwick and after an introductory tour of the establishment we were taken to our quarters, Soberton House, about five miles away. This was a large country house built around a quadrangle, which the Ministry of Defence (MOD) had taken over for the War. Most of the wrens were allotted a large cabin in the front of the house.I moved quickly to get a double bunk near the window for my new friend, Hughes, and me. We chatted and sorted out our kit. She re-read a letter from her mother, which she had only had time to glance at when she picked it up earlier that morning. It began with 'My dear Bunty' and she explained it was her mother's pet name for her as she had been such a bouncing baby. I called her Bunty, teasingly after that, but as there was another Dorothy in our crowd, the name caught on, and she was Bunty Hughes to everyone.

I admired her courage that night as she knelt beside the bunk to say her prayers. If anyone had sniggered I am sure I would have hit them. As she wasn't feeling well, I let her have the top bunk (always the favourite) without the usual toss of the coin, which was going on elsewhere in the cabin. However, when the alarm bell went off at 6.00am she forgot where she was and fell off – straight through the soft top of her suitcase. Fortunately, I had a sail-makers palm and needle and some waxed twine so was able to repair it by the time she went on leave, but she never slept on a top bunk again.

How cold it was that winter, and Soberton Towers was like a barn. The galley was officially out of bounds, but we would sneak down there at night and while one stood guard, the other made cocoa on the big Aga cooker.

I heard from my mother that they had killed a pig at home and she was sending me some faggots. They duly arrived but the problem was how to heat them and then eat them. We were not allowed to have food in the cabin. However, nothing ventured nothing gained. I posted my friend Hughes at the top of the stairs - the danger signal was a loud fit of coughing - whilst I dashed down to the galley and put the faggots in the oven. Then back to the cabin to wait for half an hour while they heated up. I explained to the interested others how they were made. Faggots had never been part of their diet, I am afraid, the same as caviar, which had never been included in mine. Time was up. I took my seaman's jersey to wrap around the dish as much to disguise it as to keep it hot. Before we reached the stairs to the galley a strong smell of onions wafted along the corridor. Panic stations! We got those faggots back to the cabin at a rate of knots, then when we were halfway through eating them the lights went out. Someone had a torch, and went to see what had happened. It turned out that Manuela Sykes, who was the helpless type, had gone to the attic to do some ironing and put the plug in the wrong socket thus fusing the lights. Falling over the ironing board and bumping her head was no more than she deserved for bringing a load of officers down on us. One came to our cabin to see if we were all right then asked what that funny smell was. I told her the window was open and it was coming from outside. Actually it was coming from under the bedclothes where I had put what was left of the faggots. When she had gone Bunty and I dissolved in fits of laughter, which soon stopped when we discovered she was sitting on the faggots.

Manuela was a very intense person. I seem to remember her mother was an author and an authority on some intellectual subject or other. Be that as it may, it happened that the son of some Dutch friends of hers came with the crew of his ship to HMS Dryad for training. As instructed by her mother, Manuela contacted him and they went out and about together when off duty. She fell in love with him. This was her first love affair and she was totally smitten. Bunty, being a good listener, got a detailed account of the effect this was having on her life.

At bedtime, sitting on her bunk rolling up her hair in paper, Manuela would pour out her feelings. No one had ever loved as she did. Then one night returning to quarters from a date, I was met by a distraught 'agony aunt Hughes'. Dot, you have got to come with me to search the ground for Manuela. The Dutchman has told her he is more or less engaged to a girl in Holland, and she is almost suicidal. More girls turned up armed with torches, and we set off in different directions. It was a horrible night, wet and foggy. I thought Sykes could have been a bit more considerate and waited for a frosty moonlit night as a branch knocked my hat off and bushes snagged precious stockings! Eventually we reached the lake, and after discussing its awful possibilities we decided to backtrack to the house and report to the duty officer, who could then organise a proper search party. This done, we went back to the cabin to dry off and await the outcome of events. I certainly did not expect to find Manuela sitting on her bunk rolling up her hair. Apparently she had shut herself up in the attic to come to terms with the most traumatic experience of her life.

Sometimes we did not take the truck back to quarters, but caught the local bus to Wickham. On the corner of the Square, there was a sweet shop-cum-café where we enjoyed a lovely pot of tea and oodles of bread and dripping. The tea cost twopence, the dripping, sixpence. The only drawback was we had to hitch a lift back to Soberton as there was no bus service.

One evening our luck ran out - not a single service truck came our way. Bunty was getting weary of walking and it was beginning to rain, when a car pulled up and an elderly lady asked if we would like a lift. "Oh yes, please, are you going near Soberton?" That was exactly where she was going. Easier said than done, the car was a little, soft-topped Austin with a very small back seat, completely occupied by a large dog. How on earth were two healthy wrens going to squeeze in? Only one way, and with great difficulty, Bunty sat on my lap in the front seat with her head wedged in the roof. We only managed this by the driver giving her a push.

Going round corners was dreadful. The door on our side was dodgy and the driving was most erratic. To add to my misery the dog put his paws on the back of the seat and proceeded to lick my face. We nearly went off the road as our driver took her hand off the wheel to try and push him back.

It was a relief when she pulled up at the bottom of our drive. Then we had another problem, how to get out? Margaret Rutherford, for that was what we nicknamed her afterwards, tried to pull Bunty out backwards, but that didn't work, she couldn't get her head down far enough. "Come and pull her forwards across the driving seat," I yelled. She did grab Bunty's feet and with a heave, pulled her. Unfortunately, the dog decided to join in, it jumped over the seat and landed on top of Bunty, barking like mad. I can't remember if we thanked the lady for the lift. Bunty couldn't, she had the breath knocked out of her and leant heavily on me as we walked up the drive, rather unsteadily, as the life had gone out of my legs. What upset us most was the fact that we were too late for supper.

On the whole, we enjoyed our work at Dryad. In fact, it could be great fun making up mock battles on the master plot in the control room, used to train the ship's crews, who worked on the plots in the replica of a destroyer and aircraft carrier.

Many of the wren plotters were from high society in civilian life. In our section were a couple of 'ladies', several 'honourables', and many with double-barrelled names, but service life is a great leveller and we really did get on well for such a mixed bunch.

It was very rural in Soberton. At night, owls hooted from the old church tower and two great Danes, left behind by the owner, padded around the corridors of the house at all hours. It was difficult to get transport to and from either Portsmouth or Fareham so we were delighted when, after a few months, new quarters were found for us in the Solent Hotel on Southsea seafront. This meant we could go to the cinemas, shows on the pier and the theatre.

Bunty was lucky and had 14 days leave over the Christmas holiday. I remember how lonely and fed up I was listening to Handel's Messiah on Christmas Day, all alone in the recreation room. The day she was due back had been one of those when everything seemed to go wrong, and I was glad to take an early evening bath (in the regulation three inches of water) then relax in my new snazzy red and black pyjamas, and thick seaman's jersey and socks. Our unheated cabin was an attic room with four double bunks and we all dressed up to go to bed.

About 8.30pm someone yelled up, "Bowdler, your friend Hughes is on the phone." Fearing she was ill or something and not coming back I dashed downstairs. "Oh, Dot, I am glad you are there, could you come and help me? I've found a young boy wandering round the street looking for his mother. She left him in the house with his two little sisters and one of them is feeling ill and keeps crying. I think she has a temperature - I don't like to leave them. Could you come and look for the mother? I think she is in a pub somewhere." "But Bunty, I am in my pyjamas," I wailed. "Put your bell-bottoms on top of them and hurry." She then gave me the name of a side street near the Guildhall and said she would get the boy to look out for me - then her money for the telephone ran out.

In a pub, I thought. Doesn't she know there is one on every corner of every street in that area? Nevertheless I did as I was bid and went as fast as I could. There was no hope of getting a bus along the Parade, up to the terraces and round by the Duke of York pub. No point going in there until I had a name and description, then I saw the boy, or rather, he saw my uniform and shouted.

There was Bunty on the sofa nursing a child with another sitting beside her. A miserable fire was smouldering in the grate. In fact the whole scene was miserable. "Could you try and find something to make a cup of tea before you go to look for the mother – I can't put this child down." Bunty could never go for long without a cup of tea! I eventually found the mother. It was a familiar story in those wartime days, her husband was in the Army. She had to have a bit of fun, didn't she - the kids were all right when she left? I didn't say a word. My friend, Hughes, said it all.

We were very quiet as we walked back to the Solent Hotel, taking it in turns to carry her suitcase, which weighed a ton. Then she spotted my red and black pyjamas hanging down below my bell-bottoms and out came the laughter, which was never very far from the surface.

It wasn't long after this incident that Bunty caught a very bad cold. It affected her right eye, which almost closed and the area round it became badly discoloured. It was arranged for her to see an eye surgeon at Queen Alexandra's Hospital, Cosham. He diagnosed a diseased antrum, and made arrangements to have her to come in so that he could operate and remove it. After the operation I went to see her, wearing my good, number one uniform and clutching a bunch of flowers. A nurse directed me to the ward – a Nissan hut – and as I started to walk down it, Bunty spotted me and called out, "Over here." Suddenly my feet shot out on the highly polished floor and I went on my bottom, ending up near her bed, having knocked a trolley over on the way. I was still clutching the flowers.

At last we were given our own quarters, Redlands, a small block of four flats overlooking the canoe lake in Southsea. Ours was a lovely front room with a bay window on the first floor. In it were four double bunks, and once again we managed to get one almost in the window. A chest of drawers was allocated to every two persons, which gave us two long and one short drawer each. The top of the chest was usually covered with personal knick-knacks, books etc which the other inmates respected.

The night we moved in was a bit chaotic, so I suppose Pam McMillan could have been excused for picking up Bunty's bible, but not for reading out loud, the dedication inside the cover. It had been given to her at the orphanage where she spent some unhappy years as a child. "Oh, how quaint," said McMillan in her affected voice. "I've never met anyone from an orphanage before, was it fun?" Utter silence. Having been a foster child myself, I could feel the fury rising in me, but Bunty with great dignity said, "May I have my bible, please? If you haven't got one, Pam, you are welcome to borrow it at any time."

111

At last it was VE Day. The captain addressed the whole ship's company of HMS Dryad from the balcony above the portico of Southwick House, which is of course where Monty and Eisenhower planned and carried out the D-Day operation. We sang the national anthem, then it was 'caps' off and 'three cheers' for the King.

The rest of the day was ours, he said, but the chaplain was conducting a communion service in the village church for those who wished to attend. Bunty and I decided to go and so did Rogers. Although it was such a wonderful day, it was also very sad. It was good to know no more lives would be lost, at least not in Germany. The War in the Far East was still going on, but it was impossible to forget all the fear and heartache of the previous six years.

My boyfriend had been a Mosquito pilot. He was killed as he tried to land his damaged plane after a pathfinder mission. Many more old school friends had gone too, and boys I had known in Combined Operations perished on D-day. I thought of them all and I am sure the other girls had similar thoughts as we travelled back to Southsea.

A very noisy Southsea it was - every ship's siren and air raid siren was going, car horns were blazing, people were singing. It was bedlam. For lunch that day there was a piece of Spam, dehydrated potatoes and a few carrots followed by a plum duff and watery custard. Several girls decided to go to London, if they could get on a train, as that was where everyone wanted to be. The First Officer came into the dining room and said that wrens in quarters had been asked to act as hostesses to foreign ships' companies in port. Four Norwegian crews had been assigned to us.

With our two strapping Norsemen, who didn't speak a word of English, Bunty and I made our way to the Guildhall, where it seemed hundreds of people were milling around singing and dancing. Not surprisingly, we became separated in the melee. My escort and I made our way to the Guildhall steps, which I thought would be a good vantage point to look for Bunty. Some marines were trying to climb on top of the stone lions. I pointed them out to my companion, who thought I was indicating that I wanted to get up there too. He grabbed me, lifted me up on to his shoulders and started climbing. Frantically I made him put me down again, but in the crush we fell, knocking over several other people. Luckily Bunty happened to notice the commotion on the steps and pushed her way through the crowd to come to my rescue. I am not at all clear how we eventually formed into some sort of parade, but with various bands leading us we finally reached the Savoy, having travelled most of the way on the shoulders of our Vikings. I think they were afraid we might be trampled underfoot.

Somehow or other, we ended up inside the Savoy and were on the balcony surrounding the dance floor when the King's speech was broadcast, but we didn't hear a word of it - the noise was too great. At night, there was dancing on the pier but when we got there it was full and there were no more admissions. This did not daunt our friends, however, they merely lifted us up and over the turnstile, then vaulted over themselves. We had hardly got inside when some crazy Yank caught hold of me and swung me round in the jitterbug. In one particularly acrobatic movement he let go of my hand too soon and I landed beside the drummer on the bandstand. That was enough. I could see Bunty was having her problems too and as soon as I could get hold of her, we decided to call it a day and make our way back to barracks and bed.

It was sometime later, though, that we got into our bunks. The cabin was full of exhausted wrens, swapping experiences. In between peals of laughter, Bunty explained the reason for my dishevelled appearance. Suddenly there was a loud knocking coming from the window. Someone opened the curtains (no more blackout) and there peering in, were our Norwegians. They had come to say goodbye, via the ropes, which went from the window to the ground as a sort of fire escape. Practically the whole crew were out there and we decided there was nothing for it but to get the duty officer's permission to take them in the galley and make them some cocoa, then hope they would make their way back to the ship. They did after giving us their home addresses, making us understand how welcome we would be there when things were back to normal.

Sometimes, Bunty would make up a foursome to go to a tea dance, otherwise she seldom if ever, made any dates. For a while, she kept up a correspondence with a boyfriend from her previous ship, but after some heart-searching decided she didn't want to keep up the relationship. That was when she told me about John - how she had met him at the bank where she worked before joining the wrens. He went in the Army, but had been taken prisoner of war. She had, to use a phrase popular at the time, made up her mind to wait and see what the future might bring. It brought them together.

Life was much more relaxed after VE Day. It was as though we had come through a long, dark tunnel into the light. People were happier and seemed to laugh and smile more easily. The popular big bands of that era performed at the pier on Sunday afternoons - Henry Hall and Harry Gold and his pieces of eight.

Bunty and I could hardly believe our eyes when we saw a man selling ice cream outside. Funds were low, and we couldn't really afford it, but how could we resist it after such a long time? Fumbling in our money belts, we came up with the cash and were given a dollop of ice cream on a ship's biscuit. Walking up the stairs in the theatre every lick was fully savoured, then a tragedy occurred! It was whilst looking for our row letter. As I bent to examine the side of a seat, my ice cream slipped off the biscuit and landed on the back of the neck of the sailor who was sitting in the seat. With horror, I watched it slowly sliding into his cotton flannel shirt and made futile efforts to retrieve it. It took a few minutes for the poor fellow to realise what had happened. Then his girlfriend sitting beside him took a hand or rather a handkerchief, in fact we all took out handkerchiefs, and started mopping him up. I was left with my rock-hard biscuit. My friend, Hughes, very generously gave me a lick or two, but she was laughing so much.

With a fortnightly pay of only 32/- (shillings) we were always short of money and travel warrants were only issued for long leave so if we wanted to go home in between, to save money, we hitched a lift. Bunty and I decided to do this one weekend and see if we could get to Cinderford. The hitches we picked up only took us a short way, then we were back on the road again thumbing it. To add to our misery it started to rain and one of Bunty's shoes had a hole in it. The only thing we could find to put in it was an old registered envelope, which didn't do much to keep the wet out. By evening we had only reached Newbury in Hampshire, so we thought it best to call the whole thing off, find a hostel and make our way back the next day. What a miserable night that was. The accommodation was a camp bed with a piece of coconut matting to cover us. We had to sleep in our uniforms because of the itchiness of the matting and to keep warm. In the morning a cup of tea and a piece of toast was our lot, but what could you expect for a shilling all-in? Two very dejected wrens eventually made it to my cousin's house in Portchester. As always, Dot gave us a warm and sympathetic welcome, with a hot meal thrown in. It was heaven to relax in front of a good fire while relating our adventures to the three children. Before we left, Dot found a rubber sole and stuck it on Bunty's shoe.

In the face of adversity, Dot's brave cheerfulness was an inspiration. Her soldier husband, John, had sailed to Singapore before her youngest child was born. When the Japanese invaded he was taken prisoner. Since then she had heard nothing except for two printed cards. After the Japanese surrendered, the ships gradually brought the prisoners home. Bunty, Rogers and I spent a Sunday at the house making flags, bunting and a 'welcome home' sign. Dot met every ship at Southampton. She refused to give up hope until the War Office eventually notified her that John had died on the infamous Burma railway, two years before. Her grief affected us all.

That winter my mother became ill and I was given a week's compassionate leave which was extended indefinitely, as her condition deteriorated. Bunty came to stay for her 14 days leave, to give me a hand nursing mum and look after the family. She loved the forest and the friendliness of the foresters. They, in turn, took a great fancy to her. It was while she was with me that Art came home from the Middle East and we first met him at his mother's house. Everyone knows everyone else in our mining village, as it was then. The environment made it a very close community. Bunty was continually surprised at the number of people who stopped to speak to her as if they had known her for years. Not long after she got back to Dryad she was sent on a course. Her letters made me feel quite envious and I missed her too.

Meanwhile, I was getting more involved with Art, mostly by correspondence, as he was stationed in Carlisle. It became obvious that my mother was going to need care and attention for a long time, so it was arranged for me to go back to Dryad and my demobilisation was brought forward. At Christmas, Art had leave, or rather he took French leave and we announced our engagement and decided to marry when he was demobilised in March. Bunty agreed to be my maid of honour, but a few days before the date of the wedding my mother had a severe haemorrhage and it had to be postponed until a month later, which was Easter. By then, Bunty had been demobilised, so she was able to stay with my mother whilst we were on honeymoon. The weather was cold and drizzling on our wedding day. The flowers, which had been kept for three days in an air raid shelter, wilted. The white fur cape, which a well-meaning neighbour had lent me, moulted. The night before, as I imagine all brides do, I started having misgivings and Bunty, who was sharing my bed, also shared my misgivings. She had not been at all keen on my marriage anyway and thought I was being too hasty. My suitcase was already packed. She said I could sneak off in the early hours, get a train to Liverpool and stay with her family. She would stay behind and explain matters to the groom and my family, but we dropped off to sleep before coming to a definite decision and in the morning it was too late.

The ceremony was a hoot. To the strains of 'Lead us Heavenly Father Lead Us', and the vicar heading the procession, we had only gone a few yards up the aisle when Bunty, her attention distracted by someone in the congregation, walked on my train causing the veil and headdress to go astray. A little further on, the heel of one of my borrowed shoes stuck in the grating. By the time we had released it, the vicar had reached the altar and everyone was looking round to see what had happened to us. All went well after that until Art said, "I will," before he should have. The vicar said, "Wait a minute, Arthur," then when he should have said it he didn't and the vicar had to prompt him again. Four months later I knew I was pregnant. Bunty was very cross because I had not been well and she envisaged all sorts of problems. She was proved right too, the biggest problem being when I had to walk 23 miles in labour to the nearest hospital, the morning after a blizzard. That was in March 1947, the worst winter on record. At the end of April, Bunty came for the christening and to be Lindsay's godmother. She made the robe almost all by hand. Aunty Ruby brought the lace in Ireland. In fact, Bunty had been so worried that my baby might have nothing to wear, I was hopeless then at knitting or sewing, she and her sisters made a complete layette, for which I was very grateful.

I was staying at Halewood with Lindsay; she was about 18 months old, when Bunty had her first date with John. The girls and I gave her all sorts of advice and she must have changed her mind a dozen times about what to wear. I stayed on to hear all about it when she came home and it was obvious she was in love and very happy.

In our conversations we often spoke of our hopes and dreams for the future. She thought she would be content with love in a cottage and two children. I wasn't sure about the cottage and wanted four children. As it happened, she had four and I was only able to have two. It was quite surprising how many things we had in common. We were the same age, semi-orphans. We both married men seven years older than ourselves. I had two daughters – one dark, one fair – so did she. She had three grandchildren named Tom, Edward and Emily and three of mine have those same names.

Little girls love to tell you about their bosom friend. Bunty was my bosom friend. She was loving and loyal with a gift for laughter and a sense of the ridiculous. I loved her.

Memories from Children

Children who stayed at home

General memories

I know that I had a ceiling come down on me in my bedroom, once when I was in bed, and thankfully, twice when I was not. We had an air raid shelter in the garden and used to go down into that, along with the next door neighbours. My dad had an allotment and one of his fellow gardeners had his onions blown up!

We had bomb sites near us for years after the War.

Everyone listened to the radio. We had to use an accumulator so listening, to the news and children's hour was rationed too. My mother didn't want to know, so didn't listen.

The children who came down from London were more aggressive.

My dad drove a tram in London in the War and some days he couldn't work until the bomb damage had been cleared and the craters repaired.

Dad was on war work making timber planes and landing craft, and when things started to get tough he decided it was time to send us to his brother's for safety. Anyway dad was right, because within a few weeks our house in Tottenham, London, was destroyed by a bomb, with just a few minor casualties. Then dad got us a new place to live. It was decided we should stay together and we moved back to London. I can remember standing in the street watching the vapour trails of the 'dog fights' in the sky, with no concern about the gun shells that would be coming down somewhere.

We used stirrup pumps and buckets for putting out incendiary bombs

We accepted everything. Sometimes, buses and tube trains used not to run. It was part of life. You couldn't do anything about it so got on with it.

I was born in Streatham, South London, in January 1935, so I was four years old when war was declared in 1939. I remember, one day, sitting with my parents and older sister, June, listening to the radio, and my parents looking very worried and upset. We were at war with Germany.

Everyone looked after everyone else in those days.

It made you grow up very quickly. We understood more. There was always fear that your father would not come back.

My father had a map behind the radio, and he would follow the war from the news and mark it. A lot of my relatives were in the war and they came back to us when they came on leave. My heart stood still when we listened to the radio in case they were killed or injured in the fighting. Vera Lynn was a famous singer and some of her songs were quite sad and we heard some of the songs were banned – too sentimental!

We lived in Dorset Road, Forest Gate, (London) my dad was a bus conductor. It was convenient for him to walk through the church grounds to get to the bus garage. He was close to work when an incendiary bomb landed on St Andrew's Church. Being fairly old, it caught fire pretty quickly and the vicar was moaning that all the church records were about to go up in smoke. My father, not a particularly religious man, ran into the church and brought them out. He received a commendation and was thought of as a hero.

If you were in a protected industry you had extra tea and sugar rations.

After the war my sister was working in the dockyard and when they took the blackout curtains down they asked if any one wanted them. She and her friends had some and made themselves skirts.

There were no silk stockings – so when they went out, ladies dyed their legs with tea and drew lines up the back to look like a straight seam.

Early on in the war, a German plane crash-landed in Parsloes Park (Essex), near to where my gran lived. The pilot was uninjured so local people took him into their house, gave him a cup of tea and a piece of cake while they waited for the police to arrive to take him away.

After the war there were German POW (prisoner of war) camps on Southampton Common and I remember when we had our school carol service they invited POWs to join. We didn't hold a grudge against them, we just accepted it. We even felt sorry for them.

After the war when the British POWs came back from Japan we went and waved to them all. They were very thin people – skeleton-like. They had been given chocolate and though they were hungry themselves, they threw us the chocolate, as they were so pleased to see British children.

Bombings and shootings

We lived near Grangemouth. It was only bombed once. On its way back to base a plane discharged its remaining explosives. Unfortunately this hit an ammunitions site. The explosion was huge and could be felt eight miles away. My gran was really fat and weighed 15 stones. She was blown from her chair across the room and landed on top of the sideboard. Other than being a little surprised, she was fine.

Two boys had a fight trying to decide who should have a rocket they had found. Later, I heard a terrific bang. The boy who won the rocket was blown up and killed by it.

Walking home from a trip with my dad to Streatham High Road in London, a German plane, which had slipped through, started firing at the guns under the railroad bridge we were approaching. Dad pushed me to the ground and fell on top of me, until the plane had turned back.

One evening, my dad was on his way to the pub when there was an air raid warning. He decided to turn back and was almost home when a bomb fell quite near – my mother was worried but then he came in and said, "Something told me to come back." That bomb fell on the pub where he was going.

Another day we were coming home from school and suddenly a door opened and a lady grabbed us and took us indoors. We thought we were being kidnapped, but she had heard the noise of the doodlebugs.

Bombs fell anywhere – doodlebugs, V1s, just dropped anywhere. It was totally indiscriminate bombing. Dreadful droning noise. Targets were oil refineries, plane and ammunition factories, particularly.

Because of the bomb damage, there was plenty of firewood about, plenty of scrap wood. Builders repaired bomb damage, so got plenty of money.

My brother died in March 1940 and I think the school was bombed about that time though it may be a little later. One bomb dropped at the beginning of School Lane and didn't explode. The second one dropped in a field to the right of the lane between the first bomb and the school and the third bomb dropped in front of the school damaging the school. I'm told that there was a fourth bomb but I didn't know about it.

It was lucky for this man – he said, "I didn't know whether to read another story or go home so I tossed up and said I am going home." He just got round the corner when the house, where he had been, went up.

We lived over our mother and father's greengrocery shop situated on the outskirts of London in North Watford. One night – with a high-pitched whine, silence, and a thunderous shaking crash – a V2 bomb demolished most of the surrounding area and with it the back of our shop.

I remember seeing the Home Guard practising for an enemy invasion. They were lying down on the pavement with their rifles. Later in the war, I heard a doodlebug coming down and running with my friends to look see. It landed a couple of blocks away on the pavement. There was water from the fire hydrant gushing out.

In 1941, a Heinkel 111 plane was hit by anti-aircraft guns and went down about 400 yards from where I lived. The next morning, two of my mates came over, and we went and found the wreckage. There was no guard, which was unusual, so we each took some bits from the plane plus a gun each and hid them in the ditch nearby. Suddenly there was a great shout from the guard. We asked if we could have a few bits from the plane – he didn't know we had a ditch full!

We were out on Horton Heath, near Southampton. We found a bomb sticking out of the ground, khaki in colour. We dug it out with a piece of metal and decided the best thing to do was to take it to our headmaster. It weighed about six stones so we took it in turns to carry it, singing as we did, "We are the boys of the BDS (Bomb Disposal Squad)!" We laid it on the lawn of the headmaster's house, about six feet from the front door. His wife, Mrs Chamberlain, answered the door whilst still chewing her dinner. "Please Miss, we've found an unexploded bomb," we said. "And where is it?" she said. We said in unison, "It's here." Mrs Chamberlain froze, stopped chewing and then passed out hitting her head on the quarry-tiled floor.

We were walking by the river Itchen near Southampton, across the water meadows, when we found incendiary bombs scattered all over the place. I picked one up, unscrewed the top and emptied it out. I then carried it home on the handlebars of my bike covered with a cloth. My mother nearly died when she saw it as she thought it was live! "No, I diffused it," I said. She was even more cross and I was severely told off.

The blitz ended and we returned to London. Memories include going with everyone else to view the mine, swinging from its parachute from a tree in the churchyard. I also remember going into a shop that didn't seem to have any goods. I asked the man behind the counter, who was wearing an apron, for something. He looked under the counter before offering the closest alternative he had - very different from today's supermarket shopping!

Soon we were treated to the V1 or doodlebug. We got used to listening to the familiar 'phut-phut' of its engine. When the noise stopped you dived for cover. This was then followed by the V2 which was much more serious. The first anyone knew of it was a large explosion as a whole street was demolished. My brother and I were evacuated again, this time to a miner in Yorkshire.

"Look at all that. It's Portsmouth burning, don't bother to get undressed. Let's get to our Annie and we will be safe there, its just over the creek." My whole family had been bombed out, so the whole family was in my front room. Between 25-30 arrived. My father called them the 'Royal' family. Everyone was poor. We were having our tea, so they were told, "Don't talk about bodies at tea time."

117

I can remember standing looking down towards the dock area. Once the Blitz started on the docks they burnt very quickly. We watched them going up.

We came home from Sherringham in Norfolk on holiday and stayed at a house near a builder's yard in Upton Park. It was very old-fashioned. It had a coal-fired washing boiler and a more or less outside toilet. Nothing much happened for the first six months. We had a cellar, which father reinforced and we slept in it. Then, West Ham was very badly bombed. Windows were blown out lots of times. We had an incendiary in our bedroom, burning through the ceiling. My dad got a metal dustbin and went to the loft. He cut through the joists so the incendiary went into dustbin.

We had to move out several times because of land mines or unexploded bombs hanging from trees.

We used to watch the doodlebugs go over, but if the engine stopped and it turned round we had to run as fast as we could and go into the shelter.

When the V2 rockets started, we had no Warning they were coming.

Later, the blitz started, as Hitler used the Luftwaffe to attempt to break us. My mother now ran a shop in Upton Park, London. During one raid, my father and I stood under the shop blind looking up at the searchlights probing the sky for bombers. A lot of bombs fell on West Ham and anti-aircraft guns had been set up to reassure us that we were hitting back. A white-hot piece of shrapnel fell into the road in front of us. I made a rush over to pick it up as a souvenir but my father stopped me. I think he thought I might burn my hand on the metal. Later, we both laughed as we realised we were sheltering under a piece of canvas, from bombs and shrapnel.

When the neighbouring street was bombed, the shelter door was wedged by the blast. Mum and I were alone, but she thoughtfully kept a hammer inside and battered the door open – our house was only one of the few to retain windows.

Another night, the door of the shelter blew in and we were all covered in dirt and dust. A bomb had dropped very close by - about 300 yards away. As we climbed out of the shelter, the girl who lived next door – and who had been sleeping indoors – ran down the garden path, screaming. Her mother followed, caught the girl, turned her round and slapped her face – and the girl stopped screaming immediately. When we went indoors to see the damage we found the window frames had all been blown in and were hanging up in the curtains. I'm glad I wasn't indoors that night – and I can quite understand why the girl next door was hysterical.

My earliest memory is of my younger brother in a pram with my mother and me running in Victoria Park. There were loud sirens and a large balloon the shape of a plane. My mum was trying to get back to safety.

I remember seeing 'dog fights' through the skylight window at night. Dad was on fire warden duty and mother was nowhere around. I am looking up at the sky when the house around the corner disappears - bombed out.

The heavy bombing raids of the Germans were beginning. Sometimes, the air raids would be in daylight, but the majority were at night – affecting our sleep. Each time the siren sounded, we would listen for the distinct throbbing of the German bombers' engines. Most of them would fly over Long Melford on their way to Coventry, Birmingham and other Midland and industrial towns and cities. Other times, they would cross East Anglia on their way to London. We would stand and watch them going over. Sometimes we saw the flash of guns, as an English night fighter attacked them. At the same time as this was happening, people were being evacuated to Long Melford!

On a Saturday in early September, the German Air Force hit London with a great force. Living in Walthamstow, we were a few miles from the docklands which were taking heavy punishment. We were able to sit in deck chairs in the garden and watch the dog fights taking place a mile or so away. Great cheers went up when a plane was seen to spiral down in flames. Unfortunately, we could not always distinguish friends from foes. When the fight was overhead, we took shelter to avoid bits falling on us.

...On one occasion, I was sitting at home when one (bomb) exploded near by. I looked up to see our rather heavy wireless set swaying on its shelf, just above my head. Fortunately, it did not fall otherwise I may have been badly injured, or killed, by a falling radio set!

<u>The house and air raid shelters</u>

The windows were covered with brown paper, then the sticky tape which looked like crosses. The idea was to stop the glass from shattering.

At first, people reacted to the air raid siren by going to a shelter. We had an Anderson shelter in the back garden. This was not very popular as it was made of galvanised iron covered in earth. We were too close to nature and all the creepy crawlies! We took to gathering in our living room, which was in the middle of the house and keeping the blackout curtains drawn. One night, I sat on the arm of the settee, playing with my stamp collection whilst my mother sat on the settee behind me reading. The head of a shell came through the roof and landed with a crash on the floor upstairs causing the plaster in the living room to fall on the table. My mother grabbed me and hauled me to her on the settee. Although uninjured by the shell fragments, I was in danger of being throttled to death by my mother holding me by the neck!

Eventually, we went back to London, a bomb had fallen three doors away so we lost windows and a couple of ceilings. We thought it was great fun to have a tarpaulin for a ceiling, as it whipped up and down when the wind blew.

We went back to sleeping in the shelter each night, and picking up shrapnel each morning, which we used to trade, keeping our favourite shaped pieces of course.

We had to get up in the night when the sirens went off. I remember my sister waking me and telling me to hurry up. We went down to the shelter in our night clothes with our coats on too. When there was a lull in the raid, my dad, who was a chef, would sometimes go indoors and make hot cocoa for us all. I also remember him making scrambled egg with dried egg powder after the raid when we were all safely indoors again.

Shortly after that incident, we were bombed out, a landmine dropped on the roof and took out the roofs of six houses. None of us was injured although I think it killed one of the neighbours. That was when we moved to Barking. My aunt Vi lived in Oulton Crescent and the house next door was vacant, the owners had moved to Manchester, so we rented it.

You had different types of shelters, I was petrified of them. One shelter was just a pile of bricks, I hated that, it was really scary. Another one, opposite my grandmother's, which was in a basement but the scariest of the lot was near where we lived, between Wandsworth Bridge and Putney Bridge. The shelters in Wandsworth Park were underground, right beside the river. This was really scary. We had to go into these every night, it was like a rabbit Warren, I was always frightened of being buried alive. Everyone was quite jolly down there. We used to have singsongs and the shop opposite made us Oxo for a penny. The absolute fear lasted until it was morning and you realised you were alive and could come out.

We always washed before going into shelter as there was no water in there.

There were no lights on buses, cars or bikes. And you could get a heavy fine if your chimney caught light - this often happened because people could not afford to have their chimneys swept regularly. Also, coal was rationed. There was no central heating – just one fire in the living room (lounge). And all our windows were blacked out.

There were public shelters too – large ones, underground. Also people slept on the stations in the London Underground. Every evening around 6.00 pm, as we played in the street, groups of people – whole families - would be making their way to the local station, wheeling prams or wheelbarrows containing bedding and food. They would take the train until it reached the Underground part of the Tube system and would sleep the night on the Underground platform, with hordes of other people.

Once the air raids started properly, June and I were put to bed in the shelter each night, which was easier for my mother than getting us up to put us in there when a raid started.

We had a paraffin heater in the air raid shelter. It was very dangerous.

In the shelter it was packed. We had hardly any sleep. My father didn't approve of everyone in the shelter so put a tent up in the garden and slept there!

We used to keep warm in the boiler room of a local boarding school as our shelter was wet and dark. My dad came home one day on leave and rushed to the boiler room. Apparently, we had nearly died from the fumes from the coke they used in the boiler. It was lucky he came when he did but we just didn't know how dangerous it was. We were pulled out, feet first, semi-conscious. I have a fear of dials to this day as they remind me of the boiler room.

We saw the mines swinging from trees in their parachutes. The gas pipes and water pipes were smashed so we had to boil water. We collected shrapnel.

We stayed then until the night the Guildhall was hit and the water mains hit and then our house caught fire. We lost everything. We had a piano and the blast of the bomb caused it to jam in the door. Afterwards we went to see it, as my aunt's rings were in the house, but it caught fire.

One particular night, they had pressed the siren button and we all rushed down to the Anderson shelter at the bottom of the garden when I realised that my youngest sister (Ann) aged about three was still in the house. I rushed back and picked her up just as the bombs were falling in the distance. When I got her to the shelter, I realised I had been carrying her upside down.

The water mains were hit and then our house caught fire. We lost everything.

Whilst at home during air raids we used to sleep in the Anderson shelter in our neighbour's garden…their name was Anderson!

Children having fun

I remember receiving little dolls made from wooden clothes pegs.

Outside we played block, hopscotch, skipping – we had a rope across the street where everyone joined in chanting rhymes. I collected shrapnel for my brother, David, to make toy soldiers when he returned from being evacuated, aged eleven.

David was the youngest of a gang. He was caught with lead from a house roof in his hands and kept at the police station until the owner of the bombed house could be contacted in London. The police received a telling-off for wasting their time over a young boy.

We loved mudlarking – you had to stand in the mud and someone threw a penny down. Everyone tried to find it and got covered in mud. Sometimes, you would be given threepence if you put your head in the mud.

We lived on a farm and painted the inside of the pigsty with white distemper and used it as our pretend house.

If you cut up a length of bicycle inner tube and fold and fold it until it is a ball shape it is brilliant. It bounces so high but it is very hard so is probably dangerous but we didn't think about that.

My brother, who is three years older than me, decided to teach me how to make a Molotov cocktail – using a milk bottle and petrol with rag in the top. One side of our house had a blank wall and my brother said, "I'll light it and you throw it." It seemed to set the whole wall alight. It didn't do a lot of damage, but I got into a lot of trouble.

We played in the street until the siren went – then we all went indoors, or into the air raid shelter. When the 'all clear' went we all came out again and carried on where we left off – just as though nothing had happened. We played the usual games – ball games, skipping, hide and seek, cowboys and Indians – but, of course, a lot of the time we were soldiers or sailors or airmen battling against the enemy! It wasn't always easy to get someone to play the enemy so sometimes we were all battling together against an invisible foe – a bit like the real thing really.

I wasn't evacuated myself, so air raids and doodlebugs were a part of our lives and taken in our stride. For instance, one day a group of us were playing cricket on Beacontree Heath when a doodlebug came over. We stopped playing and watched its' progress. When the motor cut out we walked calmly over to one of the underground public shelters on the Heath, waited at the entrance for the big bang, then went back and carried on with our game.

Childhood

It was a very extraordinary childhood but we didn't realise it at the time, just got on with it. Never any panic, people took everything in their stride.

Prior to going to Scotland we did go out to Rownhams near Southampton (about five miles from where we lived). A family we knew rented a big house. We used to walk there. We were lucky as people were sleeping in fields and ditches but we had somewhere dry to go. We came back during the day.

We went by train to a town called Gloucester. We all had to wait in this church hall to be picked by the different families who were going to look after us. Before getting on the train I fell over and had a bad scratch on the side of my face. When the choices were being made I was the only one left. I expect I looked pretty horrible so nobody wanted me.

When the bombing was all over and they picked me up they could see why I was protesting. It was not because of the planes, but because I had been thrown onto a patch of stinging nettles and all my exposed parts were covered in stings!

Ben, the lodger, was a skilled technician and was fairly handy with electrical bits. He decided some of our neighbours needed help in hearing the air raid warnings so put an extra large siren on the side of the house. Obviously we kids had better hearing and if we were not at school we pressed the siren button.

We read today about rationing during the war and the shortage of food but I can't remember ever being hungry. I did know however, that I had to eat every thing given to me. This included burnt toast and crusts, also we had to drink the small bottle of milk that was often turning sour at school, otherwise we were threatened that Lord Woolton would 'get us.' He was the Food Minister during the wartime.

I was in hospital with appendicitis, then scarlet fever and then later meningitis. Then when I came out we frequently had the gas mains blown up. My grandmother had an oven in the yard, with a gas pipe coming out the top and a tarpaulin over the top.

We always had gas masks with us but didn't put them on. After the bomb went off, Tommy Holloway, a friend of mine, went back into the classroom to collect some of his belongings. When he came back he told me that there had been quite a lot of damage to the school. We were diverted through the churchyard where we were stopped by two reporters who asked us what had happened and Tommy was able to tell them about the damage. We were both given 2s6d (half a crown) each.

Barbara was seven when war broke out. We lived in Powerscourt Road with my mum, my brother and aunt and uncle who were just married, but dad was away, We didn't really understand what the war meant. We had a shelter in the garden, it was very damp so we didn't use it. One evening a friend came rushing in, "Why aren't you in the shelter. The house over the road had an incendiary hit and it's on fire?" Our beds were downstairs and we used to go under auntie's bed when the sirens went. This time we jumped into the shelter. It was all damp and horrible. Luckily, we did, as where we had been under the bed a bomb had a direct hit and we wouldn't have been here today. That weekend my aunt's husband came home for a few days leave and he put bricks in the bottom of the shelter, floor boards and then a mattress – we children thought it was a game and went down there to sleep.

Gran used to keep me at home to do the housework. I had to scrub floors even though I was only ten years old.

The beadle came round to see why my brother wasn't at school. I had on a turban and a full apron and I was cleaning the stairs. My brother was drying the paper-round money on the clothes line as he had got soaked. The beadle didn't realise I was a child too.

Before our house got bombed my brother and I were going to the Majestic cinema in Kingston Crescent, but we couldn't get in, so we went to the Shaftsbury cinema. There was a raid and the Blue Anchor pub got bombed. Our mum was really worried thinking we had been killed. We just carried on watching the film after the all clear.

…next seeing dog fights through the skylight window at night. Dad was on fire warden duty and mother was nowhere around. I am looking up at the sky when the house around the corner disappeared – bombed out.

…we still had a good time.

People had the street door keys hung on a piece of string through the letterbox – that way we only had to have one key per family.

With my father away, my mother coped perfectly well, she could do anything. There were five kids and not much money – 15 shillings a week. I did all the shopping - the same each week, half a leg of lamb and corned beef did us for four days,

We still carried on semi-normal, I went to Brownies. There was a barbed-wire fence and I cut myself. We had barrage balloons on the Common, guns everywhere. We could see searchlights going round all the time looking for enemy aircraft.

I was in Southampton for the blitz, we were not just bombed over the weekend, but night after night. We used to go to a neighbour's opposite in his Anderson shelter. The routine was, we went to bed, got up, put on a siren suit. We went to school, but if we had a bad night we used to have a sleep during the morning. If the sirens went off at school we went into the school air raid shelter. I liked singing, so used to sing to keep everyone entertained.

We had all the troops in Southampton, they were all sitting down in the street waiting to be marched on to the docks. I was eight when war broke out. All my childhood we didn't feel deprived. My parents were exceptionally calm and I think we must have picked it up from them. We didn't feel as though we were suffering, but we probably were.

The British are so stoic. My friend had a telegram to say her brother was missing presumed dead. She cried all the way to school. We supported her. We were united.

At school I was boarded in a house opposite the main school in Petersfield. At night we were told to place our mattresses on the floor under the bed and sleep there. We had to put our bedspreads on the bed to avoid any flying glass. What we actually did, was to hang out of the windows, seeing and hearing the doodlebugs as they flew overhead, presumably aimed at London. However, we knew we were safe, if we heard the engine cut out, as the plane would then glide on for some miles.

David and Gill Stone wearing their siren suits ready to go down into their shelter. Gill thinks her suit was made from her mother's old coat

Then we went back to London, don't know why. We were all Catholics and someone realised I hadn't been baptised, so I had to go back to London, have instructions and the nuns gave me a rosary and the priest gave my mother a pound of butter! Then we went back to Woodley, but there was no Catholic church. I must have been nine or ten when we went back to Putney. We went to a small Catholic school. If there was an air raid we went into a reinforced room, called the doctor's room. There was only a handful of us, as most children were evacuated.

Because there were only two of us, mum had to have lodgers – three Russian Jewesses - for a short time, in our shelter drinking from bottles.

There was some discussion - should I go to Australia - but no. It was decided I should stay with mum. My dad was killed – he was a war correspondent.

We kept chickens and rabbits in the builder's yard – in cages, which we killed and ate – butcher next door did it, we couldn't.

I had just started at school when the War began. The whole school was evacuated. "My children are not going to be evacuated," said my dad. A Roman Catholic convent took us on which previously had only taught girls shorthand and typing. My older brother, me and John Wells had to go about a mile and a quarter from where we lived. We walked, took a trolley bus or rode a bike – one between us.

We went on holiday to Hapsburg in Norfolk. We had hired a typical seaside country shack, which it turned out was made of asbestos. We were there for VJ day. Loads of people had gone on holiday. We had a big bonfire though everything was still rationed. The land was being eroded at a very fast rate by the sea. The lighthouse had been 100 yards from the sea, but now it was in the sea. I can remember my father had an Austin 10 and it wouldn't go up the hill with us in, so we had to walk to the top of the hill.

When I was 14, I kept rabbits and chickens in the garden and collected rabbit food every evening. German prisoners of war were building houses behind where I lived, in Glenfield Avenue, Bitterne Park and I became very friendly with one called Gerard Lenz.

As a three-year-old I saw our town bombed in the Blitz, it seemed to be on fire. I was absolutely terrified of that, but not when my school was bombed.

I used to go down to an anti-aircraft gun site behind AST factory and elevate the barrel of the gun, rotating it too, pretending to fire it. The soldiers made me a spitfire plane out of wood. They probably knew that my father had just died of pneumonia.

Unfortunately, my mum died – bombed in January and she died of TB in September. We had to go to live with my gran, even though my mum's dying wish was, 'Don't let her go to live with our gran she isn't very nice'. But I did and stayed until I left home at 17/18. I then just walked out one day and left to stay at my uncle's. She wasn't a kind lady, she wasn't kind to her own children so definitely not kind to me. She was as bad to everyone.

He was away when mum died, so when his ship came in, the padre was walking towards him to tell him. They kept her for two weeks before burying her in case dad came back. A neighbour took me up to the ceremony which I watched. Meant to be 16 to go, but my brother went, as he was tall.

Some people believed that Cambridge wouldn't be bombed as they were keeping it for the education of German youths!

We had 'Jack Frost' (ice) inside the windows. The bed felt like ice it was so cold. The mattress was made of feathers. We devised a way to get the bed warmer by putting an electric light bulb in the bed.

We dressed and undressed in the airing cupboard.

Tomatoes were solid as they were frozen – in kitchen.

Only had oil stoves to keep warm.

There were people in uniforms everywhere.

We had an Anderson shelter in the back garden – dug about three feet deep into the earth. We had an old piece of lino and a bit of carpet on the floor. It was quite damp even though we had a paraffin heater. There were plenty of creepy-crawlies. It was very draughty - even though we tried to plug the gaps with cement. For a light we had a home-made light made from a shoe polish tin filled with cotton wool soaked in paraffin. The lid went on top and some of the cotton wool was pulled through a small hole in the lid to form a wick, which we lit. This was all the light we had – and we daren't let any light shine out of the shelter as the light might be seen by enemy aeroplanes.

One night, there was really heavy bombing along the Thames – aimed at the London Docks which were sited where Canary Wharf is now. The bombs dropped continuously for about two hours. The sky was bright orange because of all the fires that the bombs caused. There was a knock at the air raid shelter door and when it opened it was my uncle Doug in his Army uniform. Doug was normally a brave man – this night his eyes were like saucers and his face was bright red. He'd walked and run all the way home from Canning Town through all the bombs and fires. He'd just had the fright of his life.

The last part of the War was most scary. Doodlebugs (pilot-less, engine powered planes containing bombs that exploded on landing) used to appear in the sky overhead. We used to stand in the garden and watch them. When the engine stopped – as it was planned to do – the plane would falter and go into a dive. So, when this happened we would all scamper into the air raid shelter and hope that it wouldn't fall on us. Soon, the doodlebugs were replaced by a more deadly weapon – the V2 explosive rocket. These made no sound. They were launched like a space rocket and were targeted on London and the Thames. They just arrived out of the blue *without Warning. Fortunately, the German Army surrendered, soon after the introduction of the rockets.*

When I came back to school from Scotland, the colour of the uniforms was different, but I kept my old uniform as there were no coupons for a new one. I very quickly copied the Scottish accent, then when I came back to England I had to lose it again!

Children who were evacuated

The good times

Our stand-in parents gave us the love and discipline we needed and continued (to do so) after the war.

Before the war, a German sea captain told my father to get the family away from the docks. My grandparents had a large house in Surrey so we went there, whilst the Battle of Britain was on. We could see the dog fights from the house. Often the shelters had water in them. How we survived I do not know.

My earliest memory is of going to school, at the age of four and a half, at the village school of Ledsham in Yorkshire. This was September 1941. We were evacuated from our home in Barking. The normal age was five years old but as mum was pregnant with her seventh (and last!) child and had a toddler of three, the school allowed me to attend with my three older sisters. My teacher was Mrs Tilley and she was a motherly person. I remember playing most of the time, but probably learnt some things. There were only two classes – five to eight year olds and nine to fourteen year olds.

The Christmas of 1941 was spent there and mum managed to get some oranges. There were no shops in the village and no bus service so mum and my aunt used to walk about five miles across footpaths to the nearest shops. They were good customers, mostly because they were the only ones not to have run up a 'slate' for their groceries, which was why they were allowed to buy the oranges.

I remember we went to church and the message came through that war had been declared and the rector said no prayers. He just said "Go home!"

We were at the rectory about a month. Then we went to the Judd's. We were very happy there, only the two of us and they made us so welcome. We had nice things to eat. And we had a bath! They boiled water in a copper and then had to move it into the bath. We had to bath together and then they bathed the dog after us.

A friend was evacuated to the Isle of Wight. Someone heard the surname 'Haylet' and she remembered it so claimed this child, Joan. Joan had a very poor, hard upbringing at home. Her life became completely changed. She had a home. She stayed there and eventually married there.

One day we went up to Paddington station and were sent to Woodley, near Reading. When we got there we waited in a recreation ground with a pavilion. We stood there and people came and said "I'll have her, or him." An old man said, "I'll have her," so I went off with this bloke. We walked through a wonderful wood – I had never seen woods before. This man, Mr. Plumtree, offered me some chocolate, which I refused because I thought he was bribing me. I was only five. There was a Mrs Plumtree and a daughter, Vera. We lived in a bungalow which was really nice. My brother, Tony, was chosen to live with another family, so my mother was left with my two sisters and she went elsewhere. All in Woodley, but we hardly saw anything of them.

While there one day, June and I were sitting on a fence watching a convoy of armoured cars, tanks and jeeps come by, and busily noting how many of each there were. A jeep stopped and a very pleasant soldier asked what we were doing, so we proudly showed him our list. He asked if we would trade it for some gum, which we happily did!

We were never told what was happening. When we were evacuated we had jars of jam, tinned milk, tinned corned beef.   My brother came with me and my two sisters went somewhere else. We lived in a corrugated iron house – it was really noisy when it rained. I had to fill buckets of water using the pump from the well and we had eggs from chickens. I liked it but my mum missed us so she came to collect us.

We were with a retired headmistress in a huge house with a huge garden. She grew apples and sold them at the door. There was also lots of honey, which she sold. "Come on we will take these apples to the soldiers," she said.

We didn't have anything to do with the maids. There was a nice fat one who was jolly who spoke to you, but the other one didn't speak.

The Judds used to teach the piano. We went off with our flasks and I went with Mr Judd to collect the insurance money. Then, on Sunday he played the organ at church – I was farmed out with his father, so didn't go to church. I went for a walk with him. He always had something to show me. He always walked with his gun uncocked in case we found something suitable, such as a rabbit.

We fondly remember the black American troops based there briefly before D-day. They gave us kids rides up the hills in their jeeps and gave us chewing gum. We couldn't understand why they hung their heads and shuffled when shouted at by the white Americans.

I was evacuated with my two sisters to Morecambe Bay, Lancashire. I lived with a Mr and Mrs Tattersall, their son, Harry, and their daughter, Norah, who was the same age as me. I think I was about seven at the time. They also had an aunt living with them, so the house must have been enormous because they used to have Air Force personnel billeted there too. I remember I used to do well for pocket money from the Air Force fellows because I was a Londoner! I was lucky because one sister was in the house next door and the other was just across the road.

I remember the first night we got to Morecambe, we stayed in a church overnight and there was a thunderstorm. Several of the children were crying because they thought it was an air raid again. The next day we were taken to the houses where we were to stay. The driver said, "We don't know there is a War on here." Smarty-pants me said, "Why, haven't you got a wireless?"

We were evacuated to Three-Legged Cross, (another school!). The house owner was like the wife of a squire. Two families stayed there and then a whole lot of children came from London. My mother and another lady bathed them as they were filthy – the water was absolutely grey. They just got cleaned up and then went to other places in the village.

Sometimes a chosen child would be sent into the back garden of the house to pick up 'fallers' – pears from the ground for us to eat.

At the end of the War, when the doodlebug raids were at their height and London and the Thames were the main targets, I was evacuated to a family in the North. My aunt and my gran came too. I was there long enough to go to school but when my mother and father (on leave from the Army) came to visit, I insisted that I came home with them. My father had no money for my train fare so I sneaked on the train in Newcastle and sneaked off again when we got to London!

I was then evacuated to Reading. Whilst I was there during Christmas, the local Air Force guys picked us kids up and brought us to the Air Force base. I had my first taste of America. The Yanks handed out lots of candy and we had fun.

Mr and Mrs Armstrong were the epitome of kindly folk, reaching out a hand to those in trouble. We were a little worried to get a plate of Yorkshire pudding and gravy for our first meal. We liked it and enthusiastically consumed a second plate thinking this was all Yorkshire people ate. The meat and vegetables which followed were unexpected.

The not such good times

When we lived in Renfrewshire, the Clyde docks were bombed a couple of times. Then we stayed with my grandmother and the V1 and V2s came over, when the drone stopped you knew it would be exploding. They were really awful, no sirens, they seemed to just come over and that was it.

Two teenage boys were evacuated to Hampshire where they lived in a village on a hill. They made a huge kite and were able to fly it very well. They even managed to get different pieces that they had added, to fall off as the kite was flying. Unfortunately, someone from a nearby village saw this and was very suspicious so called the police. The police came and confiscated the kite. They said it was in case the boys were sending messages to the enemy!

The High Street was totally flattened and Edwin Jones, a department store, lost all its toys - they said afterwards - if they had known they were going to be bombed, they would have given the toys away.

In the summer of 1939, after a very long journey, we arrived at a small town in Northants. We were taken to a school hall where we were inspected by the villagers, who picked out who they would billet for an unknown time. Inevitably, someone has to be last but it is very disappointing when you are that person. The billeting officer took me to a house for one night. The following day a young couple with two small children were asked to take us. We were treated kindly but were not wanted as we disrupted their family life. My parents came once a month, on Sundays, in a coach organized specially for parents to visit their children. I returned to Walthamstow on Easter Sunday, 1940.

My next address was 16 Bowling Green Terrace, with my brother next door. There was no bedroom for me, so I slept on a mattress on a board on the bath. This was fine until summer came and paying guests arrived!

My next address I cannot recall, but it was to a woman opening a beach cafe. I think she took on sixteen London evacuees as cheap labour. At six or seven years old I was not much use to her. My two half-sisters, on leave from the Women's Auxiliary Air Force (WAAF), came to see us. They were concerned to meet me running to the Island School in the rain wearing only a shirt, shorts and plimsoles. They asked the people at 16 Bowling Green Terrace to take me back. This I didn't like as they painted my thumb with mustard to stop me from sucking it. The problem of where I slept was solved by putting a mattress in the roof space under the eaves.

I was too young to be evacuated, being only one year old when the War started, but my sister and brother left home just a few days before War was declared. It sounded like a great adventure, they said. They were separated and after a two-hour journey to a lovely seaside town, my sister was taken to the home of a pleasant lady and her husband. Perhaps not having children of their own they were rather unaware of the feelings of a nine-year-old, my sister. She was taken upstairs to sleep high up in the attic room. She says she can always remember the panic of that first night, the spooky room, the silence and being alone away from the closeness of our family.

A couple of girls I know ran away, it was so horrible. Then Mrs Smith came for her daughter, then my mum came to collect me the next week.

My sister and I were evacuated to Forfar, a small town in the north east of Scotland. We lived with an uncle and aunt, who owned a jeweller's shop and a terraced house nearby. They did volunteer work in the evenings and at weekends. Although there was no war here - no air raids, no bombs, no fear of death - we were left alone for what seemed like a really long time.

I can remember getting on a corporation bus. We were on top of the bus and the headmistress said, "When we start to move we should give a cheer." I looked down and waved. My mother was in tears so I was worried. When we went to the railway station it was bedlam. We all had labels on like Paddington Bear. When you are young anywhere is long way away. It seemed to take all day to get there. We went to Wilton in Wiltshire. We went to the school and there was a load of women inspecting us. They picked us like Belgian chocolates, 'no, don't want any boys,' until there was only us left.

There was a lot of gentry in the Wiltshire area – a Mrs Duff-Cooper took about a dozen of us including a carer. My teacher, myself and about ten of us we went to the rectory opposite to stay with the Reverend and the Honourable Mrs Campbell. Before we got to Wiltshire we were given carrier bags containing a bar of chocolate and a tin of corned beef etc. In the rectory there was a cook, two housemaids, and a housekeeper – they had everything from our bags.

They had to give us bedrooms. There was a brother and sister with us. Miss Craddock said he could not stay in the bedroom with the girls so we had to have a shift round. The four older ones went up into this dreadful attic.

They had funny apple trees. We used to eat the apples as we were hungry.

After our teacher left, there was a bit of a stir up because we were put in the attic because we were the oldest. There was one little window and our beds were four green baize doors - very spartan. We didn't like it. We were very lonely and very hungry. Then, our parents turned up and one parent said, "Where do you sleep?" "Come on, I'll show you," I said. The mums came up and were disgusted. One parent gave us a sandwich which was meant to be her lunch.

After the fuss, as a treat, we were made cocoa plus one Osborn biscuit each. Vivienne said, "I like these with cheese." Margaret said, "I like my cocoa with milk." We were told we were very ungrateful girls. We had a giggle at the end so got told off. Only one more night and then the four of us were found other billets.

Then the War got really bad. We had to go to a big school in Lavender Hill, London, for a medical. Only Margaret, Pam and me went this time. I was ten, they eight and six. We were put on a train at Paddington and ended up in Wales. We arrived in a village called Skewen, near Neath, close to a big coal tip. We lined up again to be chosen. There was an elderly lady who chose me and my little sister, Pam. Her name was Mrs Thomas. At this point my sister, Pam, started to scream so in the end she went to Mrs Thomas' daughter down the road.

They were NOT nice people. I suppose we must have been horrible cockney kids and they were not prepared for us. They fed us, but there wasn't a school so we went to the tabernacle one day and then the library the next, wherever they could find a building and a teacher. I can still sing 'Bless this House' and learnt to count up to 15 in Welsh and learnt a bit of French.

During that time I apparently did my scholarship but I don't remember doing it. Mr Thomas was not very nice, he was a miner and they got a tin bath off the wall and bathed. There was a little yard and Mrs. Thomas used to chase me round the yard with her big leather handbag and wallop me – I must have been very naughty - though I can't remember what I did.

One evening we came back from school and I noticed that there was a suitcase by the door. Mrs T gave me some money to buy some biscuits. I said, "Are we going home?" She slapped me and said that's for having big ears! We were going home.

The train journey seemed to last all night, just the three of us, then we got the tube to Putney Bridge. My father opened the door with my brother and baby sister. My mother was very ill in hospital. The Thomas's just dumped us. My father was furious, absolutely livid. It all got too much for me. We had an outside loo and I went out and sat there crying. My father and the Thomas's had an awful row because they didn't believe my mother was ill. When I went back in doors they had gone.

We had been there since February, living in a small cottage which normally housed a farm worker, but he was in the Army. My older sisters had been evacuated with their Barking schools to the west country – two to Kingsbridge and two to Dulverton, but when mum and dad visited them they were horrified to find they were being used as servants, so removed them, and arranged for them to join my aunt and cousin in Yorkshire.

Margaret was sent away because she ate with her mouth open!

I cried all the time so came home from being evacuated.

We lived in Liverpool and the whole school was evacuated to Anglesey. Where I stayed was fine, but my brother lived in this dreadful place. My grandparents went to see him and were so disgusted they brought him home straight away. They had to de-bug him as he had fleas.

Whilst walking in Falmouth High Street, an enemy plane dropped a string of bombs. A cheer went up as a parachute was seen to fall out. This quickly turned to horror as we watched a large parachute mine floating towards us. We had nowhere to shelter except the roadway. The mine drifted over the roofs and landed in the harbour without exploding. The next day, I heard the explosion which killed the diver and his support crew who were attempting to defuse the mine.

I hated the Plumtrees, even though they fed and clothed me and ensured I went to school. Vera was really, really spoilt so I resented her. They gave me a bike. They also made me eat my greens! Eventually I went back home.

We were looked after but not really welcomed. The people were only doing it for money. I was there for whole year.

On one occasion, I went to Tynemouth and then got machine-gunned on the beach within two days. Two German planes came over, they both dropped bombs and then fired at us. We went under the promenade – we got no sympathy – I cried, but my mother slapped me round the face and told me to pull myself together, as I was 14 years old.

Joan and I were evacuated to the Isle of Wight. We stayed with one couple. He was a fisherman and she was posh. We came down to breakfast. We had bread and marmalade. She said, "You will sit there until you have eaten it and can stay there until dinner and then tea." There was a thunderstorm. We were in separate beds but in the same room. I got out of my bed and into my brother's bed. This woman hit the roof. She treated us as adults not as children.

I was so confused I didn't realise it was mum and dad who had come to collect me. I thought they had come to buy apples. When I got home I didn't know who all the people were, even though I had only been away for not very long, probably no more than about six weeks.

I was next evacuated to South Wales. We had the identity tags on and a farming couple took me in. I saw a pig slaughtered in the back of the house. I never forgot the screams of the pig as the farmer was sawing it through the neck.

The evacuees had to do all the washing-up after school dinners – none of the village kids had to do it.

I don't think we bothered to change our clothes. We didn't have a bath, just a bowl of water to wash in.

My father was the billeting officer and told our family about a little boy who lost his name tag so no-one knew who he was. He went to stay with a family in the village and stayed there forever. No-one claimed him or had reported him missing, so the family brought him up as their own child. He still lives in the village to this day.

Some final thoughts

There were no air raids, so gradually children went home.

Came home to do the eleven-plus and then never went back. My mother said I was 'to take my chances with the rest of us'.

I had a very unusual childhood but we didn't realise it at the time, we just got on with it. There was never any panic, people took everything in their stride

We were lucky that all our family got through the war without being killed.

When the war was over I was so disappointed to find that my father actually wasn't a fire fighter but owned a shoe shop.

You went through the blitzed areas and accepted it as part of the day.

My brother had been in a prisoner-of-war camp in Germany and we knew he was coming home but we didn't know what day. So every day I would run home from school hoping he would be there. I can still remember the banner saying, 'Welcome Home, Charlie' and the flags from the bedroom windows tied to the wire that went along the privets. Anyway, this particular day, I ran home as usual and when I saw a soldier sitting in the house I threw myself at him to hug him, but it wasn't Charlie, it was a fellow he had saved from the hospital in the camp when it was bombed. Charlie had been in the Royal Army Medical Corps and when the hospital was bombed, the doctors said the patients couldn't be moved or they would die. Charlie said they would die if they stayed in there so he went in and got several wounded soldiers out. The soldier sitting in my house was one of the Arnhem boys he had rescued from the burning hospital. For his bravery my brother got the British Empire Medal.

The idea of keeping children safe is good. The idea of taking them away from their families is not. The sadness and longing both for the children and the parents is hard to understand. It is also hard to understand how so many people could have been so cruel. Perhaps some of them did not know any better or perhaps some people are just really unkind or unthinking.

Conclusion

1939-1945 was a dreadful time for so many people. There were the deaths of family and friends, both in conflict and at home. Some families were hungry. Some families became homeless and many lost all their treasured possessions. People were separated from their loved ones often for many years. People were scared of what might happen to their children so sent them away under the evacuation scheme.

People were also starved of information. For example they were not told that their children were being evacuated to a place only a few miles from home or even to places that were on the direct firing lines of the bombers.

Despite all of this, the camaraderie, helping hand and good nature of people shone through. If someone needed help they were helped, if someone needed a bed to sleep on they were offered one, if someone needed some food they were given it. People cared for and about each other.

Although over 60 years has elapsed since the end of the war, some people are still affected by their war time experiences – can't bear the dark, has a fear of dials, hate high-pitched noises for example. Many are also only just coming to terms with what happened.

And yet, the pride and passion of these people shines through. Their stories touch the heart

Ack Ack guns – nickname for anti-aircraft guns.

Air raid patrol Warden - the main purpose of ARP Wardens was to patrol the streets during blackout and to ensure that no light was visible. If a light was spotted, the Warden would tell the person/people responsible by shouting something like, "*Put that light out!*" or "*Cover that window!*" The ARP Wardens also reported the extent of bomb damage and assessed the local need for help from the emergency and rescue services. They were responsible for the handing out of gas masks and pre-fabricated air raid shelters (such as Anderson shelters, as well as Morrison shelters), and organising and staffing public air raid shelters. They used their knowledge of their local areas to help find and reunite family members who had been separated in the rush to find shelter from the bombs.

Aluminium - light silvery metal.

Anderson shelter - shelter built in the garden of every two or three houses where people went to keep safe when the sirens sounded. Anderson shelters were outside and Morrison shelters were inside but served the same purpose.

Asbestos - a fine-fibrous material once used as a building material but now known to cause a type of cancer.

Auxillary fireman - the Auxiliary Fire Service was formed from volunteers at the outbreak of War, to assist the regular fire brigades. Initially, many wrongly saw firemen as dodging the forces, but when the bombing began their value was realised. Fire was a huge threat to the British people.

Emergency firewater tanks were installed in many towns and where a large water supply such as a river was available, pipes were laid to provide water for fire fighting. Many of the ranks were made up of women - in March 1943 there were 32,200 women serving with the National Fire Service.

For the part time fire fighters, men were on duty every fourth night and women every sixth night.

Barracks – building, or buildings for housing soldiers.

Beadle – person responsible for making sure a child went to school.

Billet - lodgings – usually for troops - but also used for lodgings for WW2 evacuees

Black market – selling things that were not available either because they were rationed or because they were not being made.

Blackouts – the time when no lights were on in the streets and no light could be allowed to shine from a house. At night, everywhere was in a blackout. You didn't dare put a light on and if you did the air raid Wardens would have rapped on your door and shouted, *"Put that light out!"*

Blancmange - a jelly made with milk.

Civvies – non-uniform clothes

Cami knickers – sexy, silky French style knickers

Copper – a large tub used to boil water, usually used to wash clothes and laundry. Clothes and soap are put in and the washing is moved around using a copper stick.

Concentration camp – a prison camp where people are held without trial. During WW2, the Jews particularly were held there by the Germans.

Conscientious objector – someone who does not believe in fighting in a war. they refuse to fight because of their conscience.

Demobilisation (demob) – discharge from the Army.

Dog fight – close range aerial combat between enemies.

Doodlebug – see V1 and V2s.

Evacuee - someone who moved away from where it was thought to be dangerous to live to somewhere that was thought to be safe.

Faggots – a roll of internal organs of a pig mixed with bread, onions and savoury herbs, usually eaten hot.

Forage cap – military cap.

Gas masks - the British Government believed that some form of poison gas would be used during the second World War. It was therefore decided to issue gas masks to everyone living in Britain. By 1940, the Government had issued 38 million gas masks. Adult gas masks were black whereas children had 'Micky Mouse' masks with red rubber pieces and bright eye-piece rims. There were also gas helmets for babies into which mothers would have to pump air with bellows. Air raid Wardens wore gas masks with a long hose and a speaking box which was attached to the belt.

The Government threatened to punish people for not carrying gas masks. However, a study at the beginning of the War suggested that only about 75 per cent of people in London were obeying this rule. By the beginning of 1940 almost no one bothered to carry their gasmask with them. The Government then announced that air raid Wardens would be carrying out monthly inspections of gas masks. If a person was found to have lost the gas mask they were forced to pay for its replacement.

Gerry - short for German person/soldier.

GI – nick name of American forces

Home Guard - the Home Guard were volunteers who defended the five thousand miles of British coastline in the event of an invasion by Germany. They were originally called the **Local Defence Volunteers**.

Layette – baby's complete outfit.

Molotov cocktail - also known as a petrol bomb, gasoline bomb or **Molotov** bomb. It is a name used for a variety of home-made incendiary weapons.

Petty officer – PO – non-commissioned officer in the Navy

Prisoner of war – POW - A person taken by or surrendering to enemy forces in wartime.

Reserved/protected occupation – a job that was considered too important for the War effort for a person to be called up into the armed forces.

Shrapnel – pieces of metal from a bomb. Originally invented by General Shrapnel (1761 – 1842) where a shell was filled with musket balls. The idea is to increase the devastation when the bomb lands.

Siren - air raid sirens first sounded the Warning in London in September 1939. They became almost a daily part of most people's lives who lived in or near cities. When people heard the siren they would stop what they were doing and make for a shelter.

Siren suit - a siren suit was called a siren suit because that's what children often wore when the siren went off. It was a complete outfit-in-one. It had feet at the end of the legs and mittens at the end of the arms. It did up from top to toe. It was mainly worn by young children and babies.

Slate (run up or put on) - people didn't pay for the goods straight away so owed the shopkeeper or pub landlord money.

Square bashing – military slang for drill on the barrack square.

Strafing - the practice of attacking ground targets from low-flying aircraft using aircraft-mounted automatic weapons.

U-boat - German submarine

V1s – flying bombs - the Vergeltungswaffe 1 FZG-76 (V1), known as the Flying Bomb, Buzz Bomb or Doodlebug, was the first modern guided missile used in wartime and the first cruise missile. Vergeltungswaffe means 'reprisal weapon', and FZG is an abbreviation of Flak Ziel Gerät ('anti-aircraft aiming device'), a misleading name. Called the Buzz Bomb because of the noise of the engine. It caused considerable fear in the population. People would listen for the sound approaching, but then be relieved when it sounded overhead as that meant the bomb had actually passed them. It was superseded by the V2 rocket. They were silent and did great damage.

Yanks – nick-name for Americans, in this case the American forces.

Money - There were:

12 pence (d) to one shilling (/ - 1/6d was on shilling an six pence)
20 shillings to one pound (£)

Length - Approximately

one yard	= 91 cm
one foot (')	= 30 cm
one inch (")	= 2.5 cm

Weight - Approximately

2.2 pounds (lbs)	= 1 kilo
112 lbs	= 1 hundredweight (cwt)
16 ounces (oz)	= 1 lb
14 lbs	= 1 stone

Important dates during WW2

Appendix 2

Below are some important dates during WW2 plus web addresses so you can read more information if you so wish.

Day War broke out 3rd September 1939
http://news.bbc.co.uk/1/hi/special_report/1999/08/99/world_War_ii/430918.stm

Introduction of rationing 8th January 1940 with clothes rationing introduced on 1st June 1941
http://www.homesweethomefront.co.uk/web_pages/hshf_rationing_pg.htm

Introduction of slogans eg 'dig for victory', 'coughs and sneezes' October 1939
http://www.woodlands-junior.kent.sch.uk/Homework/War/campaigns.htm

First official evacuation began 1st September 1939
http://www.woodlands-junior.kent.sch.uk/Homework/War/evacuation.htm

Utility clothing including liberty bodices were introduced in 1941
http://www.worldWar2exraf.co.uk/Online%20Museum/Museum%20Docs/clothing4.htm

----

Battle of Britain July 1940
http://news.bbc.co.uk/hi/english/static/in_depth/uk/2000/battleofbritain/default.stm

Major bombings of different parts of the country including Portsmouth, Southampton, Hull, Grangemouth, Liverpool, Coventry, London, Ipswich
http://en.wikipedia.org/wiki/Strategic_bombing_during_World_War_II

The Americans joining the War 7th December 1941
http://wiki.answers.com/Q/Why_did_the_US_become_involved_in_World_War_2

D-day 6th June 1944
http://worldWar2history.info/D-day/

End of War including VE day 8th May 1945
http://www.bbc.co.uk/history/worldWars/wwtwo/veday_germany_01.shtml

V-J day 15th August 1945
http://news.bbc.co.uk/onthisday/hi/dates/stories/august/15/newsid_3581000/3581971.stm

Other major events
http://www.bbc.co.uk/history/worldWars/wwtwo/WW2_summary_01.shtml

IMPORTANT
WAR DATES

1939
Sep 1. Germany invaded Poland
Sep 3. Great Britain and France declared war on Germany; the B.E.F. began to leave for France
Dec 13. Battle of the River Plate

1940
Apr 9. Germany invaded Denmark and Norway
May 10. Germany invaded the Low Countries
June 3. Evacuation from Dunkirk completed
June 8. British troops evacuated from Norway
June 11. Italy declared war on Great Britain
June 22. France capitulated
June 29. Germans occupied the Channel Isles
Aug 8–Oct 31. German air offensive against Great Britain (Battle of Britain)
Oct 28. Italy invaded Greece
Nov 11–12. Successful attack on the Italian Fleet in Taranto Harbour.
Dec 9–11. Italian invasion of Egypt defeated at the battle of Sidi Barrani

1941
Mar 11. Lease-Lend Bill passed in U.S.A.
Mar 28. Battle of Cape Matapan
Apr 6. Germany invaded Greece
Apr 12–Dec 9. The Siege of Tobruk
May 20. Formal surrender of remnants of Italian Army in Abyssinia
May 20–31. Battle of Crete
May 27. German battleship *Bismarck* sunk
June 22. Germany invaded Russia
Aug 12. Terms of the Atlantic Charter agreed
Nov 18. British offensive launched in the Western Desert
Dec 7. Japanese attacked Pearl Harbour
Dec 8. Great Britain and United States of America declared war on Japan

1942
Feb 15. Fall of Singapore
Apr 16. George Cross awarded to Malta
Oct 23–Nov 4. German-Italian army defeated at El Alamein
Nov 8. British and American forces landed in North Africa

1943
Jan 31. The remnants of the 6th German Army surrendered at Stalingrad
May Final victory over the U-Boats in the Atlantic
May 13. Axis forces in Tunisia surrendered
July 10. Allies invaded Sicily
Sep 3. Allies invaded Italy
Sep 8. Italy capitulated
Dec 26. *Scharnhorst* sunk off North Cape

1944
Jan 22. Allied troops landed at Anzio
June 4. Rome captured
June 6. Allies landed in Normandy
June 13. Flying-bomb (V.1) attack on Britain started
June Defeat of Japanese invasion of India
Aug 25. Paris liberated
Sep 3. Brussels liberated
Sep 8. The first rocket-bomb (V.2) fell on England.
Sep 17–26. The Battle of Arnhem
Oct 20. The Americans re-landed in the Philippines

1945
Jan 17. Warsaw liberated
Mar 20. British recaptured Mandalay
Mar 23. British crossed the Rhine
Apr 25. Opening of Conference of United Nations at San Francisco
May 2. German forces in Italy surrendered
May 3. Rangoon recaptured
May 5. All the German forces in Holland, N.W. Germany and Denmark surrendered unconditionally
May 9. Unconditional surrender of Germany to the Allies ratified in Berlin
June 10. Australian troops landed in Borneo
Aug 6. First atomic bomb dropped on Hiroshima
Aug 8. Russia declared war on Japan
Aug 9. Second atomic bomb dropped on Nagasaki
Aug 14. The Emperor of Japan broadcast the unconditional surrender of his country
Sep 5. British forces re-entered Singapore

MY FAMILY'S WAR RECORD

Given to children by the government at the end of the War

135

Bibliography   Appendix 3

General

Burton Lesley, *D-day – Our Great Enterprise,* The Gosport Society, Gosport
Clamp Arthur L, based on originally by H.P.Twyford, *The Blitz of Plymouth 1940-44. The most tragic years in the city's history,* PDS Printers, Devon
Farrington, K (1995) *World War II, War Crimes and Espionage,* Abbeydale Press, Leicester
Moses, B (2002), *The War Years, The Home Front,* Hodder Wayland, London
The Evening News, Portsmouth, *Smitten City,* The Evening News, Portsmouth
Taylor Warwick (2003), *The Forgotten Conscript, A History of the Bevin Boys,* Dorset
Teague, Denis C, *Mount Batten: Flying Boat Base, Plymouth 1913 – 1986,* PDS Printers, Devon
Whitmarsh, A (2007), *Images of England,* Tempus Publishing Ltd., Stroud
Wicks B (1988), *No time to Wave Goodbye,* Stoddart Publishing Company, Toronto, Canada
Http://en.wikpedia.org/wki/Spam

Specific

---

[i] Mitchell Beasley Joy of Knowledge, (1997) History and Culture 2, Mitchell Beasley, London

[ii] Mitchell Beasley Joy of Knowledge, (1997) History and Culture 2, Mitchell Beasley, London

[iii] Herridge C (1989), *Pictorial History of World War II,* Treasure Press, London

[iv] Nemirovsky Irene, 2007 *Suite Francaise,* Vintage Books, London

[v] www.tochparticipation.co.uk/about-us

Ann Wheal was a school teacher for many years before changing career to work at the University of Southampton in the Social Science Department.

She has published widely on many different subjects relating to children and families including books on Foster Care, Leaving Care, Adolescents, Working with Parents and Children's Rights.

She is married to Peter, has two grown-up children and three grandchildren.

She was just a little too young to remember the War but has found it fascinating meeting and talking to those who do remember.